BUILDING ACADEMIC LEADERSHIP CAPACITY

A Guide to Best Practices

Walter H. Gmelch and Jeffrey L. Buller

JB JOSSEY-BASS™
A Wiley Brand

Cover Design: Wiley
Cover image: © Rudi Sebastian | Getty

Published by Jossey-Bass
A Wiley Brand
One Montgomery Street, Suite 1000, San Francisco, CA 94104-4594—
www.josseybass.com/highereducation

Jossey-Bass books and products are available through most bookstores. To contact Jossey-Bass directly call our Customer Care Department within the U.S. at 800-956-7739, outside the U.S. at 317-572-3986, or fax 317-572-4002.

Wiley publishes in a variety of print and electronic formats and by print-on-demand. Some material included with standard print versions of this book may not be included in e-books or in print-on-demand. If this book refers to media such as a CD or DVD that is not included in the version you purchased, you may download this material at http://booksupport.wiley.com. For more information about Wiley products, visit www.wiley.com.

Library of Congress Cataloging-in-Publication Data

Gmelch, Walter H.
  Building academic leadership capacity / Walter H. Gmelch, Jeffrey L. Buller.
    1 online resource.—(Jossey-Bass higher and adult education series)
  Includes bibliographical references and index.
    Description based on print version record and CIP data provided by publisher; resource not viewed.
    ISBN 978-1-118-98931-9 (pdf)—ISBN 978-1-118-98930-2 (epub)—
  ISBN 978-1-118-29948-7 (hardback) 1. Education, Higher–Administration.
    2. Educational leadership. 3. College administrators. I. Buller, Jeffrey L. II. Title.
    LB2341
    378.1'01–dc23
                                                          2014044989

Printed in the United States of America
FIRST EDITION
HB Printing   10 9 8 7 6 5 4 3 2 1

CONTENTS

THE JOSSEY-BASS HIGHER AND ADULT EDUCATION SERIES

For Val Miskin, Irene Hecht, Mary Lou Higgerson, and Peter Seldin, our dear colleagues, friends, and co-conspirators, and for Saeed M. Alamoudi, the hardest-working man in academic leadership

THE AUTHORS

WALTER H. GMELCH is one of the leading researchers in the study of academic leaders in higher education today. Formerly the dean of the School of Education at the University of San Francisco (2004–2013) and currently professor of leadership studies, he also served as dean of the College of Education at Iowa State University and interim dean of the College of Education, professor, and chair of the Educational Leadership and Counseling Psychology Department at Washington State University. Currently Gmelch also serves as director of the National Center for the Study of Academic Leadership. He has published over two hundred articles, twenty-seven books and monographs, and numerous scholarly papers in national and international journals. Gmelch is the author of three books on leadership with Val Miskin (*Chairing an Academic Department, Leadership Skills for Department Chairs*, and *Productivity Teams: Beyond Quality Circles*) and two on management and stress *(Coping with Faculty Stress* and *Beyond Stress to Effective Management*). With Irene W. D. Hecht and Mary Lou Higgerson, he coauthored *The Department Chair as Academic Leader*. Recently he has coauthored four additional books on the deanship: *College Deans: Leading from Within, The Dean's Balancing Act, The Changing Nature of the Deanship,* and *Seasons of a Dean's Life*. With John Schuh, he coauthored *The Life Cycle of a Department Chair*.

JEFFREY L. BULLER has served in administrative positions ranging from department chair to vice president for academic affairs at a diverse group of institutions: Loras College, Georgia Southern University, Mary Baldwin College, and Florida Atlantic University. He is the author of *The Essential Department Chair: A Comprehensive Desk Reference, Academic Leadership Day by Day: Small Steps That Lead to Great Success, The Essential College Professor: A Practical Guide to an Academic Career, The Essential Academic Dean: A Practical Guide to College Leadership, Best Practices in Faculty Evaluation: A Practical Guide for Academic Leaders, and Positive*

Academic Leadership: How to Stop Putting Out Fires and Start Making a Difference. Buller has also written more than two hundred articles on Greek and Latin literature, nineteenth- and twentieth-century opera, and college administration. From 2003 to 2005, he served as the principal English-language lecturer at the International Wagner Festival in Bayreuth, Germany. More recently, he has been active as a consultant to the Ministry of Higher Education in Saudi Arabia, where he is assisting with the creation of a kingdom-wide Academic Leadership Center. Along with Robert E. Cipriano, Buller is a senior partner in ATLAS: Academic Training, Leadership, and Assessment Services, through which he has presented numerous training workshops on developing leadership in higher education.

PREFACE

THOSE OF US WHO serve as academic leaders often come to our positions in an unusual way. Whereas in most professions, people train specifically for that career, receive a credential that signifies their mastery of the basic skills needed to succeed in the field, and then become more acquainted with the practicalities of their professions through internships or entry-level positions, academic leaders tend to be selected in a different and rather idiosyncratic way. They devote many years to advanced learning and research in a particular academic field, enter the professoriate where many of their responsibilities (such as teaching, serving on committees, and developing curricula) have little or nothing to do with the actual courses they took in school, and then, if they are successful at that, they are selected for even more tasks for which they have received no formal training whatsoever: proposing and implementing budgets, mediating disputes, setting priorities, managing facilities, hiring staff, supervising employees, evaluating peers, and engaging in countless other administrative tasks.

It is largely due to this strange career pathway that campuses and university systems decide to create their own leadership development programs. But these programs also have a few peculiarities. Rather than borrowing from successful practices developed by similar programs at other schools, they reinvent the wheel. In many cases, they assume that just as anyone who is a skilled researcher in an academic discipline can teach that discipline, those who are effective as administrators can train others to be like them. They also assume that this training will produce meaningful results even though the administrators who provide it have no background in how effective training is done and may never have given serious reflection to why their own practices have been successful.

Developing Academic Leadership is intended to remedy that situation. This book is a guide for those who want to begin or improve a program that prepares others for leadership roles and draws on best practices as they are found in model programs all over the world. We have worked extensively with administrators who have built successful programs and have established programs at the institutions where we work. We have also conducted research into effective training procedures, the results of which we present in the pages that follow. At the end of most chapters, we have included a section designed to help readers reflect systematically on how they might apply certain concepts to their own programs. These sections—called "Clarifying the Style," "Clarifying Shared Values," and the like—are intended to provide a bridge between theory and practice at the same time that they review several of the key principles of that chapter.

We are grateful to earlier researchers into effective leadership development programs at colleges and universities whose work provided invaluable background to this study:

- Gailda Pitre Davis whose study of leadership development programs is available through the American Council on Education (www.acenet.edu/news-room/Pages/On-Campus-Leadership-Development-Programs-A-Sampling-of-.aspx)
- The Education Advisory Board whose April 10, 2008, research brief, *In-House Leadership Development Programs for Faculty and Staff*, is available to subscribers only
- The University of California report *Preparing Faculty for Academic Management* published in January 2007
- John Schuh, Robert Reason, and Mack Shelley who collaborated with Walt Gmelch to conduct a year-long study for the Center for Academic Leadership and Research Institute for Studies in Education that resulted in *The Call for Academic Leaders: The Academic Leadership Forum Evaluation Project*

Most important, we thank the many organizers and directors of successful leadership development programs who were so generous in sharing information about their program's goals, structure, history, staffing, and budget. Among those to whom we owe a debt of gratitude are:

- Larry Abele, former provost of Florida State University and the director of the Institute for Academic Leadership of the State University System of Florida
- Kevin Gecowets, director of the Center for University Learning at Kennesaw State University
- David Kiel, leadership coordinator in the Center for Faculty Excellence at the University of North Carolina at Chapel Hill

o Nancy LaGuardia, teaching and learning consultant for the Center for Teaching of Capital Community College and director of the Schwab Institute

o Libby Roderick, associate director of the Center for Advancing Faculty Excellence at the University of Alaska Anchorage

o Pamela Strausser, senior consultant in organizational development for faculty and staff for the Leadership Development Academy at Cornell University

o Christina (Tina) Hart, vice president of institutional effectiveness at Indian River State College in Florida

o Brent Ruben, executive director of the Center for Organizational Development and Leadership at Rutgers University

o Former deans Ben Allen and Jim Melsa and executive assistant Heidi Eichorn who cocreated and delivered the Academic Leadership Forum program at Iowa State University

o John Schuh, the director of the Emerging Leader Academy at Iowa State University

o Blannie Bowen, vice provost for academic affairs, who has led programs for academic leaders at Penn State University for over two decades

o David Diehl, director of the Center for Teaching and Learning Excellence, Houston Community College

o Val Miskin, professor of management at Washington State University, who has blended his business leadership expertise with the needs of studying department chairs

o Mimi Wolverton, professor emeritus of educational leadership at the University of Nevada, Las Vegas, who has done so much to advance the research on and knowledge about academic deans in the United States

o James C. Sarros, professor of management at Monash University, for his collaboration in undertaking comprehensive studies of deans and heads of departments in Australia

Finally, we are grateful to Sandy Ogden, Megan Geiger, and Selene Vazquez for research and editorial assistance.

No matter whether you are just considering the creation of an academic leadership program or already have one that you would like to make even better, we hope that this study of best practices and emerging paradigms will be useful to you. Certainly we have enjoyed communicating with so many dedicated directors of creative centers and programs; universally they were passionate about what they did and committed to making their institutions even better. As you read this book, remember that what you do when you prepare others for academic leadership is critically important. We wish you the greatest possible success in your work to develop academic leadership in higher education.

December 2014   WALTER H. GMELCH
San Francisco, California

JEFFREY L. BULLER
Jupiter, Florida

I

THE CALL FOR ACADEMIC LEADERSHIP DEVELOPMENT

WHERE HAVE ALL THE leaders gone? Have they ever really been here? In the corporate world, some of the most widely quoted experts in management have complained that advances in leadership simply have not kept up with achievements in other areas:

> We have learned a great deal over the last decade about designing more sophisticated interventions to educate our future leaders. Yet in other ways, we have simply progressed from the Bronze Age of leadership development to the Iron Age. We have advanced, but we have yet to truly enter the Information Age. (Conger and Benjamin, 1999, 262–263)

If the situation is that dire among the Fortune 500, we in higher education must be in severe trouble indeed. Business may not yet have made it into the Information Age, but colleges and universities should count themselves lucky if they have progressed beyond the Stone Age. In 1996, more than two thousand academic leaders were surveyed, and only 3 percent reported that they had any systematic leadership development programs on their campuses (Gmelch, Wolverton, Wolverton, and Hermanson, 1996). Not much has changed in the past two decades. A 2013 study by Robert Cipriano and Richard Riccardi found that only 3.3 percent of department chairs came to their positions with formal course work in the administrative skills they need.

The same sorry state of affairs is likely to be true of deans as well. Many of them rose to their leadership positions because of their success at committee work and their duties as teachers and scholars, not because they had any formal training in the best way to run a program. Presidents and provosts may fare a little better. Although practically everyone in higher

I

education knows of upper administrators who came to their positions as the result of political appointments or successful careers in the military or corporate worlds, most university chief executive officers and chief academic officers have practical, on-the-job experience in academic settings. Most, too, have probably participated in formal leadership training programs like those run by the Harvard Institutes in Higher Education, Higher Education Resource Services, the American Council on Education, and others that are profiled throughout this book. In short, many administrators, at least at the college or department levels, begin their positions without:

○ Formal training
○ Significant prior experience
○ A clear understanding of the ambiguity and complexity of their roles
○ A solid grasp of what it means to lead within a system of shared governance
○ A realization that full-time administrative work requires not a mere shift in focus but a metamorphic change from what their perspective was as a faculty member, as well as a corresponding change in their self-image (the "Who am I now?" question)
○ An awareness of the full cost that administrative assignments will have to their careers as scholars, artists, and researchers
○ Preparation to balance their personal and professional lives

To put it bluntly, academic leadership is one of the few professions one can enter today with absolutely no training in, credentials for, or knowledge about the central duties of the position.

As a result, while institutions of higher education become increasingly complex, many academic leaders begin their jobs woefully unprepared for the challenges awaiting them. Only the very rare graduate program, like the PreDoctoral Leadership Development Institute at Rutgers University (www.odl.rutgers.edu/pldi/), makes a sustained effort to provide leadership training to potential faculty members before they receive their PhD. And it is not as though the dangers of a lack of administrative training have not been identified. For years, blue ribbon commissions and executive reports from such organizations as the American Council on Education (Eckel, Hill, and Green, 1998; Kim and Cook, 2013), the Kellogg Commission (Beinike and Sublett, 1999), the Association of Governing Boards of Universities and Colleges (Eckel, 2012), and the

Global Consortium of Higher Education (Acker, 1999) have been calling for bolder and better college and university leadership. Nevertheless, little has changed. Despite the high profile given these white papers when they are released, there is still no universally accepted credential or certification process that indicates who is qualified to deal with the opportunities and challenges of higher education today. Even on the campus level, the literature is all but silent on best practices for developing deans, directors, and department chairs. There is simply no broad consensus as to what effective leadership training looks like at the level of the system, institution, program, or individual discipline.

The sheer magnitude of this problem is all but overwhelming. Nearly fifty thousand people currently serve as department chairs in the United States, with about a quarter of them being replaced each year. Deans, on the average, serve six years. The training programs provided to most of those who will fill the resulting vacancies may charitably be described as episodic and well intentioned. In-house programs are often only half a day long, with more extensive retreats rarely extending beyond two or three days. Many sessions at these workshops are devoted to legal and fiscal issues; the goal, it would appear, is to keep the institution out of trouble (and out of the *Chronicle of Higher Education*) rather than to develop well-rounded academic leaders. Even some very good programs, which hire a skilled trainer or experienced administrator for an intense, multiday workshop, often deal with only general issues. Outside consultants may be experts in their areas, but they cannot be expected to know the local culture of every institution they visit. (We know: we are those consultants.) For all these reasons, it is not an exaggeration to conclude that the development of academic leadership is one of the most misunderstood, least studied, and most critical management challenges that exist in higher education today.

The Cost of Poor Administrative Preparation

Our failure to provide adequate training for leaders at colleges and universities affects us in several important ways.

Programs Suffer

Higher education is undergoing a period of intense change. Academic programs are facing increased competition for resources, including students (whom we often describe as our most important resources), as for-profit universities, nonprofit universities, and online universities all compete with one another for the same tuition dollars. Moreover, low-cost or no-cost sources of higher education—such as MOOCs (massive open online courses), iTunes University, academic podcasts, the Teaching Company, Rosetta Stone Language Courses, and the like—mean that potential students have a far greater menu of educational choices than they ever had before. In order to be nimble enough to respond to all the challenges their programs face, chairs, directors, and deans cannot afford to approach administration with the belief that "I'll be able to pick it up as I go along." If these administrators do not hit the ground running, their programs will suffer, perhaps irreparably, because their competitors will be succeeding while they are still winding their way up the learning curve.

Institutions Suffer

Because of their complexity, colleges and universities are governed by what sometimes seems to be a bewildering array of rules and regulations. There are institutional policies, state educational guidelines, state and federal laws, accreditation requirements for both the school as a whole and individual programs, trustee or legislative initiatives, and more. Administrators who are unaware of how all these policies fit together might act in a way that leaves their institutions liable for fines, damages, and other sanctions. For example, someone who is unfamiliar with where academic freedom ends and protection against hate speech begins could make a decision that results in a lawsuit that proves disastrous to the institution and its reputation. Members of a governing board sometimes place pressure on administrators to act in a way that would violate the principles of academic freedom and thus put the school's accreditation in jeopardy. With legislatures and governing boards taking more of an activist approach in their treatment of universities, even one poor decision—no matter how pure the administrator's intentions may have been—could set back the goals of the entire institution. Administrators need to know not only where these potential land mines are, but also what effective strategies exist for negotiating their way through them.

Individuals Suffer

Not being adequately prepared for the challenges of leading a college or department can wreak havoc with an administrator's career. It is not uncommon in higher education to hear about university presidents who either resign or are forced out of their positions in fewer than three years because they were not fully prepared for the job and the public scrutiny that came with it. While one article in the *Chronicle of Higher Education* describes university presidents as "Bruised, Battered, and

Loving It" (Glassner and Schapiro, 2013), another calls their occupation a "Precarious Profession" and notes that their time in office "is shrinking rapidly" (Fethke and Policano, 2012). That same sort of career damage occurs elsewhere on the institutional hierarchy as well. By not being adequately trained for the challenges they face, chairs, deans, and provosts sometimes experience votes of no confidence from the faculty that result in a swift and painful exit from their positions. Finding another administrative appointment after a public and humiliating failure is difficult. Even returning to the faculty can have its challenges. It can be difficult to restart a research agenda once it has been interrupted for several years. As a result, many well-intentioned administrators find their careers stalled because they got in far over their heads in terms of leadership challenges. Even worse, their personal lives may suffer in the meantime because they end up spending so much time trying to address a rapidly spiraling series of problems that they stint their obligations to their family and other loved ones. They come away from their brief administrative careers convinced that becoming a chair or dean was the worst mistake they ever made.

But Don't Current Programs for University Administrators Already Fill This Need?

It can seem a little hard to reconcile our claim that leadership training is lacking in higher education with the numerous advertisements found in professional journals that promote conferences, consultants, and publications intended to help administrators improve their performance. Certainly a broad range of programs and resources exists, and these opportunities can be a valuable component in a comprehensive program for academic leadership development. The following are examples of just a few of the programs and services available for training administrators in higher education:

- o A number of organizations like the American Council on Education (www.acenet.edu/leadership/Pages/default.aspx) and the Committee on Institutional Cooperation (www.cic.net/faculty /academic-leadership-development) offer well-established programs to groups ranging from potential faculty leaders all the way to university presidents and system chancellors.
- o IDEA Education offers a feedback system for department chairs (ideaedu.org/services/department-chairs), as well as access to consultants in a wide variety of administrative areas (ideaedu.org/services/consulting-services).

o Kansas State University sponsors the annual Academic Chairpersons Conference that assembles experts on a variety of topics related to leadership issues in higher education (www.dce.k-state.edu/conf/academicchairpersons).

o Each summer Harvard University conducts three well-established and intense programs in academic leadership development. The Institute for Educational Management is intended for senior-level administrators like presidents and vice presidents, the Management Development Program is intended for midlevel administrators, and the Institute for Management and Leadership in Education is intended for deans and academic vice presidents who are roughly in the middle of their careers (www.gse.harvard.edu/ppe/programs/higher-education/portfolio /index.html).

o Publishers that specialize in topics related to higher education, such as Jossey-Bass (www.departmentchairs.org/online-training.aspx) and Magna Publications (www.magnapubs.com/online/seminars/), regularly sponsor webinars on academic leadership and offer short DVD courses.

o Private training firms, such as the Center for Creative Leadership (www.ccl.org), ATLAS: Academic Training, Leadership, and Assessment Services (www.atlasleadership.com), the Center for the Study of Academic Leadership, the Academy of Academic Leaders (www.academicleaders.org), and Elite Leadership Training (www.eliteleadershiptraining.com) conduct workshops on site at host universities or at regional conferences or both. They also offer the services of consultants who can coach individual administrators on possible solutions to their most pressing problems.

We give more examples of national programs in academic leadership development in the appendix.

The fact is that there is no dearth of expertise available on ways in which academic leaders can be more effective in their jobs. The programs we listed are among the resources we return to repeatedly throughout this book as we explore best practices in developing leadership. But there is a difference between a short-term leadership development opportunity and a sustained, ongoing program that provides the infrastructure administrators need in order to learn how to do their jobs better, enough consistency for them to receive reinforcement in their efforts, and a well-scaffolded structure that helps them move from an introductory to a more advanced level of understanding. What academic administrators need is not a program that lasts for a day, a week, or even a month but a career-long development program that meets them where they are and carries them wherever they need to be.

As Mike Myatt, managing director and chief strategy officer at N2growth, concludes in an article aptly titled "The #1 Reason Leadership Development Fails":

> You don't train leaders; you develop them—a subtle yet important distinction lost on many.... Don't train leaders, coach them, mentor them, disciple them, and develop them, but please don't attempt to train them. Where training attempts to standardize by blending to a norm and acclimating to the status quo, development strives to call out the unique and differentiate by shattering the status quo. Training is something leaders dread and will try and avoid, whereas they will embrace and look forward to development. Development is nuanced, contextual, collaborative, fluid, and above all else, actionable. (www.forbes.com/sites/mikemyatt/2012/12/19/the-1-reason-leadership -development-fails/)

In other words, the standard approach to leadership training in higher education tends to be short term and task oriented; it emphasizes strategy, tactics, and techniques and bases its approach on the assumption that if we can only teach administrators the best methods of leadership, then administrators will become the best leaders. But as important as it is in higher education for deans, chairs, and others to master such processes as strategic planning, program review, budget management, and outcomes assessment, these processes are really only the tools that leaders use; they are not keys to leadership itself. The development of genuine academic leadership must be much more comprehensive. It must combine a task orientation (What is our goal?) with a people orientation (How are we treating our stakeholders?). It must build on what administrators already know and who they already are rather than attempt to replace their current knowledge with a universal secret to administrative success. It should avoid giving people false impressions like the belief that all academic leaders fit a specific Myers-Briggs profile. It must, in short, emphasize development rather than training, growth rather than the mastery of technique.

A New Paradigm for Developing Academic Leaders

If higher education is to create a new, more effective paradigm for developing academic leaders, its most important requirement will be a commitment to take the time to do the job right. The transformation from successful faculty member—which involves one set of highly developed skills and attributes—to effective academic leader—which involves an entirely different set of highly developed skills and attributes—cannot be accomplished by reading a book or attending a seminar. In the corporate world, as well as in such pursuits as athletics and the fine arts, K. Anders Ericcson, Ralph Krampe, Clemens Tesch-Römer, and others have suggested that it takes roughly ten full years of preparation to achieve a world-class level of success (Ericsson, Krampe, and Tesch-Römer, 1993; Ericcson, 1996). In his 2008 book *Outliers*, Malcolm Gladwell popularized these findings, arguing that it takes ten thousand hours of practice (the equivalent of five years' worth of forty-hour workweeks) to become an expert in most fields. That timetable is one we should be quite familiar with in higher education. Most American universities, for example, expect that it will take faculty members six or seven years to attain the level of expertise expected for them to receive tenure, with an additional five to seven years required before they can be considered for promotion to the rank of full professor. Moreover, all that preparation comes only after the faculty member has already spent between three and ten years as a graduate student and postdoc. So if we assume that it takes ten to twenty years for a highly intelligent person to become an expert in an academic discipline, why do we assume that we can train academic leaders in a three-day workshop?

Case Study: The Academic Leadership Forum

As a way of understanding how a new paradigm for developing academic leaders might work at a college or university, we consider the example of the Academic Leadership Forum (ALF), a pilot program run by three deans—Walt Gmelch, Jim Melsa, and Ben Allen—at Iowa State University from 2000 until 2004 (Gmelch, 2013). The idea behind ALF was to incorporate learning about academic leadership with applying the concepts learned over an extended period of time. The program would thus be a workshop, learning laboratory, mentoring environment, and support group simultaneously, providing its participants with a more comprehensive understanding of how to be effective administrators than they would have received from course work alone. Its initial goals were:

1. To help its participants develop a better understanding of various leadership styles, motives, and roles played by department chairs and deans

2. To acquire the key leadership skills required to be an effective academic leader

3. To build a peer coaching system that could support academic leaders at the institution

4. To help department chairs and deans deal with the professional and personal challenges inherent in their positions

To achieve such ambitious goals, the developers of the program adapted appropriate elements from a corporate concept known as the 7-S model (Peters and Waterman, 1982; Stevens, 2001). The name of the model is derived from seven core components that can be divided into two subsets as follows:

THE THREE HARD S'S

1. Strategy
2. Structure
3. Systems

THE FOUR SOFT S'S

4. Staff
5. Skills
6. Style
7. Shared values

In order to understand how these seven elements work together to create an effective program of academic leadership development, we examine each of them individually.

Strategy

The originators of the ALF program based their strategy on existing research about the best ways to help new department chairs make the transition from faculty to administration (Gmelch and Miskin, 2004, 2011), new deans move through the various stages of their careers (Gmelch, Hopkins, and Damico, 2011), and new school administrators become socialized into their positions (Ortiz, 1982). This research suggested that any successful strategy for developing academic leaders must consist of three ingredients:

1. *A conceptual understanding of the unique roles and responsibilities that are associated with academic leadership.* Conceptual understanding involves the knowledge that administrators need in order to do their jobs effectively. It includes understanding the organizational culture and mastering the dynamics that distinguish the university from

other work environments. In addition, successful academic leaders have to know the perspectives or frameworks different stakeholders will use in order to understand their relationship to the college or university and how this affects their interactions with other institutional constituencies. In the area of academic leadership, development programs need to address two major aspects of conceptual understanding. First, as faculty members move from teaching and research to positions of administrative leadership, their understanding of their relationship to the institution, their work, and their colleagues will change in ways they may not anticipate. They need to be better prepared for what their new assignments, responsibilities, and relationships will entail. Second, the role that managers and leaders play in higher education is distinctly different from the role that bosses, supervisors, commanders, and directors play in other types of organizations (see Buller, 2013). In the approach developed by Lee Bolman and Terry Deal (2013), we may speak of four major frames through which organizational culture can be examined: its political, symbolic, human, and structural dimensions. As faculty members assume administrative roles, they approach their work in terms of the human and structural aspects of their leadership roles: Who are my primary stakeholders? Where does my area of authority begin and end on the organizational chart? But as they grow in their positions, the political and symbolic aspects of the job assume far more importance: Who possesses more power or influence at the institution than that person's title would suggest? What are the traditions and values of our institution that affect the way we see things and make decisions? Universities have a great deal of experience in how best to teach students about leadership. That body of conceptual knowledge can also be used to improve the effectiveness of administrators. We can begin by teaching them, for example, what it means to build a community, empower others, and set direction in the distinctive organizational culture of higher education (see Gmelch, Hopkins, and Damico, 2011).

2. *Regular practice in the skills necessary to be an effective leader, particularly in how to work successfully with diverse stakeholders, such as faculty, staff, students, other administrators, and external constituencies.* In order to perform their roles and fulfill their responsibilities effectively, academic leaders need to hone their skills. While there is much that they can learn through clinical approaches such as seminars, workshops, and lectures, conceptual understanding alone does not guarantee successful leadership. They must then practice what they've learned by means of simulations, case studies, role plays, action planning, and on-the-job training. Many of the training opportunities we mentioned are designed

for institutions that can afford to send their administrators off site for a three- or four-day program. While these efforts can be highly effective in conveying the knowledge needed for skill development, Jay Alden Conger (1992) found more than twenty years ago that leadership training has only limited value unless there is appropriate follow-up. Conger discovered that the most effective approach is to provide training in work teams (e.g., a chair along with faculty members from his or her department or a dean with several of his or her chairs and associate deans). The work team would attend the same program, use simulations and role plays to practice what they learned, and then continue supporting and reinforcing each other's efforts after they returned to campus. Incorporating these ideas, the founders of the ALF program designed it so that it included teams of deans, associate deans, and department chairs in an ongoing activity that would provide sufficient practice of the concepts discussed. (For an example of a leadership development initiative that has skill development as a central focus, see the discussion of Cornell University's Leadership Development Academy in chapter 5.)

3. *A formal process of reflection that helps leaders learn from their mistakes, base their decisions on solid core values, act with greater integrity and transparency, and continue to grow as dedicated professionals.* Even when administrators understand their roles and possess the skills needed to perform their duties, they are not yet in a position to make the leap that Jim Collins (2001) calls the transition "from good to great." Leadership development is first and foremost an inner journey. Self-knowledge, personal awareness, and corrective feedback must be part of the strategy for each leader's development. In *The Reflective Practitioner*, Donald Schön (1983) asked, "What is the kind of knowing in which competent practitioners engage? How is professional knowing like and unlike the kinds of knowledge presented in academic textbooks, scientific papers, and learned journals?" (p. viii). Schön's thesis is that effective professionals engage in what he calls reflection-in-action, an attempt to understand what can be learned from situations that do not go as planned. Results that deviate from our expectations cause us to question our underlying assumptions and, Schön concluded, successful leaders develop by allowing these underlying assumptions to evolve continually. Merely engaging in activities by rote or enforcing policies "because that's what the manual says" results in stagnation, not personal growth. The goal for college administrators therefore should be to reflect continually on what it is they are trying to do, why they made that decision, whether their actions lead to the desired results, and how they might respond differently to similar situations in the future.

In our conversations with directors of various leadership development programs around the world, we found that these three ingredients recur frequently in highly effective initiatives. We will encounter them again in our discussion of best practices in preparing faculty members for leadership roles.

An important aspect of the strategy behind the ALF program was a consideration of how each of these three ingredients related to the other two. For instance, at the intersection of developing conceptual understanding and practicing leadership skills, participants in the program would be required to apply what they learned to real situations. By reflecting on how their leadership skills were improving, they would discover new ways to incorporate these skills into their regular practices. And by reflecting on the insights gained from their development of conceptual understanding, they would find new ways to ground leadership theory in application. Putting all these elements together, the participants in ALF would, it was hoped, emerge from the program with a much more nuanced approach to academic administration, one we might call comprehensive academic leadership (CAL; see figure 1.1).

Figure 1.1 Academic Leadership Development

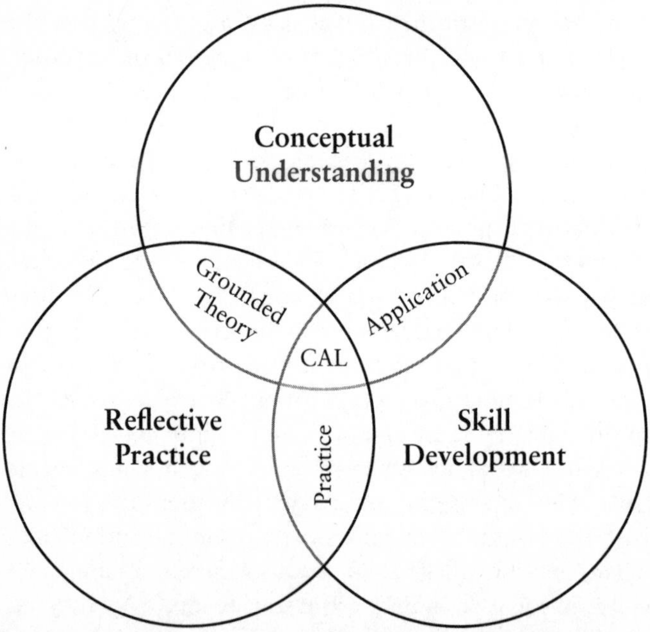

Note: *CAL = comprehensive academic leadership.*

Structure

When we talk about the structure of a leadership development program, what we are referring to is its operating procedure and basic principles of organization. In the case of ALF, this structure was determined by a steering committee consisting of the deans, administrative assistants, and one department chair from each of the three colleges represented. The charge of this group was to determine how content for the program would be selected, what form the group's various activities would take, and which research design would be used to determine the project's effectiveness. After exploring several options, this steering committee recommended that the program start with a series of monthly three-hour sessions devoted to topics that were identified as important by the participants themselves. This core structure would be supplemented with workshops, guest presentations, and seminars that were available either through the university or in the community. For example, early in the program's operation, Peter Senge, the director of the Center for Organizational Learning at the MIT Sloan School of Management, was visiting the local education community to discuss systems thinking; that opportunity was incorporated into ALF. Between sessions, the participants expanded their knowledge by reading a set of resources they developed, including articles, handouts, websites, and books. The goal of this structure was to provide regularity to the program, giving it substance and a predictable schedule, while preserving momentum between formal activities through "homework assignments" and the chance to put theory into practice on the job.

Systems

A key system developed to improve the effectiveness of ALF was the creation of peer support pairs that were called partners in academic leadership (PAL). Each PAL consisted of two administrators who held comparable positions in different colleges. The goal of this initiative was to provide a system in which participants could examine each other's administrative decisions in a supportive and nonjudgmental manner. The PALs met periodically to expand their understanding of college administration by offering a small platform in which the members could discuss their leadership challenges and opportunities in a practical way, provide honest assessment of each other's strengths and weaknesses through candid but collegial feedback, offer a high degree of confidentiality when sensitive matters needed to be considered, and provide participants with a chance to focus on issues that were too specific to individual situations to be explored by the whole group. Each PAL was also charged with creating a learning experience or leadership development session devoted to one of the topics selected by ALF participants. This system had the benefit of bringing the PALs together around a common task and taking full advantage of each member's expertise. To enable them to try out new ideas, each participant received a stipend of $250 to use as he or she deemed appropriate. The participants could thus pilot training materials or acquire books on academic leadership without cost to themselves or their academic units.

Staff

In designing an effective program for developing campus leadership, certain personnel questions arise immediately. Who is the program's target audience? Who will develop and supervise the program's activities? How many participants should be included in the program so that it will reach the critical mass needed for meaningful interaction and exchange of ideas without becoming so large as to be unwieldy?

At Iowa State, it seemed most appropriate to pilot the project in three colleges: Business, Education, and Engineering. As professional colleges, these units had missions more similar to one another than those of some of the other colleges. In addition, these three colleges had what struck the developers of the program as the right number of deans, associate deans, and department chairs to make the program viable. It would be large enough for the pilot project to make a noticeable difference in the quality of the university's academic leadership, but it was small and nimble enough to respond quickly if midcourse corrections proved to be necessary. Finally, the three colleges chosen for the pilot were those in which the administrative staff members were most supportive of the idea. This last factor proved to be the most significant. Every complex initiative encounters rough spots during its implementation. As workloads increase and other issues arise throughout the academic year, it is easy for leadership development to be placed on a back burner. Having an initial set of participants with a strong personal commitment to the idea became essential. Activities ended up being successful because they mattered to those who engaged in them. This, then, became an important insight into building an academic leadership program that is truly effective.

> The staff of pilot programs should be people who are strongly committed to its success. While there may be a temptation to pilot a concept with a representative sample of academic disciplines, if the first group of participants is not heavily invested in the program's success, it is likely to die on the vine.

There was also one unanticipated advantage derived from ALF's original staffing: the colleges of Business, Education, and Engineering were units in which there was a great deal of disciplinary expertise in such areas as management, strategic planning, budgeting, education leadership, benchmarking, and entrepreneurial approaches to new opportunities. By being able to draw from a large pool of knowledge and experience, the program could act as an in-house think tank. Expenses were low since there was little need to hire external consultants who might know a great deal about relevant topics but not about the distinctive organizational culture of Iowa State University. In terms of staffing, therefore, launching a successful leadership development program is a matter of exploring where three major factors come together:

1. Which units have the strongest interest in such a program?
2. Which units have the type of expertise that this program needs?
3. Which units are sufficiently similar to one another that they'll be able to learn from each other's mistakes, best practices, and past experience?

Skills

In terms of the content of the program, the ALF participants needed to identify the skills that they regarded as most important for successful academic leadership. This information was provided through focus groups and a survey similar to one administered to academic leaders nationally (Gmelch and Miskin, 2004, 2011) and internationally (Gmelch, Wolverton, Wolverton, and Sarros, 1999). Use of this instrument allowed a high degree of reliability and validity, as well as an opportunity to draw comparisons between the ALF participants and the national sample. The survey consisted of five general sections:

1. Background and demographic information
2. Job satisfaction as an academic leader: Cronbach standardized alpha (.90)
3. Stress: Cronbach standardized alpha (.96), including role conflict and ambiguity
4. Perceptions of preparation and training
5. Measured levels of reflective practices including six subsections on leadership identity and self-evaluation

(Note: The Cronbach standardized alpha is a measure of internal consistency. The goal on a survey of this kind is to get as close as possible to 1, indicating that respondents were consistent in their answers to different survey items that asked essentially the same question. In general, any score equal to or greater than .9 is considered excellent.) The survey addressed thirty-six common administrative tasks and yielded useful information about the skills ALF most needed to address. Chief among these needs were:

1. Managing time properly, particularly the ability to maintain currency in research while performing administrative duties
2. Providing genuine leadership, not mere management, within the distinctive organizational structure of higher education
3. Instituting effective faculty development programs
4. Strategic thinking and creating a compelling vision for the future
5. Coaching and counseling faculty members so as to improve their performance
6. Making sound decisions
7. Communicating effectively with stakeholders
8. Managing conflict
9. Working harmoniously with upper administrative levels
10. Promoting teamwork
11. Building community
12. Leading change

As a further validation of the importance of these topics, it was discovered that they mirrored those found in most leadership development programs available at that time (Conger and Benjamin, 1999).

Style

Every organization, large and small, has its distinctive culture or style. From the frugal environment at Amazon.com where everyone's focus is expected to be on work all day long to the mixture of work and play at Google, where massages are subsidized and the food is free, organizations develop a style based on both the personalities of their leaders and the needs of their industries (efficiency versus innovation, swift execution versus long-term development). Leadership initiatives are no different from any other. Some express clarity of organization—detailed workshop plans every month, online request forms for mentors, constantly updated libraries of new resources—while others encourage a more relaxed approach to leadership—an informal agreement to have lunch once or twice a month to discuss leadership issues, a website that's updated whenever someone has something new to contribute, a swap-and-share system for exchanging books rather than a highly organized library.

The style of ALF may best be described as business casual. It relied on a regular series of programs and meetings that helped provide structure to the endeavor but did not find the need for more elaborate rules, bylaws, votes, and even the keeping of minutes. Each leadership development initiative will have its own style that reflects the personalities of the participants, the needs of the institution, and the leadership philosophy that led to its creation.

Shared Values

One book that guided ALF's conceptual framework was *Common Fire* (1996), in which Laurent Parks Daloz, Cheryl Keen, James P. Keen, and Sharon Daloz Parks posit that the pace of modern life has robbed people of "hearth time"—time to sit in front of the fire, reflect, and engage in meaningful conversation. In a similar way, families have lost "table time," the time to sit together and share their experiences, and communities have lost "plaza time," the time to engage in conversations about what occurred that day and why it should be regarded as important. A major goal of ALF was to reverse this trend and create "commons time" for deans and chairs that would help them reflect on their experiences and learn from each other's successes and failures. To some extent, the PALs helped achieve this goal. Twice a month, these pairs would meet to talk informally about what went well, what got in the way, and what that person may have done differently if given a chance for a "do over." But in a larger sense, it also became apparent that the entire program provided an opportunity for administrators to explore shared values and recognize how these values, even more than the skills and techniques they learned, helped guide their administrative practice. In fact, institutions that are developing their own programs in academic leadership would do well by considering the following principle:

> No one has ever transformed a college or university by adopting a clever technique. They transformed it by embodying worthy values.

But if that is the case, which values should leadership programs be promoting? And is it really possible to instill these values in someone who does not already have them? There are several ways of answering these questions. In one sense, of course, our answer must be that the values leaders should follow as they seek to develop their own leadership skills are those they truly believe in and already have. In other words, one aspect of leadership development requires us to find out who we really are and what our core principles are. Almost any set of values a person currently has can open the door to effective academic leadership—for example:

o If you are the sort of person who always sticks up for the underdog, you can base your leadership on giving a voice to the voiceless.

o If you are a natural-born teacher who only reluctantly accepted an administrative role, you can be the type of leader who mentors others on the best ways to succeed in their own teaching.

o If you find yourself aggravated by even minor examples of carelessness and insignificant typographical errors, you can be the type of leader who sets and embodies the highest possible standards for accuracy.

o Even if you regard yourself as the most self-centered person on the faculty, you can be the type of leader who encourages others to act independently without relying on others to clean up the mistakes they themselves made.

In short, leadership development does not require administrators to embrace any specific set of core values. But it does require them to be candid with themselves about what their own core values are. A good leadership development program helps administrators find the best possible way to advocate for their stakeholders that remains true to the values he or she regards as most important (Cashman, 2008).

But, as we said, that is only one way of answering the question of which values should be promoted in a leadership development program. Another school of thought claims, to paraphrase George Orwell, that all values are equal, but some values are more equal than others.

> Various researchers argue that certain values are essential to the value systems of good leaders. These primarily include honesty and integrity, but also encompass other important values such as concern for others, fairness, and justice.... Honesty is the most admired characteristic of leaders, followed by their forward-looking nature, ability to inspire, and competence. (Russell, 2001, 77, citing Kouzes and Posner, 1993, and Posner and Schmidt, 1992)

James Kouzes and Barry Posner surveyed fifteen hundred managers in many fields, not merely in higher education, and found three most important values they wanted in their supervisors:

1. *Integrity* (is truthful, is trustworthy, has character, has convictions)
2. *Competence* (is capable, is productive, is efficient)
3. *Leadership* (is inspiring, is decisive, provides direction) (Kouzes and Posner, 1993)

Moreover, when Kouzes and Posner broadened their study, surveying more than seventy-five thousand people in 1987, 2002, and 2010, they discovered great consistency in the values people wanted their leaders to demonstrate. In order of preference, these are the top five adjectives people say they want their leaders to be:

1. Honest
2. Forward looking
3. Inspiring
4. Competent
5. Intelligent

It is interesting to note that these characteristics consistently ranked far higher in Kouzes and Posner's survey than other traits we might expect to head the list, such as being cooperative, courageous, caring, and loyal. For this reason, it might be preferable to conclude that while there's no single list of values that determines which academic leaders succeed and which fail, most people expect their leaders to demonstrate integrity, honesty, transparency, and reliability. If leaders make a mistake, admit it, and indicate what they have learned from the process, most faculties tend to be forgiving. But once leaders violate the trust of the faculty, it is all but impossible to heal the rift.

As a way of helping leaders align their decisions more fully with their core values, ALF was designed to guide administrators toward becoming more intentional about their decisions before they made them (How does the action I'm about to take reflect the values that I deem important? How does it benefit my stakeholders?) and more reflective about those decisions once their consequences were clear (Were there any unintended and undesirable outcomes of my action? Is it appropriate to make a midcourse correction to produce better outcomes?). The question then arose: How could the creators of the program determine whether their efforts in making these improvements were successful?

Assessment Methodology

The impact of ALF was measured using a value-added approach. Various assessments were made of the participants before the beginning of the program in order to obtain baseline data: What was their current level of knowledge, skill, and use of established best practices? Then those same assessments were conducted again as the program continued in order to determine whether it was making a difference. One of the methods used in this assessment was the survey described in the "Skills" section above. An additional method was the use of focus groups, which began being conducted four months after the completion of the ALF program's first year. Staff from the Research Institute for Studies in Education (RISE) conducted two focus groups, one of department chairs and the other of deans and associate deans, to help determine what impact (if any) participation in the program had on their leadership. Using the same theoretical framework that guided other ALF activities, the questions posed to the participants focused on their conceptual understanding, skill development, and use of reflective practice in their professional activities (Gmelch, Reason, Schuh, and Shelley, 2002).

Information obtained from surveys was examined using the Wilcoxon signed-ranks test (Green, Salkind, and Akey, 2000) in order to determine where statistically significant patterns arose. In addition, responses made in the focus groups sessions were transcribed, coded, and examined for consistent themes. The interpretation of these results focused on themes that emerged within each transcript, a process that Elliot Mishler (1986) called interpretive coding. Themes across the two transcripts were also identified, using a process known as inductive coding (Strauss, 1987) in which the researcher does not force the data to fit into preselected categories (a priori coding) but allows themes and connections to emerge logically from the responses themselves. Finally, these repeated themes were verified independently by two professional staff members from RISE using the approach pioneered by Richard Krueger (1998).

Leadership Development Results

Before participating in ALF, nearly half of the participants (47.6 percent) described themselves as "equally a faculty and an administrator." A third of the respondents (33.3 percent) considered their professional identity to be solely "academic faculty members," while only 19 percent (none of them department chairs) indicated that they saw themselves entirely as administrators. One interesting effect of the program was a change in this self-perception. Once ALF was under way, 74 percent of the respondents indicated that they were "equally" faculty and administration, and approximately a fifth (21 percent) indicated they were administrators alone. Only one respondent (5 percent) saw his or her sole professional identity as a member of the faculty. That conclusion was corroborated by the survey results. When the Wilcoxon signed-ranks test was applied to the data, it was clear that the program had produced a significant change ($Z = -2.236$, $p < .05$) in terms of how the participants viewed their professional identities: Overall the participants experienced a shift away from viewing their roles primarily as faculty members and toward an identity that balanced faculty and administrative components. In the focus groups as well, analysis of their comments indicated that the participants were demonstrating a more sophisticated understanding of their academic leadership roles as the program continued.

When the survey responses were examined in terms of the Bolman and Deal (2013) four frames model described earlier, the self-identified strengths of the administrators fell into distinct frames of leadership. For example, leaders with a structural frame tended to emphasize the importance of organizational goals, rules, polices, and hierarchies. Those with a human resources frame recognized the interdependence between the organization and the people composing it and gave priority to the issue of how each individual fit into the overall organization. Leaders with a political frame tended to view power, the formation of coalitions, and bargaining to advance their work, while those with a symbolic frame relied more heavily on the emotional impact of images, traditions, and rituals.

On the presurvey, the participants as a whole scored highest in the human resources frame, followed by the structural frame, the symbolic frame, and the political frame. While no statistically significant differences were found between the pre- and postsurvey results, the symbolic and political frame somewhat increased both their raw scores and their relationship with the other frames; consequently, the structural frame demonstrated the largest decrease in importance. Bolman and Deal (2013) and Tierney (1987) highlight the importance of symbolism in leadership, especially in leadership that truly transforms an organization. For this reason, the movement from the structural and human resource frames toward the political and symbolic observed in ALF participants, although minor, was regarded as a sign of progress. In addition, Tierney suggested that symbolic communication is essential to communicating organizational values, a vital component of transformational leadership. Finally, the movement toward political and symbolic leadership indicates that the participants were developing a more sophisticated conceptual understanding of leadership (as opposed to mere management of their programs) as a result of their participation in ALF. That sophistication was demonstrated through a shift in the participants' emphasis on transactional motivations (career advancement, financial gain, power) to transformational motivations (the chance to contribute to an organization, influence faculty development, experience personal growth).

Participation in ALF appeared to demonstrate a strong correlation with increases in such skills as time management and achieving work-life balance. Respondents reported that they felt more prepared and effective in thirty-two of the thirty-six administrative tasks addressed in the pre- and postprogram survey. They also reported a greater ability to balance their own professional needs with the needs of the institution. Nevertheless, ALF participants reported little progress in being able to better integrate scholarly activity into their administrative duties. Fully two-thirds of the respondents reported they were "dissatisfied" with the level of their scholarship and believed that it suffered after they assumed their leadership positions.

Perhaps the greatest progress indicated by the participants came in the area of reflective practice. The conceptual understanding part of the program increased the participants' awareness of the importance of reflection, and their work in the PAL groups gave them an opportunity to put these ideas into practice. Survey results indicated that the participants were highly appreciative of the networking component of ALF and the opportunity it provided to reflect on the experience from a broader perspective. In fact, one of the most salient findings of the ALF study related to the participants' increased job satisfaction. The administrators left the program with a renewed commitment to and enthusiasm for their academic leadership positions. They reported statistically significant increases in satisfaction with the pace of their work, administrative workload, and overall job satisfaction.

Conclusion

Although ALF served only a limited group of administrators for a limited period of time, the lessons learned from this pilot provide valuable insights into other academic units, institutions, and university systems as they proceed to develop their own academic leadership programs. In the next chapter, we outline these lessons and what they can tell us about ways of helping administrators become more effective at their jobs. Then we proceed to apply those lessons to the 7-S model described earlier, relate them to the best practices in use in other academic leadership programs, and provide a flexible blueprint for how others can create their own programs for developing academic leadership.

REFERENCES

Acker, D. G. (1999). *Proceedings of the Inaugural Conference of the Global Consortium of Higher Education and Research for Agriculture.* Ames: Iowa State University Press.

Beinike, J. A., & Sublett, R. H. (1999). *Leadership lessons and competencies: Learning from the Kellogg National Fellowship Program.* Battle Creek, MI: Kellogg Foundation.

Bolman, L. G., & Deal, T. E. (2013). *Reframing organizations: Artistry, choice, and leadership* (5th ed.). San Francisco, CA: Jossey-Bass, 2013.

Buller, J. L. (2013). *Positive academic leadership: How to stop putting out fires and start making a difference.* San Francisco, CA: Jossey-Bass, 2013.

Cashman, K. (2008). *Leadership from the inside out.* San Francisco, CA: Berrett-Koehler.

Cipriano, R. E., & Riccardi, R. L. (2013). A continuing analysis of the unique department chair. *Department Chair, 23*(4), 20–23.

Collins, J. C. (2001). *Good to great: Why some companies make the leap—and others don't.* New York, NY: HarperBusiness.

Conger, J. A. (1992). *Learning to lead: The art of transforming managers into leaders.* San Francisco, CA: Jossey-Bass.

Conger, J. A., & Benjamin, B. (1999). *Building leaders: How successful companies develop the next generation.* San Francisco, CA: Jossey-Bass.

Daloz, L. A., Keen, C. H., Keen, J. P., & Parks, S. D. (1996). *Common fire: Lives of commitment in a complex world.* Boston, MA: Beacon Press.

Eckel, P. D. (2012). Prescriptions for change: Can ideas from health care cure higher education's ills? *Trusteeship, 20*(4), 22–25.

Eckel, P. D., Hill, B., & Green, M. (1998). *On route to transformation.* Washington, DC: American Council on Education.

Ericsson, K. A. (Ed.). (1996). *The road to excellence: The acquisition of expert performance in the arts and sciences, sports, and games.* Mahwah, NJ: Erlbaum.

Ericsson, K. A., Krampe, R. T., & Tesch-Römer, C. (1993). The role of deliberate practices in the acquisition of expert performance. *Psychological Review 100*(3), 363–406.

Fethke, G. C., & Policano, A. J. (2012, July 23). The precarious profession of university president. *Chronicle of Higher Education.* Retrieved from http://chronicle.com/article/The-Precarious-Profession-of/132987/

Gladwell, M. (2008). *Outliers: The story of success.* New York, NY: Little, Brown.

Glassner B., & Schapiro, M. (2013). College presidents: Bruised, battered, and loving it. *Chronicle of Higher Education*. Retrieved from http://chronicle.com/article/College-Presidents-Bruised/137227/

Gmelch, W. H. (2013). The development of academic leaders. *International Journal of Leadership and Change, 1*(1), 26–35.

Gmelch, W. H., Hopkins, D., & Damico, S. (2011). *Seasons of a dean's life: Understanding the role and building leadership capacity.* Sterling, VA: Stylus.

Gmelch, W. H., & Miskin, V. D. (2004). *Chairing the academic department.* Madison, WI: Atwood.

Gmelch, W. H., & Miskin, V. D. (2011). *Department chair leadership skills.* Madison, WI: Atwood.

Gmelch, W. H., Reason, R. D., Schuh, J. H., & Shelley, M. C. (2002). *The call for academic leaders: The academic leadership forum evaluation report.* Ames: Iowa State University, College of Education.

Gmelch, W. H., Wolverton, M., Wolverton, M. L., & Hermanson, M. (1996). *The 1996 National Survey of Academic Deans in Higher Education.* Pullman, WA: Center for Academic Leadership.

Gmelch, W. H., Wolverton, M., Wolverton, M. L., & Sarros, J. C. (1999). The academic dean: An imperiled species searching for balance. *Research in Higher Education, 40,* 717–740.

Green, M. F., Salkind, N. J., & Akey, T. M. (2000). *Using SPSS for Windows: Analyzing and understanding data.* Upper Saddle, NJ: Prentice Hall.

Kim, Y. M., & Cook, B. J. (2013). *On the pathway to the presidency 2013: Characteristics of higher education's senior leadership.* Washington, DC: American Council on Education.

Kouzes, J. M., & Posner, B. Z. (1993). *Credibility: How leaders gain and lose it, why people demand it.* San Francisco, CA: Jossey-Bass.

Krueger, R. A. (1998). *Analyzing and reporting focus group results.* Thousand Oaks, CA: Sage.

Mishler, E. (1986). *Research interviewing: Context and narrative.* Cambridge, MA: Harvard University Press.

Ortiz, F. I. (1982). *Career patterns in education.* New York, NY: Praeger.

Peters, T., & Waterman, R. J. (1982). *In search of excellence: Lessons from America's best-run companies.* New York, NY: Warner Books.

Posner, B. Z., & Schmidt, W. H. (1992). Values and the American manager. *California Management Review, 34*(3), 80–94.

Russell, R. F. (2001). The role of values in servant leadership. *Leadership and Organizational Development Journal, 22*(2), 76–84.

Schön, D. A. (1983). *The reflective practitioner: How professionals think in action.* New York, NY: Basic Books.

Stevens, M. (2001). *Extreme management*. New York, NY: Warner Books.

Strauss, A. (1987). *Qualitative analysis for social scientists*. Cambridge: Cambridge University Press.

Tierney, W. G. (1987). *Symbolism and presidential perceptions of leadership*. Washington, DC: Office of Educational Research and Improvement.

RESOURCES

Bolman, L. G., & Gallos, J. V. (2011). *Reframing academic leadership*. San Francisco, CA: Jossey-Bass.

Gardner, J. W. (1987). *Leadership development*. Washington, DC: Independent Sector.

Jackson, E. (2012). *The seven habits of spectacularly unsuccessful executives*. Retrieved from http://www.forbes.com/sites/ericjackson/2012/01/02/the -seven-habits-of-spectacularly-unsuccessful-executives/&

2

STRATEGY

IF WE WERE TO regard Iowa State University's Academic Leadership Forum (ALF) program as a test case for what institutions should consider as they develop strategies for their own programs in academic leadership development, what conclusions would we draw from this experiment? Certainly we would need to take into consideration the unique cultural, political, and social climates of each institution or university system when planning an effective leadership program for administrators. In addition to that important principle, we may cite the following twelve lessons learned from ALF as a flexible blueprint that most schools can use in launching or improving an academic leadership initiative:

Lesson 1: Cohort groups can play a key role in most leadership development programs. Since leadership by its very nature involves relations with others and cannot be practiced in a vacuum, a successful leadership development program should offer numerous opportunities to confer, work, and interact with colleagues who are experiencing similar challenges. In fact, a combination of different sized cohort groups is probably the best possible solution. Very small groups, like the partners in academic leadership (PALs) developed at Iowa State, give the program an opportunity for peer-to-peer mentoring and allow participants to discuss issues they would prefer not to mention in front of the full group. Larger groups, like the monthly three-hour sessions scheduled for ALF, can bring a broader perspective to the issues addressed in the program and reinforce the participants' understanding that no one is alone in facing administrative challenges.

Lesson 2: Leadership development programs should not merely serve as training programs; they should also act as support groups. There is a great deal more to academic leadership development than mastering a body of knowledge and honing administrative skills. Many participants in ALF believed that the most important benefit they received from the program was the support network it provided across campus. By having regular opportunities to discuss significant issues with others who were affected by them, the participants developed a sense that "we're all in this together." That sense of camaraderie serves as an antidote to administrative burnout. For example, the transition to an administrative position can be very difficult for a newly appointed chair who, while serving as a faculty member, had often socialized with other members of the faculty on a level of equality. The leadership development program offers access to a set of colleagues who "get it." Moreover, the higher up the administrative hierarchy one goes, the more isolating it can feel. Leadership development programs serve to counteract this sense of loneliness by providing a peer group that understands what the person is going through and can offer sympathy even when it can't offer solutions.

Lesson 3: Leadership development must be an ongoing process. As educators we understand why learning that occurs in easily digestible amounts over an extended period of time is often retained better than learning that occurs in high concentration within a very confined period. That is why most students tend to retain what they learn in foreign language classes better if the course meets an hour a day all year rather than three hours a day all summer. In much the same way, immersion-based leadership training workshops, regardless of whether they take place over a weekend or an entire summer, frequently fail to change people's behavior. There just is not enough follow-through. After the chair or dean returns from the workshop, new priorities arise, and the lessons that seemed so life changing only a few weeks before are quickly forgotten. To be truly successful, a leadership program should adopt a systems approach that builds on continual, progressive, and sequential development, offering frequent constructive feedback and opportunities for ongoing reflection. Management consultant Peter Bregman suggested in his blog for the *Harvard Business Review,*

> There is a massive difference between what we know about leadership and what we do as leaders. I have never seen a leader fail because he or she didn't know enough about leadership. In fact, I can't remember ever meeting a leader who didn't know enough about leadership. What makes leadership hard

isn't the theoretical, it's the practical. It's not about knowing what to say or do. It's about whether you're willing to experience the discomfort, risk, and uncertainty of saying or doing it. (http://blogs.hbr.org/bregman/2013/07/why-so-many-leadership -program.html)

Developing the ability to live with that discomfort, risk, and uncertainty does not come about through lectures and reading. It comes about through ongoing reflective practice and skill development on the job; shortcuts simply are not possible. If participants are going to commit themselves to effective leadership development, they must be prepared to engage in a long-term process.

Lesson 4: Leaders can create and deliver their own learning opportunities. Although training opportunities provided by external consultants and organizations can be valuable components of a comprehensive development program in academic leadership, they should never constitute the entire program. Each institution and university system includes numerous experts who, because of either their extensive experience or academic training, can provide administrators with valuable insights into conflict management, team building, strategic planning, budget supervision, faculty recruitment, and other issues central to academic leadership. Moreover, local experts possess something that even the most accomplished consultant does not have: an intimate knowledge of the local culture and the people who compose it that makes each college or university different from every other. It is not uncommon in higher education to encounter a consultant who provides excellent advice that will not work in one setting or another. The systems are different, and the people who make up those systems are different. For this reason, making use of experts on your own faculty and staff provides a useful counterbalance to the tendency of outside experts and professional organizations to assume that academic leadership works in the same way everywhere.

Lesson 5: Successful leadership development programs require a supportive culture. It was established long ago that institutional change processes almost always fail if they do not receive a high level of commitment from the upper management. (See, e.g., Eckel, Hill, and Green, 1998.) The ALF program, while not dependent on resources from the university's central administration, did receive enthusiastic endorsements from the president and provost. That level of support can prove to be invaluable when the pressures of administrative work threaten to distract academic leaders from the program. Without overt recognition from upper administration that leadership development activities are worth the time and expense they require, participants may soon begin to drift away from the program or participate in its activities only halfheartedly. There are several ways in which this high level of support can be demonstrated. Most commonly, the CEO of the institution or university system will convene and provide a formal welcome at the group's opening meeting. But it is also possible for the upper administration to look favorably on continued leadership training when evaluating administrators under its supervision or lead by example through attendance at training programs itself. For instance, in the Academic Leadership Center, an initiative in which both state and private universities in the Kingdom of Saudi Arabia participate, the minister of higher education attends and is actively involved in all training sessions for university rectors (the presidents or chancellors). He makes a point of saying how useful he finds the sessions and how much he learns from them. As a result, almost all the rectors throughout the university system attend these sessions (their conclusion being, "My boss is going to be there, so I guess I'd better go too"), take them seriously ("My boss thinks these programs are important, so I guess I'd better be an active participant too"), and recommend leadership training to other administrators at the university ("My boss is always pleased when I attend these programs, so I'll be pleased if my deans and chairs attend them as well").

Lesson 6: Leadership programs tend to be most successful when they capitalize on small wins as they proceed. Karl Weick, the Rensis Likert Distinguished University Professor in the Ross School of Business at the University of Michigan, described a "small win" as a "concrete, implemented outcome of moderate importance" (1984, 43). When each small win builds on the previous one, participants in a program feel a sense of progress they would never experience if they were forced to wait for a single "transformative experience" after the training is complete. In addition, those who support the program are repeatedly galvanized because they can point to positive results that occur on a regular basis. Those who may have opposed the program for whatever reason find that they can no longer argue that leadership development is a mere intellectual exercise; they recognize that the program is producing results that have been documented. In the case of ALF, a focus on practicality and a willingness to experiment with different approaches produced recognizable small wins from the beginning. As the participants reviewed their activities, they found that they were able to identify concrete lessons they learned and to document the improvements that resulted from their participation in the training sessions.

Lesson 7: Leadership development is most effective when it occurs within a specific context. No one ever leads in isolation. At the very least, leaders have followers and many times peers (not to mention their own leaders to whom they themselves are responsible). The systematic study of leadership has demonstrated that training programs that ignore the context in which the leader works tend to be limited in their success and impact (Beineke and Sublett, 1999). In an academic setting, leadership development programs need to pay close attention to the individual culture and mission of specific institutions, units, and programs because strategies that are highly effective in one environment may be completely ineffective in others. Moreover, because academic administrators grow in leadership by discussing experiences with mentors, partners, peers, and coaches, a leadership program that occurs within that specific context—as opposed, for instance, to an off-campus retreat sponsored by a national organization or another university—has a higher potential of leaving a lasting impact.

Lesson 8: Setting aside time and space for the administrators' reflection is indispensable. Reflection-in-action is central to the art by which academic leaders deal with the uncertainty, instability, frustrations, and conflict inherent in the changing environment of higher education. (On the concept of reflection-in-action, see chapter 1 and Schön, 1983.) Sharing those reflections with peers and mentors who can correct, reinforce, or expand on the leader's impressions helps draw global lessons from isolated incidents. But since, as we have seen, academic leaders frequently feel isolated in their positions ("I used to be a colleague among many faculty members/chairs/deans/vice presidents, but it's lonely in my current position because I have fewer peers with whom I can talk about my concerns"), the typical environment of a college or university works against this shared form of reflection-in-action. A well-designed leadership development program provides formal time and space for reflection on leadership issues and offers a structure in which these reflections can be shared with colleagues.

Lesson 9: Regardless of institutional mission or personal beliefs, effective leadership development must have moral, ethical, and (in many cases) spiritual dimensions. While faith-based colleges and universities readily embrace the notion of leadership as a spiritual journey, secular institutions often find this idea a bit uncomfortable. Nevertheless, it has long been established that leadership development involves finding one's individual voice and that this type of self-knowledge requires an honest assessment of one's own value system (see, e.g., Kouzes and Posner, 2012). In addition, certain approaches to administrative development, such as positive academic leadership, which we explore later in this chapter, require participants to identify their core values and develop an administrative philosophy that incorporates those core values (Buller, 2013). Although people may define their spiritual dimensions in very different ways, that dimension of the self is all but essential to each administrator's leadership journey.

Lesson 10: Leaders must leave campus occasionally to gain a broader perspective and vision. One of the basic tenets of Peter Drucker's *The Effective Executive* (2011) is that many leaders are limited in what they can see in the world because they work within an organization. In order to avoid developing the blinders that come from viewing issues only as they are understood locally, leaders need to get off-campus periodically and seek opportunities where they can develop a national or even global perspective. For this reason, even though we just said we believe that leadership training programs like those mentioned in chapter 1 are not a substitute for institution-based academic leadership centers, we want to make it clear that we believe they can be a valuable component in an administrator's leadership development. In addition, many innovative ideas originate beyond the ivory tower itself. Since many academics have not left the setting of higher education since they arrived as undergraduates, they can benefit from participating in a "boundary span" that takes them beyond the college or university in order to achieve a much broader view of the issues affecting colleges and universities, exposes them to how academics are viewed by their stakeholders, and introduces them to alternative strategies for making decisions.

Lesson 11: Much of the value of leadership development is lost if institutions do not provide incentives for administrators to stay long enough to make a difference and sustain the change. Academic administration is a field with a high degree of turnover. Some academic leaders burn out due to the pressure. Others are replaced when new governing boards or chief executive officers decide to start fresh with a new team. And still others feel that the only way they can move up the organizational hierarchy is to switch institutions. But research into institutional change suggests that a certain degree of stability in leadership is essential in order for new initiatives to become part of the local culture (Eckel et al., 1998). Some turnover is desirable, since it brings new ideas into an institution or program. But excessive turnover is a waste of a school's investment in its academic leaders. Merely the existence of a formal leadership development program and the availability of mentors or a support group may alleviate some of this turnover. But it is also in the long-term best interests of the institution to consider mechanisms for making longer tenures for administrators possible and desirable in order to sustain the change.

Lesson 12: Leadership development programs work best when they are built around a single, well-delineated model of leadership development. New ideas about leadership develop all the time. Many administrators want to remain current with the latest thinking about academic leadership in much the same way that they keep abreast of new developments in their academic disciplines. But constantly shifting the focus of a leadership development program based on the latest book on college administration can make participants feel that the program as a whole lacks coherency. It also feeds into the suspicion certain participants may have about the program that it is based merely on what's trendy instead of what's useful. For this reason, it is highly advisable for the first of the 7 S's in a leadership development program—strategy—to be based on a clear concept of what leadership is, how academic leadership differs from leadership demonstrated in other organizational settings, and why the institution is pursuing a specific approach to academic leadership.

The Definition of Leadership

As lesson 12 makes clear, it is almost impossible to create an effective leadership development program unless you decide what leadership is. It can be tempting to say that leadership is a concept that defies being constrained by definition or to resort to Potter Stewart's famous dodge about the definition of pornography: "I know it when I see it." The fact remains that if we fail to specify what it is we mean by leadership when we create our strategy for a leadership development program, every participant and every presenter will tacitly adopt his or her own definition. To one person, leadership will mean administrative efficiency. To another person, it will be inseparable from strategic visioning. A third might view leadership as a series of traits that administrators need to develop, and a fourth might believe that it is a set of practices that must be followed. The result will be that the program will not have any focus, and it will begin to unravel almost as soon as it begins. For this reason, it is advisable to decide what you mean by leadership from the beginning and then structure a program that seeks to develop approaches that meet your definition.

Fortunately, there are many excellent definitions of leadership, and you will almost certainly find one that you can adopt or adapt so that it suits the individual needs of your school or system. In fact, after his own survey of how people describe leadership, Ralph Stogdill (1974), the director of the Program for Research in Leadership and Organization at Ohio State University, concluded that there are "almost as many definitions of leadership as there are persons who have attempted to define the concept" (259). That observation certainly may be true, but it does not require us to despair that there's no possible definition to help guide our strategy. So in the interest of bringing some order to the welter of competing definitions, let's begin by noting that several patterns emerge when people attempt to define what leadership is. As a way of illustrating these patterns, we have selected a website that quotes many different definitions of leadership, Adeoye Mayowa's Leadership Definitions by Scholars (adeoyemayowaleadership.blogspot.com/), stripped out common English words (such as *and*, *the*, and, for our purposes *leader* and *leadership*, which appear in every definition), and used Wordle.com to generate a word cloud of the results (see figure 2.1). If you have never used word clouds before, the key idea is that the larger a word is, the more frequently it appears in whatever text is being analyzed. From the image that we created, it becomes clear that the terms commonly repeated in various definitions of leadership are *people, influence, process, group, others, vision, direction, goal, towards*, and *direction*. Putting these elements together, we might adopt the following as our consensus definition of leadership:

Leadership is the process of influencing a group of people to move in a common direction toward a (frequently visionary) goal.

Although this definition is far shorter than many of those on which it has been based, it does contain six key elements that are important in formulating the strategy of a leadership development program.

Figure 2.1 Leadership Word Cloud

1. Leadership Is a Process

If you start a conversation about leadership with a randomly selected group of people, some will argue that it is an innate quality that cannot be developed if you do not already have it ("Just look at any group of children on the playground: you can already tell who's naturally born a leader and who isn't"), while others will say that it is a set of skills that anyone can learn ("Good leaders are effective communicators, efficient organizers, careful planners, and successful motivators. It doesn't take a genius to learn these things; they just require practice."). Our consensus definition falls somewhere between the two. It says that leadership is a process, something that we can learn more about and strive to improve, even though we may be constrained by our own natures and personalities in terms of how much better we can become. Think of weightlifting as a similar sort of process: with work, we can get better at it, even though the physique we are born with may limit the extent of our improvement. Figure 2.2 illustrates this idea. Visualize a spectrum on which the most ineffective leader we can imagine is on the left and the perfect, most effective leader we can envision is on the right. If your natural range of leadership ability—based on your temperament, intelligence, personality, and all the other factors observed by our hypothetical speaker who spotted "natural-born" leaders on the playground—falls rather near the left end of the spectrum, it is highly unlikely that even the best leadership development program in the world can shift your natural ability substantially to the right (figure 2.2a). But what leadership programs can do is

Figure 2.2 What Leadership Development Programs Can and Cannot Do

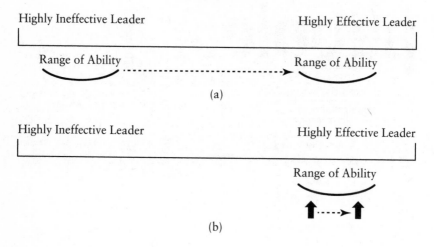

help you increase your effectiveness within your natural range of ability (figure 2.2b).

That degree of improvement is possible largely because leadership is a process, and we can improve both the process itself and our facility with practicing it. Nevertheless, different observers may view what that process entails differently. Wilfred Drath and Charles Palus (1994) regarded leadership as "the process of making sense of what people are doing together so that people will understand and be committed" (4), while Peter Northouse (2012) defines leadership as "a process whereby an individual influences a group of individuals to achieve a common goal" (15). Both definitions were included on the website that helped create our consensus definition.

2. Leadership Involves Influence

Like our consensus definition, Northouse notes that leadership does not just involve any type of process we can imagine. It involves a process that influences a group of individuals. Another way of expressing this idea is to say that leadership is always about persuasion and change. If you are not bringing about change, you are not leading anyone anywhere; you are simply managing resources and preserving the status quo. That said, there are a lot of times where managing resources and preserving the status quo is the best thing you can possibly do, but that is not really what most people mean by leadership. Certainly good leaders have to know when to stop leading and start managing their resources properly so that their organizations will be able to take advantage of the next opportunity that arises. Yet when such an opportunity does arise—or, less happily, when a significant challenge or disaster occurs—leadership returns to the fore. By means of persuasion, influence, and example, the leader begins to bring about whatever change the organization needs. That is why David Buchanan and Andrzej Huczynski (1997) define leadership as "a social process in which one individual influences the behavior of others without the use of threat or violence" (606) and why James Gibson, John Ivancevich, and James H. Donnelly Jr. (1985) define it as "an attempt at influencing the activities of followers through the communication process and toward the attainment of some goal or goals" (362). Without influence, leaders are either powerless (and thus not actually leaders at all) or compelled to rely on force or fear (and thus tyrants, not the sort of leaders the best administrators aspire to be).

3. Leadership Affects a Group of People

If you combine the area covered by the word *people* on the word cloud in figure 2.1 with that covered by the words *others, person, group,* and *individual* (all of which are largely used as synonyms for *people* in the various definitions of leadership Mayowa cites), you end up with a space that occupies nearly half the entire diagram. Leadership is, by almost everyone's definition, a process that involves working with groups of people. In fact, leadership is often about helping each individual find his or her place within a larger group of people. You cannot lead alone in your office, although many academic administrators try to do exactly that. You cannot lead a department, college, or university simply by imposing your vision and your will on others, although some academic administrators (almost always highly unsuccessful ones) try to do that too. Without other people willingly participating in the journey with you, you are not really a leader; you are just a loner who may or may not have a good idea. There is a wonderful video available on YouTube and elsewhere in which Derek Sivers follows an entire movement from "start to finish in under three minutes" (sivers.org/ff). Sivers narrates an episode in which a "shirtless dancing guy" begins to respond to the music at an outdoor event, seemingly oblivious to the rest of the crowd. He begins as a "lone nut" (Sivers's term) who seems to be mocked by everyone else until one, then two, then dozens of other people join him. This short video introduces a large number of excellent insights into leadership—including the all-important role of "the first follower"—but one of its conclusions seems inescapable: many times the biggest difference between a "lone nut" and a "charismatic leader" is simply the number of people who happen to be following.

4. Leadership Takes Those People in a Shared Direction

Similarly, if we combine the area covered by the word *group* on the word cloud with that covered by the word *direction*, we identify another key element of our consensus definition: leadership involves inspiring people to move in the same direction. If, as we have seen, influence and change are essential parts of leadership, then it is not enough simply to think about exerting that influence or plan for that change. You have to put ideas into effect; you have to move the organization from where it is now to a better or more improved state. As Jay Alden Conger (1992) says in his definition of leadership, "Leaders are individuals who establish direction for a working group of individuals, who gain commitment from these groups of members to this direction, and who then motivate these members to achieve the direction's outcomes" (18).

Notice in our consensus definition that we have not narrowed the focus to say that leadership takes people in the leader's direction. Although it may often be the case that the leader is the one who sets the course for an institution's journey, we do not believe that element of leadership to be universal. Leaders sometimes are effective because they provide the group with an ability to move toward a goal that the group itself has long wanted but been unable to achieve. In other words, a leader is not always a drum major, heading off in the direction that everyone else will follow. Frequently he or she will be a catalyst, speeding up the process of a needed change or making it more effective, even though it was another individual or group who originally charted that direction (Buller, 2013).

5. Leadership Results in Movement toward an Established Goal

The direction in which the group moves takes them closer to an important objective. We can easily imagine someone asking, "Isn't this part of the definition simply a restatement of the last part? If you are moving in a direction, aren't you always moving toward a goal?" Not necessarily. There are many aspects of life in which the journey itself is the destination. People often go on cruises simply for the pleasure of the experience. The cruise does not necessarily go anywhere. In fact, passengers usually disembark at the same port from which they originally embarked. In the same way, families stroll through a park not to reach a particular place but to enjoy their time with one another. In each case, people are moving in a direction, but that direction does not lead them to any goal other than their starting point. Leadership, however, needs to have both of these ingredients: a shared direction and an established goal. The pursuit of change for its own sake, just to "stir things up and see what happens," is rarely good for either the organization or the leader. Members of the organization will soon become disengaged as they see scarce resources devoted to changes that are unnecessary, sometimes even ill advised. Support for the leader will diminish as people realize that they are merely being led in a giant circle or, worse, nowhere at all. In his novel *A Hologram for the King* (2012), Dave Eggers has a wonderful description of an impressive-looking gateway that leads nowhere: "It was as if someone had built a road through unrepentant desert, and then erected a gate somewhere in the middle, to imply the end of one thing and the beginning of another. It was hopeful but unconvincing" (40).

Too many leadership initiatives on college campuses are similarly "hopeful but unconvincing" for precisely the same reason: a great deal of attention is paid to external appearances, with little or no thought given to the ultimate destination. Perhaps for this reason, Ralph Stogdill (1950) focused his entire definition of leadership on the identification and attainment of goals: "Leadership may be considered as the process (act) of influencing the activities of an organized group in its efforts toward goal setting and goal achievement" (4).

6. Leadership Engages Others Most Effectively When It Guides Them toward a Visionary Goal

Finally, many people believe that the best sort of leadership is visionary in nature and helps others achieve goals they once thought impossible. You will notice a slight hesitancy on our part here. In our consensus definition, we placed the words *frequently visionary* in parentheses and remarked that many people believe leadership is best when it is visionary. What we wish to convey is that no leader can afford to be visionary all the time. Sometimes you just have to make sure that the lights come on and the bills get paid. But what many people mean by *leadership*, and what campus leadership centers tend to emphasize, is not the mundane day-to-day decision making that executive positions inevitably require. When no one in a group can make up his or her mind about where to have lunch, the person who steps forward and says, "We're having Italian!" is exerting a kind of leadership. After all, making that decision does involve influencing a group of people to move together toward a common goal. However, it is not the kind of leadership that profoundly affects the future of an organization. (It just profoundly affects the future of lunch.) So the ability to be visionary at the appropriate time and when it is truly useful can be extraordinarily valuable to leaders, but not unless their vision is somehow tied to practicality. In the video mentioned earlier, Derek Sivers says, "We're told we all need to be leaders, but that would be really ineffective" (sivers.org/ff). An organization where everyone leads and no one follows is one that ends up in chaos, going nowhere at all. And in a similar way, we could say, "We're told leaders always need to be visionary, but that would be really ineffective." As Paracelsus famously said about drugs and poisons, the only real difference is in the dosage (Borzelleca, 2000).

> If you have a headache and take an aspirin, it's good for you. If you take the whole bottle, it's not. A similar principle applies to being visionary as a leader. Too much vision accompanied by too little attention to paying the bills and getting courses taught is a recipe for disaster. The key when it comes to visionary leadership is moderation: sufficient imagination to see what is possible, coupled with sufficient practicality to turn those dreams into reality.

Bennis and John Scully may well have been right to observe that leadership "revolves around vision, ideas, direction, and has more to do with inspiring people as to direction and goals than with day-to-day implementation" (Bennis, 1989, 139). But the person who says, "It's my job to dream the dream. It's your job to get us there," is really only cheerleading, not team leading. And while colleges and universities always need cheerleaders, they want their chairs, deans, and presidents not merely to set the goal for others but also to guide the way.

Academic Leadership

By selecting a consistent definition of what leadership is, you create the basis for what your development program will be helping others achieve. That is the first step in planning your strategy. For example, if you adopt our consensus definition of leadership, certain aspects of what your program needs to do will immediately become clear. You will need to provide guidance in interpersonal relations since leadership involves working with groups of people. You will need to discuss effective goal setting and the creation of inspiring but attainable visions for an academic program. You will need to provide opportunities for participants to learn how to use influence as a way of promoting consensus, and so on. If you select a different definition or write your own, that decision too will begin to guide your strategy. To phrase this principle another way:

> You can't really help others develop their leadership until you first decide what leadership is.

That observation leads us directly to the next question you will need to answer: Even after you decide what leadership is, what would you say constitutes effective *academic* leadership?

The reason this question is important is that colleges and universities have such different organizational cultures from corporations, armies, churches, clubs, and families. While higher education has its own sense of hierarchy—ask any associate professor who has been called an instructor, any member of the faculty who has been mistaken for a member of the staff, or any provost who has been introduced as a dean—the concepts of collegiality and shared governance assume a much more important role in an academic setting than elsewhere. In many cases, all the people who report to an academic leader have terminal degrees in their field. They are experts in subjects the academic leader may know only peripherally and have scholarly achievements that far surpass those of the academic leader. Moreover, George Mobus, an associate professor of computer science at the University of Washington, Tacoma, has observed that leadership entails followership:

> A basic problem in considering the meaning of leadership in an academic setting is that very few academics think of themselves as followers. Yet, by definition, leaders lead and followers follow that lead. I now suspect that the vast majority of academics think of themselves as independent contractors, especially if they have tenure. This attitude is not wrong, per se. Academics function best when they have academic freedom, but that also fosters a strong sense of independence from the possible dictates of administrators as well as from their colleagues and peers. (questioneverything.typepad.com/question_everything/2010/04/what-do-we-mean-by-leadership-in-an-academic-institution.html)

Nurturing that independence requires a very different type of leadership from that exerted by the general of an army, the manager of a department store, or the parent of small children. Indeed, most people who work in higher education seem to feel that academic leadership means something different from leadership in other environments. So what is that difference?

Unlike leadership in general, academic leadership does not benefit from having been defined so often by people with so many different perspectives that we can create a word cloud and develop a consensus definition from it. But we can do the next best thing. In the 1990s, Mimi Wolverton and Walt Gmelch conducted a study they discuss in their book *College Deans: Leading from Within* (2002). As part of this study, Wolverton and Gmelch surveyed over thirteen hundred academic deans at 360 universities in the United States, with a 60 percent response rate (Wolverton and Gmelch, 2002; Gmelch, Wolverton, Wolverton, and Hermanson, 1996). The results of that survey, combined with their review of other major leadership studies that were then going on, led them to propose the following definition of academic leadership (Wolverton and Gmelch, 2002, 33):

> The act of building a community of scholars to set direction and achieve common purposes through the empowerment of faculty and staff.

If we examine this definition closely, we find that it has three important aspects:

1. *Academic leadership builds a community of scholars.* As we have already seen, the concept of community is integral to the organizational culture of higher education. Professors and administrators grapple with concepts like shared governance and collegiality to an extent not found in many other institutions. As a result, academic leadership is not effective—or at least it does not tend to be effective for very long—if people try to exert their authority in a rigid, top-down manner. Building a community, particularly one that respects scholarly values like academic freedom and the importance of research integrity, is essential for success as a president, provost, dean, or chair and lies at the heart of what most people mean when they discuss academic leadership.

2. *Academic leadership sets the direction for either an entire institution or a unit of that institution.* Our consensus definition of leadership noted that leaders help others move in a shared direction toward a common goal. In higher education, the direction or vision toward which the organization is moving could occur on levels ranging from an entire university system to an individual program or even a single emphasis within a larger department. But the most important thing to observe about this

element of academic leadership is that, by saying leaders "set" the direction, we do not mean that they dictate, impose, or control that direction. To do so would be to violate the other distinctive elements of academic leadership: the creation of a community of scholars and the empowerment of others to help achieve significant goals.

3. *Academic leadership empowers others.* "Delegation involves the assignment of responsibility; empowerment involves the assignment of authority" (Buller, 2013, 137). Central to shared governance is the recognition that tasks are performed much more effectively and creatively at a college or university when the authority to perform those tasks is not confined to a narrow circle of administrators but truly distributed throughout the organization. Moreover, allocating authority to others requires much more than merely assigning others responsibility for things you do not want to do yourself. It means putting people in charge of making their own decisions, understanding that, by doing so, you are surrendering control over the exact direction of the process and giving people an opportunity to learn by making their own mistakes. Finally, it means not merely tolerating the involvement of others in these processes, but openly welcoming them and recognizing their value.

In their own definition of academic leadership, Christopher Gould, director of the Center for Faculty Leadership, and Len Lecci, professor of psychology, both at the University of North Carolina Wilmington, describe it as "the ability to build and maintain a highly productive department, college, or university while sustaining morale" (Gould and Lecci, 2011, 16). If we were to update our earlier definition by incorporating these ideas (while not duplicating those already included in our earlier consensus definition of leadership), we might posit a definition that looked something like the following:

Academic leadership is the act of empowering members of the faculty and staff by working with them collegially to achieve common goals, build a community of scholars, and sustain a high level of morale.

As you develop a strategy for your own academic leadership program, you are free to borrow this definition or create an alternative that fits the precise mission and goals of your institution. But just as we saw in this chapter that it is possible to develop a strategy for improving leadership only if you first decide what leadership is, so will your strategy be more effective and your task less challenging if you base that strategy on a clear understanding of what academic leadership means.

Should Your Strategy Include a Distinctive Focus?

Most institutions discover that merely having agreed on definitions of leadership and academic leadership provides all the guidance they need in developing the strategy for their academic leadership center or program. Some institutions, however, may want a more distinctive focus for their strategy, developing not just academic leadership in general but a specific type of academic leadership, one that reflects a particular set of values or beliefs. For instance, it might be appropriate for your college or university to assume one of the following as a theme for your leadership development program (Cockell and McArthur-Blair, 2012):

○ *Academic servant leadership*, the philosophy that administrators exist not to manage stakeholders or head an academic unit but to serve the needs of their constituents (Wheeler, 2012).

○ *Positive academic leadership*, the strategy of directing one's energy toward expanding successes and rewarding productive colleagues rather than solving problems and punishing unproductive colleagues (Buller, 2013).

○ *Academic appreciative inquiry*, the technique of investigating the causes of what's already working well and then doing more of it. It "involves, in a central way, the art and practice of asking questions that strengthen a system's capacity to apprehend, anticipate, and heighten positive potential" (appreciativein -quiry.case.edu/intro/whatisai.cfm).

○ *Authentic academic leadership*, the approach of emphasizing candor, openness, and constructive social values over bottom-line strategies such as tracking outcome metrics, including student credit hours and graduation rates. Authentic leaders focus on building relationships with stakeholders and exert influence through the trust they inspire rather than the power they wield (George, 2003; George and Sims, 2007).

There are both advantages and disadvantages to basing your strategy on a particular approach to leadership. On the positive side, having a tight focus will make it much easier for you to decide what topics to include as you plan workshops, faculty learning communities, guest speakers, and other activities. On the negative side, having a focus that's too narrow can cause you to exclude certain perspectives that could have been of great value to your academic leaders. The participant who could benefit most from practicing appreciative inquiry will not hear about it if your program deals solely with servant leadership. Moreover, your end result may be to produce administrators whose leadership skills aren't as flexible as you might like because they resort to adopting only one philosophy or strategy in every situation. Remember the old adage that the person whose only tool is a hammer sees every problem as a nail. A compromise approach might be to incorporate into your strategy the practice of changing themes every semester or year so that participants have ample time to consider an approach in sufficient depth while not being limited to a program that considers academic leadership only from a single point of view. (We discuss the concept of developing a distinctive focus for your program in greater detail in chapters 7 and 8.)

The Three Habits

In our consideration of Iowa State University's ALF program in chapter 1, we noted that the organizers found three ingredients of singular importance as they developed their strategy: content in the form of conceptual understanding, practice in the form of providing opportunities to apply various skills, and integration in the form of reflecting on the outcomes of their decision. We can generalize from these three ingredients of an effective leadership development program to describe three essential habits for all college administrators to have: habits of mind, habits of practice, and habits of heart. (On these three habits, see also Gmelch, Hopkins, and Damico, 2011.)

Habits of Mind: The Development of Conceptual Understanding

Certain aspects of higher education administration are so important that academic leaders need to know about them. For instance, administrators need to understand how a university operates and how they can make use of the distinctive organizational, political, and social culture of higher education. They need to understand effective ways of running a meeting, building consensus, accommodating dissent, and reconciling differences. At different administrative levels, they will need to master additional concepts in order to remain effective as their responsibilities change. For example, department chairs have to have intimate knowledge of their program's curriculum and course offerings, as well as the effect that the institution's calendar is likely to have on their units. By the time they are deans, provosts, and presidents, however, just knowing those things will not be enough: they will also need a broader understanding of fundraising, the best ways to deal with external constituents (including legislators and members of the governing board who may not have a good grasp on the organizational culture of higher education), and how to serve most effectively as chief cheerleader for the programs they represent (Gmelch, Reason, Schuh, and Shelley, 2002).

It is not uncommon—and not even surprising in light of how graduate students are educated—that certain administrators reach positions of authority without a clear understanding of the larger structure of colleges and universities or the overarching issues challenging higher education today. Development of conceptual understanding can remedy this situation by providing annual updates on current issues in higher education and offering an immersion experience for new chairs and deans that gives them the information they need in order to do their jobs effectively. Since many successful organizations have learned that it is often better to "grow their own" executives instead of hiring them from the outside (Collins and Porras, 1994), colleges and universities can do the same by using leadership development programs to provide faculty members with the conceptual understanding they need to move into administrative positions.

Habits of Practice: The Development of Skill

It is one thing to know how to ride a bicycle from reading a book about it. It is something else entirely to be able to ride a bicycle because of your practical skill. Something similar can be said of academic leadership. Reading all the books in the world on best practices in college administration and attending dozens of seminars in every aspect of what a provost, dean, or chair does in their jobs will not guarantee your success. The problem is that opportunities for skill development, except for actual experience in the trenches, are few and far between. The result is that many administrators develop their skills only gradually and haphazardly, with access to sporadic training, inadequate feedback, and occasional mentoring. Even worse, since many administrators are not familiar with the resources available to them with regard to the content and conceptual understanding of academic leadership, the skills they attempt to practice are often drawn from ideas developed in a corporate setting. Those skills may or may not be appropriate to the organizational culture of higher education, and so skill development truly becomes a process of trial and error.

While colleges and universities sometimes have programs to develop academic leadership, most of these opportunities confine themselves to improvement of conceptual understanding. They provide few if any opportunities for administrators to polish their skills. Since skill development is precisely the element of administrative growth that is unlikely to be addressed at a conference or off-site workshop, it is particularly important that the strategy for a campus center or program include some practical and applied opportunities. Well-designed skill development strategies might take into account one or more of the following components:

○ Complex case studies that require academic leaders to address challenging ethical dilemmas and difficult choices, not merely the topics like personnel practices, legal issues, and details of budget development that are usually covered in the habits of mind component of the program.

○ In-house mentorships that pair a more experienced administrator with someone who is starting out and encourage the consideration of multiple possible paths that lead toward particular goals.

○ Peer-level confidants, similar to the partners in academic leadership initiative at Iowa State described in chapter 1, which provide an environment in which administrators can discuss concerns with someone who is likely to be having the same experience. Mentors and confidants fill different needs. A mentor can be a great source of advice, while a confidant more commonly provides moral support. Both are vital, particularly when administrators are still developing their skills.

○ Outreach to external programs that can integrate institutional skill development with the specific academic programs for which the administrator is responsible. Many disciplinary groups, such as the Council of Colleges of Arts and Sciences (www.ccas.net) and American Assembly of Collegiate Schools of Business (www.aacsb.edu), offer training programs tailored to professionals in their fields, and many professional organizations include workshops for chairs at their national conferences.

○ A formal leadership transcript that outlines not only the content mastered by the participant through habit of mind opportunities, but also the skills he or she developed through practical application of this content. Such a transcript can help an academic leader document his or her professional growth for evaluation purposes and plan future development goals based on areas where gaps in experience and training can be identified.

○ An administrative portfolio, such as that proposed by Peter Seldin and Mary Lou Higgerson (2002), to help academic leaders document their achievements, reflect on their areas of strength and weakness, track their growth in the position, and illustrate the ways in which they are unique in their approaches to administrative challenges.

Habits of Heart: The Development of Reflective Practice

Understanding the role of an academic leader and possessing the requisite skills, while important prerequisites for administrative success, are still not enough for effective academic leadership. In order for the strategy of a leadership development center or program to be complete, it should also consider how administrators will pursue a lifelong learning approach in their positions. Self-knowledge, personal awareness, and openness to corrective feedback are all part of the ongoing process of leadership development. In addition, many administrators find their work enhanced through attention to the moral, ethical, and spiritual dimensions of leadership. For many academic leaders, these reflective practices come naturally and have long been included in their administrative tool kits. For others, however, guidance is valuable in learning how to distinguish between a healthy level of reflection and an unhealthy amount of self-reproach or the inability to let things go. As James Kouzes and Barry Posner suggest in *The Leadership Challenge* (2012), leadership development is very much about finding one's voice. Doing so often requires a process of reflection on the motives that guide one's decisions and the relationship between one's professional actions and one's personal values. Even when this type of reflection occurs, too many academic leaders engage in it only as a solitary practice. They don't share these thoughts with peers and colleagues who can help them place their reflections in a larger context. As a result, many academic leaders feel isolated. They assume that the issues they are struggling with are unique to them, that they are dealing with ethical dilemmas unlike those of their colleagues, and that they must be doing something wrong as a result.

A useful practice that an academic leadership program or center could incorporate into its strategy therefore is a mechanism for making reflection-in-action more systematic, shared, and forward looking. One way of doing so was the subject of a series of experiments conducted by Sonja Lyubomirsky, the author of *The How of Happiness* (2008).

By trying various combinations of exercises and their frequency, then comparing the results with a control group, Lyubomirsky found that people who regularly took time once a week to record five good things that happened during that week tended to be measurably happier, more content with their jobs, and even healthier:

> Those participants who counted their blessings on a regular basis became happier as a result. Compared with a control group (i.e., people who did not practice any kinds of exercise), the gratitude group reported significantly bigger increases in their happiness levels from before to after the intervention. Interestingly, this effect was observed only for those who expressed gratitude every Sunday night. The participants who counted their blessings three times a week didn't obtain any benefit from it. This finding might seem puzzling at first, but we believe there is an explanation: the average person made to express his or her gratitude every Tuesday, Thursday, and Sunday appeared to have become bored with the practice, perhaps finding it a chore, whereas the person made to express gratitude only once a week likely continued to find it fresh and meaningful over time. (92)

A reflective exercise of this sort helps administrators avoid losing track of the good things that are resulting from their leadership. While it can be useful to reflect on what did not go well and what you would do differently next time, making the exercise as positive as possible tends to create the most significant demonstrable effects over time.

Group reflections can also become a valuable component of a leadership development strategy. By providing administrators with a safe and supportive environment in which to share their feelings about their work, administrative support groups build closer bonds among leadership teams and end that sense of isolation that many administrators regard as one of the greatest drawbacks to their jobs. For many academic leaders, also having a confidant outside the institution provides the greatest opportunity to vent, see matters from a broader perspective, and share information that they feel uneasy revealing to others inside the institution.

Clarifying the Strategy

To close this section on how to develop an effective strategy for a leadership development center or program, we offer the following set of guiding questions that can assist institutions in developing the most appropriate strategy for their own leadership development efforts:

1. How will the center or program define leadership? How will that definition guide you in the opportunities and services that it provides?

a. How will the center or program define academic leadership? How will that definition guide you in the opportunities and services that it provides?

b. Will your center or program adopt a particular approach to academic leadership (such as servant leadership, positive leadership, or appreciative inquiry)?

2. How might your initiative's strategy incorporate the twelve lessons learned from Iowa State University's ALF program, as described at the beginning of this chapter? Are there any of these lessons with which you disagree and thus want to construct your program differently?

3. What will success look like for the program you are creating?

- What will your institution have more of than it has now?

- What will your institution have less of than it has now?

- If you were to phrase your goals as learning outcomes, what would those outcomes be? What will participants in your program be able to do at the conclusion of their leadership development activities that they can't do now?

- What do you most want to occur? What's the best-case scenario?

- What do you most want never to occur? What's the worst-case scenario?

4. What specific approaches will your initiative take to address the three habits discussed in this chapter: conceptual understanding, skill, and reflective practice?

REFERENCES

Beineke, J. A., & Sublett, R. H. (1999). *Leadership lessons and competencies: Learning from the Kellogg National Fellowship Program*. Battle Creek, MI: Kellogg Foundation.

Bennis, W. G. (1989). *On becoming a leader*. Reading, MA: Addison-Wesley.

Borzelleca, J. F. (2000). Paracelsus: Herald of modern toxicology. *Toxicological Sciences, 53*(1), 2–4.

Buchanan, D. A., & Huczynski, A. (1997). *Organizational behaviour: An introductory text* (3rd ed.). London, UK: Prentice Hall.

Buller, J. L. (2013). *Positive academic leadership: How to stop putting out fires and start making a difference*. San Francisco, CA: Jossey-Bass.

Cockell, J., & McArthur-Blair, J. (2012). *Appreciative inquiry in higher education: A transformative force*. San Francisco: Jossey-Bass.

Collins, J. C., & Porras, J. I. (1994). *Built to last: Successful habits of visionary companies*. New York, NY: HarperBusiness.

Conger, J. A. (1992). *Learning to lead: The art of transforming managers into leaders*. San Francisco, CA: Jossey-Bass.

Drath, W. H., & Palus, C. J. (1994). *Making common sense: Leadership as meaning-making in a community of practice*. Greensboro, NC: Center for Creative Leadership.

Drucker, P. F. (2011). *The effective executive: The definitive guide to getting the right things done* (Rev. ed.). New York, NY: Routledge.

Eckel, P., Hill, B., & Green, M. (1998). *On route to transformation: On change*. Washington, DC: American Council on Education.

Eggers, D. (2012). *A hologram for the king*. New York, NY: Vintage.

George, B. (2003). *Authentic leadership: Rediscovering the secrets to creating lasting value*. San Francisco, CA: Jossey-Bass.

George, B., & Sims, P. (2007). *True north: Discover your authentic leadership*. San Francisco, CA: Jossey-Bass.

Gibson, J. L., Ivancevich, J. M., & Donnelly, J. H. (1985). *Organizations: Behavior, structure, processes* (5th ed.). Plano, TX: Business Publications.

Gmelch, W. H., Hopkins, D., & Damico, S. B. (2011). *Seasons of a dean's life: Understanding the role and building leadership capacity*. Sterling, VA: Stylus.

Gmelch, W. H., Reason, R. D., Schuh, J. H., & Shelley, M. C. (2002). *The call for academic leaders: The Academic Leadership Forum*. Ames: Iowa State University, Center for Academic Leadership.

Gmelch, W. H., Wolverton, M., Wolverton, M. L., & Hermanson, M. (1996). *National study of academic deans in higher education*. Pullman, WA: Center for Academic Leadership.

Gould, C., & Lecci, L. (2011). Leadership and personality: What the NEO five-factor inventory tells us. *Department Chair, 21*(3), 16–18.

Kouzes, J. M., & Posner, B. Z. (2012). *The leadership challenge: How to make extraordinary things happen in organizations*. San Francisco, CA: Jossey-Bass.

Lyubomirsky, S. (2008). *The how of happiness: A scientific approach to getting the life you want*. New York, NY: Penguin Press.

Northouse, P. (2012). *Leadership: Theory and practice* (6th ed.). Thousand Oaks, CA: Sage.

Schön, D. A. (1983). *The reflective practitioner: How professionals think in action*. New York, NY: Basic Books.

Seldin, P., & Higgerson, M. L. (2002). *The administrative portfolio: A practical guide to improved administrative performance and personnel decisions*. San Francisco, CA: Jossey-Bass/Anker.

Stogdill, R. M. (1950). Leadership, membership and organization. *Psychological Bulletin, 4*(1), 1–14.

Stogdill, R. M. (1974). *Handbook of leadership: A survey of theory and research.* New York, NY: Free Press.

Weick, K. E. (1984). Small wins: Redefining the scale of social problems. *American Psychologist, 39*(1), 40–49.

Wheeler, D. W. (2012). *Servant leadership for higher education: Principles and practices.* San Francisco, CA: Jossey-Bass.

Wolverton, M., & Gmelch, W. H. (2002). *College deans: Leading from within.* Westport, CT: American Council on Education/Oryx Press.

3

STRUCTURE

AFTER DECIDING ON THE strategy your institution or unit will take toward academic leadership development, your next goal will probably be to decide on the best structure with which to implement this strategy. Should your initiative be a program or a center, have its own staff or make use of those with assignments in other areas, be highly programmed or aim for maximum flexibility, report to another office or be an independent unit, seek external funding or tap into existing resources, and so on? As with so many aspects of leadership development, the answers to these questions are best done at the local level in response to your individual needs. In other words, rather than concluding that a leadership development initiative should always be an independent center that reports to the provost, have a full-time director and an administrative assistant, conduct at least one formal program per month, and control its own budget, it is better for you to structure your initiative in a way that works best for what you hope to accomplish.

The structure you choose should flow logically from the strategy you have developed, reflect the genuine needs and political realities of your institution, and be inspired by, not limited by, some of the best practices that we discuss throughout this book. What a multicampus university with more than fifty thousand students will expect from its leadership development initiative will be quite different from a residential liberal arts college with an enrollment under one thousand. As you explore this chapter, try to consider each idea and case study as it relates to your own environment. As they say in advertisements, "Individual results may vary."

Champion the Cause

We have a principle that often guides us in our administrative work:

> A task that is the responsibility of everyone is really the responsibility of no one. For this reason, it will be done poorly if it is done at all.

In other words, no matter whether you intended to establish a fully staffed center with weekly programs, its own budget, and a prominent physical location on campus or a more loosely organized program that conducts only a few events each year, consists of only members who volunteer their time, and maintains no ongoing budget, it is very important that someone is charged with seeing this initiative through. Otherwise, as other demands for people's time begin to grow, the focus of your leadership development efforts will begin to blur and the entire project will soon become moribund.

For this reason, no matter whether the director of the initiative holds a paid, full-time position or simply contributes time as part of his or her service to the institution, it is important for there to be someone in charge—a person whose face becomes associated with the project and is the first person others contact when they have questions or suggestions about academic leadership. The exact title of the position is not important. Throughout this book, we call this person the director of the initiative, but other titles—such as coordinator, chair, manager, organizer, or liaison—may better fit your structure. The director becomes the point person for professional leadership development at the institution. Anytime people have questions about the best books and videos to use for improving their leadership skills, want to know about useful training programs off campus, need some advice about a difficult decision, or are interested in discovering new ways of becoming a better leader, the director is the person they will contact. Naturally, being the face of the program does not mean that the director has to lead all the sessions, know all the answers, and provide all the mentoring on his or her own. But the director does provide a single point of contact that makes it easier and quicker for people to find the resources they need in order to engage in leadership development.

Championing the cause also means receiving strong support from the upper administration for the activities of your leadership development initiative. We saw in chapter 2 how important it was for the Academic Leadership Forum (ALF) program at Iowa State and the Academic Leadership Center in Saudi Arabia to receive the active support and involvement of senior administrators. If you find that the person you report to (as well as his or her boss) is indifferent to the idea of a formal leadership development initiative—or, worse, regards it as a waste of time and resources—it does not mean that you cannot proceed, but your challenge becomes infinitely greater. Try to relate the goals of your center to some of your supervisor's priorities. For example, if your boss seems reluctant to support the initiative because "all our energy ought to be going into teaching and research, not a lot of trendy management training for administrators," present your program or center as a means of improving teaching and research. "I agree," you might say. "But we have to remember that deans and department chairs are often the ones who need to provide guidance to faculty members as to how to improve their teaching and research. And most of them reach their positions with absolutely no training in how to do that. The kind of leadership development initiative I have in mind is one that's going to make administrators more effective at helping faculty. Besides, we've kept expenses to the bare minimum by relying heavily on talent we have right here at the university. In fact, we were hoping to take advantage of your own experience as a successful academic leader by ..." In addition to all the other planning that you do in order to make your efforts successful, it can be a very helpful practice to reflect on three questions:

1. Which priorities and core values of my supervisor (and his or her supervisor) will make that person likely to support this initiative?

2. Which priorities and core values of my supervisor (and his or her supervisor) will make that person likely to resist this initiative?

3. Where is there the greatest amount of overlap between my own goals for this initiative and the goals of the upper administration?

We have much more to say about priorities and core values in chapter 8.

In the late 1990s, the American Council on Education (ACE) conducted the Project on Leadership and Institutional Transformation, a study funded by the W. K. Kellogg Foundation. Of the nine strategies they found that made change processes successful in higher education, one-third of them had to do with building support among stakeholders who would then champion the cause (Eckel, Hill, Green, and Mallon, 1999):

○ The senior leaders at the institution were fully behind the proposed change and actively involved in seeing it through.

○ A clear and compelling case was made to stakeholders as to why the change was necessary.

○ Those in charge of the change made alliances with people and programs throughout the institution in order to create support, develop
synergy, and maintain momentum.

Plan Comprehensively

Once there is support from the upper administration and at least some
degree of buy-in from other groups of stakeholders, the next important
component of your initiative's structure is the development of a detailed
but flexible plan for moving forward. For example, will the initiative be
designated a center, institute, program, or something else? Some institutions and university systems have clear guidelines for what terminology
can be used for different kinds of activities (Buller, 2007). For example,
at some schools, centers have to be self-supporting, while institutes do
not have this restriction. At others, centers are regarded as more complex organizations than institutes, and at other schools, it is the reverse.
At still other institutions, institutes are credit-offering units, while centers are not, and so on. So plan to choose a designation that reflects your
institution's specific terminology and conveys to your stakeholders what
type of endeavor you are undertaking.

The second important issue to consider as you develop your comprehensive plan is whether your development initiative would benefit from
having a steering committee or leadership team. Many institutions find
that an advisory body—with representation from various academic units
as well as such offices as human resources, student affairs, and upper
administration—is useful in generating ideas and building broad support.
But a group of fifteen or more people is difficult to schedule for regular
meetings and poses a real challenge when it comes to reaching consensus. For this reason, a subset of the larger group, perhaps consisting of
three to five people, can be effective in setting the agenda for larger meetings, making day-to-day decisions, proceeding quickly when time is of the
essence, and making decisions when the larger advisory group becomes
gridlocked. We saw in chapter 1 that the ALF program at Iowa State
began as an initiative of three deans who continued their role on this
type of steering committee or leadership team throughout the existence
of the initiative. At Florida Atlantic University, the Center for Leadership
and Professional Development arose as a proposal developed jointly by
a dean, an associate vice president of human resources, and the director
of the Center for Teaching and Learning, who similarly continued to provide leadership for the endeavor even after a far larger advisory committee
was selected.

There are both advantages and disadvantages to naming someone to be the director of the leadership development program or center. On the one hand, recall what we said about the task of everyone soon becoming the task of no one: if there is not someone who is put in charge of the activity and held responsible for it, progress is likely to be slow and fitful. However, establishing a full-time director for academic leadership development may undermine the very purpose of the activity. In other words, if one of the goals of your program is to demonstrate to people that leadership in higher education does not have to follow a rigidly hierarchical model, why create a leadership center that has its own hierarchy? If you have ever attended a presentation on active learning where the speaker lectured endlessly about how ineffective lecturing is as a pedagogical technique, you are already aware of the irony that can result when your medium does not fit your message. For this reason, your comprehensive plan for your leadership program or center should be a natural outgrowth of the leadership philosophy you want your initiative to have. If the idea is to help people understand that academic leadership is everybody's business, then avoid structures that are inherently top-down, chain-of-command in nature. Consider having the activity led by a rotating chair or coordinator rather than a permanent director. Delegate planning to a steering committee or executive board. But do not convey the message that you attach so little credence to your initiative's leadership philosophy that you do not even bother following it in your own organizational structure.

Take Stock

Taking stock as you develop a campus leadership initiative is a matter of using your existing resources in the most cost-effective and innovative manner. In other words, rather than starting from scratch or believing that every aspect of a leadership development program needs to be outsourced, take an inventory of your institution and identify the existing resources that will be valuable as you structure your initiative. Go back to what you decided in chapter 2 about your overall strategy and definition of (academic) leadership and use that insight to guide you toward those individuals, offices, and programs at your institution where expertise in these areas already exists. Keep these important offices in mind:

- o *President and provost.* Most presidents and provosts have many years of experience as academic leaders. Many of them may have served in the ACE Fellows Program (see www.acenet.edu/leadership/programs/Pages/ACE-Fellows -Program.aspx), other academic leadership programs like those outlined in chapter 1 or the appendix at the end of the book, or training workshops offered by their professional organizations. They may have served as mentors to other academic leaders and gained a great deal of insight from their own practical experience. By involving the president and provost as resources in your initiative, you both capitalize on this experience and encourage them to champion the cause.

o *Business office.* Budgeting is an important part of nearly every leadership position. Representatives from the business office can offer insight into institutional practices related to planning and administering budgets, best practices in cost accounting, and technical details (such as the difference between transferring funds and transferring costs) that many deans and department chairs do not know. They can offer strategies of financial sustainability and resilience that can help make limited resources go further.

o *Office of research.* Offices devoted to grants or sponsored research can benefit a leadership development program in several ways. First, they can put you in touch with sources of seed money or even ongoing funding that can help support your program. In addition, since writing grants and obtaining external funding is an increasingly important expectation of academic leaders, this office can assist with workshops on refining research projects, identifying new sources of funding, grant writing, and grant supervision.

o *Office of human resources.* Professionals in departments of human resources frequently conduct training sessions for members of the staff. Not all of their offerings correspond well with faculty and administrative work, but others—such as how to provide constructive criticism, conduct a fair but thorough performance evaluation, and mediate disputes among employees—are quite relevant to the work of academic leaders. Moreover, the insights they can provide into institutional policies and procedures make them valuable partners in leadership development programs.

o *Law school or office of legal counsel.* Higher education law is so complex that it is extremely valuable to have representation from the law school or your campus attorney's office in your leadership development program. Lawyers with a specialty in higher education law can help explain the role that the Americans with Disabilities Act, the Family Educational Rights and Privacy Act of 1974 (the Buckley Amendment), Title IX, the Health Insurance Portability and Accountability Act of 1996, and other major laws have on our rights and responsibilities as academic citizens. If your institution is unionized, they can help academic leaders become more effective while reducing the likelihood of successful grievances. They can explain the limitations of tenure rights that many academic leaders do not understand and review case law relating to the extent to which issues of collegiality may be addressed in personnel decisions. They can also help academic leaders work through such complex issues as where limits may occur on free speech, academic freedom, and faculty governance.

○ *Health center or counseling center.* Academic leadership positions are often highly stressful. In order to be effective as academic leaders, we have to understand the best ways of dealing with that stress and not allow it to interfere with our work or our personal lives. Campus health centers and counseling centers are experienced in dealing with stress-related issues since many of the problems students have also stem from the pressure that they are under. For this reason, these offices can provide expertise into stress management, work-life balance, and maintaining a healthy lifestyle even when working long hours. The same offices can also provide training in how to deal with students in crisis and what to do when you suspect that a faculty member might have mental health problems, be engaging in substance abuse, or neglecting his or her own health or hygiene.

○ *Department of management.* Management departments regularly deal with leadership strategies, strategic planning, benchmarking, labor relations, managerial economics, and project management. Although the organizational culture of higher education is distinctly different from that found in the corporate world, the faculty members in management departments with training and experience in both environments understand these differences. As a result, they can help administrators apply appropriate best practices from the business world to challenges in their own programs.

○ *Department of marketing.* A surprising number of administrative challenges are marketing challenges. We have to know how we can be most effective in marketing programs to prospective students, donors, funding agencies, and even internal stakeholders during such processes as program review. Faculty members with marketing expertise can assist academic leaders with best practices in disseminating the message they want to convey to target audiences in a cost-effective manner.

○ *Department of educational leadership.* Colleges of education are indispensable resources when it comes to launching a leadership development project. Faculty members in the department of educational leadership will deal directly with the issues that the initiative will address. While some of them will undoubtedly focus on leadership topics at the precollege level (teaching courses that help prepare future principals rather than future deans and department chairs), they have the advantage of being familiar with current research in this field. They can help provide a theoretical framework for the knowledge, skills, and attributes developed in your program. Furthermore, if the college of education at your school has a program in higher education leadership or pedagogy, you'll have the advantage of access to experts who specialize in precisely the areas that your center or program will address.

○ *Department of communications.* As almost everyone learns in any academic leadership development program, effective leadership is almost inseparable from effective communication. While we may initially think that leaders spend much of their time developing inspiring visions for their programs, making difficult decisions, and securing additional resources, the fact is that much of academic leadership involves communicating in memos, at meetings, and through public events. Faculty members with specialties in communications can help administrators do that more effectively. They can provide training in how a leader communicates in a system of shared governance as opposed to in a rigidly hierarchical environment such as a corporation or military unit. Faculty members in communications are also experienced in providing guidance in such areas as collegial communication when emotions are running high, improving teamwork skills, and conducting effective negotiations.

○ *Department of psychology.* Psychologists can assist faculty members and administrators in understanding how students learn best and thus how to build environments most conducive to student success. They can provide advice on how best to help faculty members who are coping with a personal tragedy or a family problem that is affecting their work. They can offer insight into human development that allows leaders to be more effective in dealing with the challenges of returning adult students from those that traditional-aged students are dealing with. Since many of them also are highly trained in statistical analysis, they can assist with interpreting the results of surveys and polls conducted by the initiative (as well as recommending when approval should be sought from an institutional review board before a survey or poll is conducted).

o *Department of political science.* Departments, colleges, and institutions are political constructs. Even the flattest administrative structure has power differentials, and even in the most congenial academic environment there are undercurrents of distrust and disagreement. If you are working in a more politicized environment, these factors become more important. Political scientists can help a leadership development program by providing insights into how political challenges are best addressed. They can also discuss how pending legislation affects higher education and whether issues of international concern are likely to have an impact on programs at the institution.

o *Department of sociology.* Sociologists provide insight into group behavior, including at institutions like colleges and universities. Including sociologists in a leadership development initiative can help participants better understand group dynamics, how issues of culture and subculture affect social interactions, gender issues related to leadership, the role of symbols in group dynamics, the interplay of language and social interaction, and so on. Together, faculty members in management, political science, and sociology can help academic leaders adopt a systems approach to their thinking rather than see their units as a random collection of discrete individuals and problems.

o *Department of curricular design/distance learning.* Just as not every college course is best taught in person, so is there no need for every aspect of a leadership development program to be provided in a series of meetings. Faculty members in curricular design or with experience in distance learning can help administrators create a virtual leadership center in which modules related to budgeting, institutional policies, best practices in evaluation, and the like can be addressed at the individual's own pace and on his or her own schedule. In addition, their insight into the most effective ways of structuring lessons and making them interactive can improve the quality of the leadership development as a whole.

o *Division of student affairs.* While our focus in this book is on leadership development for faculty members and administrators, most leadership development efforts will be in close contact with the division of student affairs. For one thing, many such offices run their own leadership development programs for students; sharing resources and even conducting a certain amount of cross-programming is cost-effective and can enhance the value of both initiatives. Second, many administrators working in student affairs have themselves attended programs in leadership development and can thus be useful resources when a workshop series is being planned. Third, the insight that student affairs professionals can provide is a useful corrective to the tendency of many administrators and faculty members to see university issues only from their own perspective, not the perspective of the students they are seeking to serve.

o *Department of public administration.* Faculty members in public administration programs can provide insights into nonprofit management that can help academic leaders become more effective at their jobs and possibly even discover new sources of supplemental funding. Many specialists in public administration also teach courses in servant leadership, appreciative inquiry, and similar topics that can provide a broader focus to a leadership development program. Performance management, quality assurance, managing people in the public sector, managing volunteers, administrative ethics, program evaluation, fiscal administration, and many other topics covered in public administration courses are also highly relevant to a leadership development program.

o *Faculty senate.* An institution's faculty governance structure, such as a faculty senate or assembly, has intellectual resources that can be valuable in building your program. These groups regularly deal with such issues as parliamentary procedure, conflict resolution, civil engagement, and enforcement of standards and policies. In many cases, their members can provide a faculty eye view of administrative approaches that will help academic leaders see themselves as others see them. Moreover, many faculty senators have had their own leadership roles for many years and can provide valuable insights into the practical aspects of academic leadership.

As should be apparent from this very long list, the expertise that most institutions have to draw on in planning their leadership develop efforts runs deep. The director or leadership team should not feel they need to provide every workshop, webinar, or mentoring session on their own. In fact, the more carefully you take stock of the resources that already exist, the greater the amount of buy-in you will have throughout the institution. People will feel that they are invested in the initiative's success because they have contributed to it in a substantive way. Training programs that are imposed on institutions from the upper administration are often met with resistance because participants feel that the activities are intended to "make us do it *their* way." But if people contribute their own ideas and expertise to the program, they will feel that they own it and want to be sure it succeeds.

Staff the Program Adequately

We have already seen that supervision for a campus leadership initiative can take a number of forms: a director (a model that tends to be very efficient but runs the risk of the program becoming too focused on whatever issues the director regards as most important), a steering committee (a model that provides broader buy-in and balance of topics but can be far slower in getting things done), or some combination of the two. But there are also other staffing needs to consider. Who will reserve rooms and audiovisual equipment? Who will make sure that handouts and other materials are prepared properly? If there is a library of resources available, who will track the items that have been checked out? If external experts are brought in, who will make travel arrangements for them? And who will take care of minor details like making sure that coffee and snacks or wine and cheese are where they need to be for various events?

Because leadership development initiatives often become far more complex than they were originally envisioned to be, it is important that the structure of the project include some attention to personnel and organization. Most leadership development initiatives discover that they need at least some type of part-time administrative support in order for their efforts to be successful. But deciding on staffing solves only part of the problem. You also need to decide to whom the administrative support person will report. Particularly if your effort is led by a leadership team or steering committee, who is ultimately in charge? That question may not seem very pressing until two people both claim to have major priorities that require the staff member's time immediately and someone has to decide what gets done first. Or it may arise when the staff member has to undergo an annual performance review and the leadership team is divided on how effective the person has been. It is better to decide from the start who the support staff's direct supervisor will be (which most human resource departments will require anyway) rather than for there to be ongoing uncertainty over this issue. While it may seem to be an easier matter if the support person is merely dividing his or her time between the initiative and other duties at the institution, that very division can create more problems. If the head of the leadership program isn't the same person as the staff member's other supervisor, whose needs receive priority? Is there a set time when the person will work on the leadership project—such as every Friday from 8:00 a.m. until noon—or merely a more flexible schedule—such as four hours per week? If the latter system is in place, who tracks those hours, and what happens if (or, more likely, when) significantly more or significantly less time is needed?

Matters of organization also become involved when you are attempting to decide on the physical location of the leadership program. If it is placed in a facility clearly associated with one specific function of the university (such as the provost's office, human resource office, or a particular college), it may come to be identified with that function even if that was never the intention. Someone might say, "Oh, I didn't know I could bring a problem involving a conflict between my administrative assistants here," or, "I thought we were only dealing with academic leadership in this program." For this reason, many campuses decide to locate the office of their leadership development initiative in the library, adjacent to the president's suite, or in some other location that signifies its relevance to all campus areas. Remember Bolman and Deal's (2013) concept of the symbolic frame, which we mentioned in chapter 1. The location for your center or program sends a signal about what your initiative means and what issues it addresses. The most tempting solution is always to locate an office wherever on campus space happens to be available. But keep in mind the symbolism attached to a location like the student union, business office, or development office, and people will draw conclusions about your initiative's intent based on where it happens to be.

This entire question of developing appropriate staffing and properly locating your effort in the institution's overall organization is so significant that chapter 5 is entirely devoted to this issue.

Allocate Sufficient Resources

In their urge to get leadership development initiatives under way as soon as possible, some administrators think, "Let's just get started by taking this project on in addition to our current efforts. Once we're successful, we can make a strong case that we need additional resources." That approach is usually a mistake. For one thing, if you demonstrate that you can put on a program without additional resources, what you are really demonstrating is that you can put on a program without *needing* additional resources. The program will simply become an expected part of your job, and you will end up spreading yourself too thin. For another thing, even a leadership development program that is entirely staffed with current personnel is going to require some supplies. Photocopies will need to be made, web pages may need to be created, books will need to be purchased, and facilities will need to be reserved. It may not be a strain on anyone's budget when the effort is just starting out, but what about when the program begins building on its success and starts involving five to ten times the original number of participants?

For both of these reasons, planning the structure for a leadership development initiative needs to address the question of resources. While we initially think of financial resources in this regard, it is important to remember that other kinds of resources exist as well. In addition to the staffing resources we just explored, there is the matter of allocating time, facilities, equipment, and information. In order to make sure that none of these considerations is overlooked, here is a resource checklist to use in developing the budget and structure of your leadership initiative. You may decide that certain of these suggestions are not needed for your initiative, but going through the checklist is a useful exercise anyway: It helps ensure that you are omitting an item intentionally, not merely through oversight.

Leadership Development Initiative Resource Checklist

Financial Resources

- Stipends for in-house presenters
- Stipends for guest presenters
- Stipends for program participants
- Salaries for executive staff/directors/organizers
- Salaries for administrative and clerical staff
- Funding for expenses (photocopying, telecommunications, computers, office supplies)
- Funding for refreshments during programs
- Funding for web page development

Personnel Resources

- Someone to plan the calendar of events
- Someone to book the rooms for events
- Someone to process expense payments and reimbursements
- Someone to update web notices

- ☐ Someone knowledgeable about audiovisual resources
- ☐ A director or leadership team to set the general direction of the initiative
- ☐ Presenters who are able to conduct a sufficient number of workshops and presentations
- ☐ Someone to invite the presenters and participants to each program
- ☐ Someone to handle the logistics of each program

Time Resources

- ☐ Blocks of time identified when participants are most likely to attend
- ☐ A calendar of events sequenced in a logical order
- ☐ Sufficient time for presenters to prepare each program
- ☐ Time for both presenters and participants to reflect on the progress of the program
- ☐ Release time for the leadership of the program

Facilities Resources

- ☐ Office space for administration of the program
- ☐ Suitable meeting space for workshops and presentations
- ☐ Socializing space for refreshments and informal discussions among participants
- ☐ Storage space for supplies and resources

Equipment Resources

- ☐ Computers or tablets for running presentations
- ☐ Digital projectors
- ☐ Remote presenters
- ☐ Laser pointers

Information Resources

- ☐ Library of books on academic leadership
- ☐ Subscriptions to *Academic Leader, Department Chair, Dean and Provost, Change, Academe, Chronicle of Higher Education,* and other periodicals relevant to academic leadership

> ❑ Subscriptions to publications that regularly deal with leadership such as the *Harvard Business Review*, the *International Journal of Leadership and Change*, the *Journal of Leadership Studies*, the *Journal of Leadership Education*, and *Executive Leadership*

Leadership initiatives often stall because other priorities come along after the initial burst of enthusiasm for the project, and the resources that seemed sufficient when the program began are now required elsewhere at the institution. Resource planning is thus an important part of improving the likelihood of success for your initiative, even if you start by seeing it merely as an informal activity to which a number of volunteers are going to contribute their time.

Sustain the Charge

After that initial burst of enthusiasm has subsided, leadership initiatives can struggle because their charismatic founder leaves the institution or becomes caught up in other work. For this reason, part of the structural planning for the project should include the questions, "How are we going to keep this going?" and "What is our long-term plan?" By doing so, you will reduce the likelihood that your efforts will begin with great anticipation but soon decline because grandiose ideas far outstripped the institution's ability to sustain the charge. If in the first year of your initiative's operation you find that you yourself end up conducting most of the workshops and serving as the program's primary mentor, will you have that amount of time to contribute every year for the foreseeable future? It is probably not realistic to assume that someone else is going to step forward and fill that gap once you "show them how it's done." If the leadership initiative is too much your own passion and pet project, other people may feel that it is up to you to keep it going. After all, they have got their own passions and pet projects to consider.

Walt Gmelch—capitalizing on the work of the Kellogg Foundation, the Institute for Electrical and Electronics Engineers Deans' Summit, and Karl Weick, the Rensis Likert Distinguished University Professor at the Ross School of Business at the University of Michigan—developed the following inventory of best practices in sustaining institutional change. A number of these principles are also based on the change model that John Kotter described in *A Sense of Urgency* (2008) and *Leading Change* (2012). As you review the structure you have developed for your leadership development project, see how many of these ten best practices in sustaining change strategies apply to your concept.

Inventory of the Top Ten Strategies for Sustaining Change in Higher Education

		Yes	No
1.	Does a sense of urgency exist at your institution (or in your program) that this initiative is truly necessary at this time?	☐	☐
2.	Have academic leaders (such as chairs, deans, and the upper administration) made a clear and compelling case as to how the initiative addresses a currently unmet need?	☐	☐
3.	Have opinion leaders among the faculty come to accept the need for this initiative?	☐	☐
4.	Have opinion leaders among the faculty promoted support for this initiative among other stakeholders across the institution?	☐	☐
5.	Do the people you report to support this project?	☐	☐
6.	Are the people you report to actively involved in this project?	☐	☐
7.	Are key leaders among the administration and faculty likely to remain at the institution long enough for the project to get well under way?	☐	☐
8.	Have adequate support structures, incentives, and resources been set aside for this project?	☐	☐
9.	Does your institution (or program) generally have a climate of goodwill and trust?	☐	☐
10.	Do you have a clear plan for celebrating this project's "small wins" as well as its major achievements?	☐	☐
	TOTAL	___	___

If, after completing this inventory, you have more no than yes answers, it seems highly unlikely that your initiative will be sustainable over the long run. Use the inventory then to identify the areas where you will need to make a stronger case, gain wider support, or include more people in order to increase your initiative's odds for success. It is better to take these steps while you are planning your project's structure than to get a few months into your effort and discover that you have been moving toward a goal that is ultimately unsustainable.

Clarifying the Structure

Here again is a set of guiding questions you can use to determine the overall soundness of the structure that you've created for your leadership initiative and whether you need to reconsider any elements before proceeding.

1. If you were to identify the three strongest champions of this project, who (besides yourself) would they be? Does that core group have enough influence and respect among your institution's various constituencies to build a broad base of support for your effort?

2. Why have you chosen the leadership structure that you have? After looking at the advantages and disadvantages of having a director as opposed to a leadership team or steering committee in charge, which arguments seemed to you to be most compelling? If you decided on a structure that includes neither a director nor a leadership team, why were these two options not suitable for your needs?

3. Which individuals and offices at your institution will be your primary resources as you plan the activities of your center? Whom have you asked to review your list of internal resources to make sure that you are not overlooking an important component of your activity?

4. After you completed the Resource checklist and the Inventory of the Top Ten Strategies for Sustaining Change in Higher Education, did you go back to fill in any significant oversights or omissions?

REFERENCES

Bolman, L. G., & Deal, T. E. (2013). *Reframing organizations: Artistry, choice, and leadership* (5th ed.). San Francisco, CA: Jossey-Bass, 2013.

Buller, J. L. (2007). *The essential academic dean: A practical guide to college leadership*. San Francisco, CA: Jossey-Bass.

Eckel, P., Hill, B., Green, M., & Mallon, B. (1999). *On change*. Washington, DC: American Council on Education.

Kotter, J. P. (2008). *A sense of urgency*. Boston, MA: Harvard Business Press.

Kotter, J. P. (2012). *Leading change*. Boston, MA: Harvard Business Review Press.

RESOURCES

Berke, D., Kossler, M. E., & Wakefield, M. (2008). *Developing leadership talent.* San Francisco, CA: Jossey-Bass/Pfeiffer.

Kelly, R. (2013). Preparing future academic leaders in graduate school. *Academic Leader, 29*(10), 3–4.

Kotter, J. P., & Rathgeber, H. (2006). *Our iceberg is melting: Changing and succeeding under any conditions.* New York, NY: St. Martin's Press.

Weick, K. E., & Sutcliffe, K. M. (2001). *Managing the unexpected: Assuring high performance in an age of complexity.* San Francisco, CA: Jossey-Bass.

4

SYSTEMS

"LEADERSHIP IS A TRICKY BUSINESS. Perhaps that is because no one is quite sure what it is, also because successful leadership practice can vary so much from one situation to another" (Mintzberg, 2004, 213). That conclusion by Henry Mintzberg, Cleghorn Professor of Management Studies at McGill University, is less a cry of despair than an insight into the sheer complexity of leadership as an object of study. It is reminiscent of James MacGregor Burns's remark that "leadership is one of the most observed and least understood phenomena on earth" (Burns, 1978, 2). But these observations are perfectly understandable. Consider not only how varied the environment is in different sectors of the economy (from corporations to the military to nonprofit organizations to primary schools to colleges and universities) but also within higher education itself. Anyone who has worked at a community college, an elite liberal arts college, a Research I university, and a regional university can attest that the leadership environment, challenges, and issues are very different in each of these academic settings. Although we speak of "leadership in higher education" as though it were a single entity, it is not. Leadership is not the same for the chair of a faculty curriculum committee as it is for the vice president of business affairs, and it is not the same in the college of engineering as it is in the college of arts and sciences. The fact is that it often makes little sense to talk about leadership in the abstract without a careful look at how it plays out in any individual system.

Throughout the 1990s, Jay Conger (1992, 1999) conducted an extended study of formal leadership programs. From his examination of the programs that truly made a difference in the overall quality of leadership in their organizations, Conger concluded that in order to be effective, leadership initiatives had to incorporate elements of four major approaches:

1. Personal growth experiences
2. Conceptual development

3. Regular feedback

4. Skill building

As individual components, these elements are similar to the three habits (mind, practice, and heart) that we explored in chapter 2. But the important lesson Conger adds is that however we parse the constituent elements of leadership development, none of them is particularly effective on its own. They reach their full potential only when they are combined in an overall system. In other words, rather than seeing knowledge about leadership development as one thing, our reflection on our own experiences as something else, our skills of time management and consensus building as yet a third component, and the values we bring to our leadership positions as a fourth element unrelated to the first three, effective leadership tends to result when we see how all these habits and approaches relate to one another. As a result, successful leadership development programs tend to be those that foster this type of integration by providing a unified and meaningful experience rather than a series of independent and unrelated workshops.

Systems and Leadership Development

Organizing your initiative in such a way that it provides this kind of unified and integrated experience for the participants means thinking about your program or center as a type of system. How do the different components work together to achieve a desired goal? How do the three habits that we discussed in chapter 2 reinforce one another? How do you relate theory to practice and practice to reflection in the opportunities you provide? This type of systems thinking is important for determining both the best content to include in your program and the best format in which to provide that content. In fact, we can identify four ways to speak about academic leadership development in terms of a systems approach:

1. We can discuss the unique system in which the participants' leadership will be demonstrated. (How is this institution different from others?)

2. We can consider systems approaches to leadership itself. (How do certain leadership theories cause us to treat our unit or institution as a system?)

3. We can examine the method of delivery that will be used to provide the leadership development activity for the participants. (What delivery system will best meet the needs of our participants?)

4. We can identify the network of principles and beliefs that the leader brings to each opportunity. (In which belief system is our approach to leadership grounded?)

We delay our discussion of the fourth perspective until chapter 8 where we consider the notion of the academic leader's values and their significance in some detail. For the purposes of the discussion in this chapter, let's see how the first three perspectives affect how an institution might want to design its leadership development program.

The Leadership Environment as a System

We can define a system as "a series of independent entities that affect and are affected by one another in a significant way." Familiar examples include:

- A computer system, in which the monitor, CPU, storage unit, keyboard, mouse, and printer all have separate functions but must work together effectively in order to develop, interpret, and disseminate information

- The circulatory system, in which the heart, blood, arteries, capillaries, and veins all have separate functions but must work together effectively in order to sustain life

- An HVAC system, in which the furnace, air conditioner, thermostat, vents, and ductwork all have separate functions but must work together effectively in order to maintain a desired temperature and level of humidity

The environment in which we work as academic leaders is similarly a type of system. In fact, it is several systems at once: we act simultaneously within the global system of higher education, our national system of higher education, our state system of higher education, and the complex system that is our individual institution. At each of those levels, entities remain separate and yet affect and are affected by other entities. For example, although our institution may be far from a university in another country, we may still accept transfer credits from that school, hire faculty members who received their credentials there, and compete with them for the same grants, students, and employees. In our own country, community colleges, large research universities, for-profit schools, online schools, and state colleges all have distinct missions and identities, but all can affect the national debate about what higher education is for, how much students should be charged and professors be paid, and what the standards of accreditation should be. And at our own schools, the division of academic affairs has a different focus from the divisions of student affairs, financial affairs, community relations, and athletics, but each division has a strong impact on the work that is done in all other divisions.

Leadership development programs have to be aware of and relate to all of these different levels of system. After all, the type of leadership that a dean or department demonstrates is very different from that of a corporate vice president or a colonel in the military. That difference affects everything from the way in which decisions are made to the way in which instructions are given, information is shared, success is rewarded, and unacceptable behavior is addressed. Despite the tendency of organizational charts to depict universities as traditional pyramid-shaped cultures and for certain trustees and legislators to describe higher education as a business, those parallels break down rather quickly. A dean or provost who consistently gives direct orders to a subordinate will soon be far less effective than a military officer who does so, and a department chair who bases scheduling decisions solely on the bottom line will inevitably fail while a store manager who does the same thing might well succeed. As a result, you cannot simply develop academic leadership in others by adopting the jargon of the latest management fad or reading the latest book on how to succeed in the corporate world. The type of leadership development we provide has to make sense for the system in which higher education operates. (For more on how the organizational culture of higher education affects the type of leadership administrators must demonstrate, see Buller, 2013.)

Of equal importance is training that is cognizant of the exact leadership environment in which the administrator will operate. We speak of the unique culture of a given university, a division within that university, and a department within that division. Anyone who has ever moved from one school to another knows how significantly different cultures can be, even among, for example, a group of midsized state-supported, teaching-focused comprehensive universities. What is forbidden at one school is sometimes mandatory at another, and the leader who does not respect that difference may be in for a rude awakening. Moving from a unionized to a nonunionized environment often entails a complete change of culture, modes of interpersonal communication, and operating procedure. Even within the same university, being a dean of a college of liberal arts and humanities usually requires very different strategies from being a dean of a college of business administration, and being a chair of English often requires very different skills from being a chair of classical studies, even within the same college. An important component of effective leadership development programs is introducing the participants to the practice of viewing their work from a systems perspective. Programs can begin this process by inviting participants to engage in exercises like the following:

Defining My Leadership System

1. Choose five adjectives to describe our institution that would not apply to the institutions where you worked previously or where you received your degrees.

2. Choose five adjectives to describe the unit where you work (such as a college or department) that would not apply to other departments at this institution.

3. Identify the ten people with whom you work most closely. If possible, these should be people who report to you and with whom you interact daily. Completely ignoring their job description, academic discipline, title, or credentials, identify the following for each of these ten people.

   - What is the one thing that this person most contributes to your work environment that you would not have if this person did not work with you?
   - What is the role (e.g., class clown, parent figure, drama queen, archnemesis, and so on) that this person tends to play most often?
   - With which of the other ten people on the list does this person have a positive relationship?
   - With which of the other ten people on the list does this person have a negative relationship?
   - With which of the other ten people on the list does this person have no relationship?
   - Which of the ten is most highly respected as an opinion leader?
   - Which of the ten is most widely regarded as the weakest link?

4. Within these same ten people, are there any groups of people who tend to form subunits? In other words, can you identify any groups of two or more people who regularly:
   - Have lunch or dinner together?
   - Socialize with one another?
   - Have spouses, partners, or children who are close friends?
   - Sit together at meetings?

- Vote with one another as a bloc?
- Share dislike or disdain for the same individual or group outside their subgroup?

5. When you identified the ten people with whom you work most closely, how many of them were within the unit where you work (such as a college or department)?

  - Is there anyone in your unit who is *not* on that list? Why is that the case?
  - If you were to include people from your unit who were not on your original list of ten, would your answers to questions 3 and 4 be any different?

6. What are three things that the person you report to most needs from you? What are three things that you most need from the person you report to?

7. If you were to propose an idea at work (the precise content of the idea does not matter), who is likely to support you regardless of what you propose? Who is likely to oppose you regardless of what you propose?

The purpose of this exercise is to help the participants understand their work environments from a systems perspective. Without a reflective exercise of this sort, many academic leaders tend to view the people who work at their institutions in terms of either their titles or their credentials. The exercise encourages the participant to avoid categorizing people as administration, faculty, or staff or regarding them simply in terms of the classes they teach or the type of research they conduct.

When we see our colleagues differently in terms of their roles outside their work environment, their contributions to our institution that fall outside their job descriptions, and their relationships with others, we understand better how the systems around us operate. We recognize how we can better help others when the advice they need to hear might be ignored or regarded as suspect if it came from us. We develop relationships with them that are more three-dimensional than if we regard people as merely the sum total of their résumés. By so doing, we become not only better at doing our jobs, but we become better colleagues as well. For this reason, it is a good idea to conclude this exercise by asking the participants to identify at least one thing they will do differently because of the insights they gained from the activity. By so doing, you will help them bridge the gap between an intellectual understanding of how effective leaders work and the actual practice of how they themselves do their jobs on a daily basis. For example, they will see more clearly how ideas that are good in principle might at times be completely impractical due to political realities and how people's job descriptions do not even begin to encompass the actual role they play at an institution.

Systems Approaches to Leadership

Our consideration of the unique environment in which each academic leader functions also reinforces for us an important truth: since all leadership takes place within a system, it is essential for us to examine it by using a systems approach. In other words, we can go only so far in our study of leadership in terms of the traits that leaders have, the behaviors they exhibit, the skills they possess, and the backgrounds they tend to have. As we saw in chapter 2, all leadership takes place within a group, and so those group dynamics become important in any attempt to develop current or future leaders. If we try to study leaders in isolation from their organizations, the needs and personalities of their followers, and the overall context of their actions, we end up with a highly distorted view of what leadership is.

In *Leadership: Theory and Practice* (2012), Peter Northouse discusses several major approaches to understanding leadership that take account of the system or environment in which the leader is acting. Unlike theories that posit that leadership is dependent on individuals having certain traits or engaging in certain behaviors, these theories suggest that leadership can be understood only in terms of the interactions between a leader and other members of his or her organizational system. The following are some of the most common systems-oriented leadership theories (Northouse, 2012):

Situational theory	The concept that different types of leadership are required in different types of situations. The goal is to adapt to the system.
Contingency theory	The concept that a leader's success is contingent on how well his or her style fits the style of the unit or organization the person is leading. The goal is to match to the system.

Path-goal theory	The concept that leadership is about finding suitable paths to the various goals of the organization. The goal is to motivate those within the system.
Leader-member exchange theory	The concept that effective leadership results from the interrelationship between the leader and his or her followers. The goal is to recognize those within the system as individuals and relate to their individual needs.
Team theory	The concept that leadership involves helping followers make the transition from a loosely organized group to a tightly interconnected team. The goal is to inspire and unify those within the system.

Developing opportunities to learn about these approaches to leadership (as well as the many other theories that Northouse discusses) helps participants realize just how complex a phenomenon leadership is. It is surprising how many people who ought to know better still think of leadership in terms of telling people what to do, exerting the maximum amount of control over the people who work for them, and assuming that people will not perform adequate work unless they fear what the boss may do. Systems approaches provide a strong antidote to these misconceptions. They demonstrate that the leader's success is rarely, if ever, the result of the leader's actions alone.

Moreover, by considering these systems approaches as you plan the activities for your leadership development initiative, you are far less likely to fall into a trap of thinking that teaching people about leadership is about giving them knowledge or skills only. It is also important to recognize that leadership development cannot be directed at just the usual suspects alone. In addition to those who are already in administrative positions or have significant responsibilities among the faculty or staff, leadership development can also have a role for all the stakeholders in the system. Reflect, for example, on such questions as the following:

- What can members of a department or college do to make the work of the chair or dean in their area more successful?
- What types of information should members of the faculty and staff share with their supervisors in order to help them serve the area better?

○ If a problem arises with the president, provost, dean, or chair, what are the best ways of addressing this issue so that the problem can be resolved without fear of reprisal?

○ What do the stakeholders in a system need from their leaders that they are not currently receiving?

○ How would the stakeholders in a system describe the optimal relationship with their supervisors and the opinion leaders in their area?

Delivery Models as Systems

In chapters 1 and 2, we examined the three key ingredients for any strategy to develop academic leaders and how those ingredients become the three habits effective leaders demonstrate. (See figure 1.1.) Those three ingredients and habits also tell us a great deal about how our initiatives can create well-designed delivery systems for academic leadership development.

DELIVERY SYSTEM I: HABITS OF MIND, OR CONCEPTUAL UNDERSTANDING
The first system we explore, conceptual understanding, is based on the notion that administrators need to understand leadership from a conceptual or cognitive perspective. That perspective might include such dimensions as Bolman and Deal's four frames of leadership (see chapter 1) or the various leadership theories presented by Peter Northouse in *Leadership* (2012). As might be expected, cognitive approaches have been developed and studied extensively by scholars (Marion and Gonzales, 2014; Lussier and Achua, 2013; Bolman and Gallos, 2011; Bess and Dee, 2008; March, Simon, and Guetzkow, 1993; Birnbaum, 1992; Bennis, 1989), and they tend to provide the vast majority of the content in most campus leadership programs. It is important for key concepts in the organization and culture of higher education to be understood as both barriers and as lifesavers when navigating the whitewaters of academic leadership. As we saw in chapter 3, faculty members in the college of education can be excellent resources for helping current and prospective academic leaders understand current theories of leadership and how they can lead to effective policy and practice. For instance, workshops, online courses, or webinars could be developed around such topics as these:

○ What does it mean to lead an organized anarchy, loosely coupled system, or collegial culture?

○ What do researchers mean when they talk about a learning culture, and what relevance does this topic have for higher education?

○ What are some of the major theories of effective decision making, such as the garbage can theory, stepladder model, and Gårdenfors-Sahlin's decision-making method (Harrison and Lomi, 2012; Williams, 2013; Gärdenfors and Sahlin, 1982)?

Academic leaders benefit from having these and other key concepts within their conceptual understanding because it helps them avoid mistaking an issue for being more or less complex than it actually is, reinventing the wheel when faced with a problem that is new to them, and approaching each new situation on an inconsistent, ad hoc basis.

DELIVERY SYSTEM 2: SKILL BUILDING The skill-building component of leadership development helps participants make the transition from knowing about effective leadership to actually leading effectively. We can think of it as the spring training or golf clinic of leadership development initiatives in that it allows academic leaders to practice certain competencies before they actually apply them during the "season games" or "conference tournaments." (On this concept, see Conger and Benjamin, 1999.) For example, training in conflict management might be designed around a simulation or role-playing scenario in which the participants practice their skills in negotiation, active listening, and interest-based resolution, a technique discussed by Fisher, Ury, and Patton in their work *Getting to Yes* (1991).

As might be expected, success in skill-based leadership development depends almost entirely on how teachable any given leadership skill or competency happens to be. Complex competencies such as visionary thinking or charismatic communication may not be easily taught and may require a long gestation period involving multiple skills if your center or program wishes to address them (Conger, 1992; Westley, 1992). Skill building also involves a second significant challenge: time. To develop true expertise in a skill may not take the full ten thousand hours Gladwell talks about in *Outliers* (2008), but it does take experimentation, coaching, feedback, and the willingness to make improvements and refinements (Ericsson and Smith, 1991).

There are two important points to consider when deciding whom to include as participants in a leadership development program. First, retention of administrative skills is highly dependent on a participant's opportunity to practice and receive active support from colleagues. For this reason, as we saw in chapter 1 when we were reviewing Iowa State's Academic Leadership Forum program, "training is more effective if intact work groups with their superiors attend the same program"

(Conger, 1992, 178). Second, in higher education as in industry, more senior managers often send their middle managers to skill-building programs, assuming they themselves already possess such skills or simply do not have enough time to perfect them. At many universities, provosts think that leadership development is important for their deans but not themselves, or deans want their chairs to participate although they believe their own skills are good enough as they are. In fact, including an entire team in a program is much more effective for skill development than is individual participation with no involvement of the person's supervisor. (For more on skill building, see chapter 6.)

DELIVERY SYSTEM 3: REFLECTIVE PRACTICE The ancient maxim "know thyself" appears to have originated with the philosopher Thales of Miletus, became associated with the Delphic Oracle when an image of Thales bearing this statement had been dedicated, and was reinterpreted as an antidote to the unexamined life by Socrates. But despite its long and convoluted heritage, it is a principle that should be part of every academic leadership program. You cannot lead without knowing yourself: who you are, what values guide you, and why you are trying to lead others in any given direction. Outside of academia, personal growth and leadership development programs from the NTL Institute (www.ntl.org) and Werner Erhard's once popular EST (Erhard Seminars Training) to Outward Bound and the Center for Creative Leadership have made great use of reflecting and the pursuit of self-awareness as strategies for individual improvement. While many pop psychology fads have faded, institutions of higher education have had great success with programs that promote reflective practice through reading, discussion, and mutual exchange of feedback. One university, for example, sponsored two separate academic leader groups—the first consisting of the president, provost, and vice presidents and the second consisting of deans, associate deans, and directors—to read and collectively engage in a year-long discussion of Kevin Cashman's *Leadership from the Inside Out: Becoming a Leader for Life* (2008). During this process, the university's leadership team was guided through a "reflective journey to grow as a whole person in order to grow as a whole leader" (19).

Contract renewals for many academic leaders require some type of evaluation by superiors, colleagues, faculty, staff, and other stakeholders. This 360-degree feedback approach provides campus leaders with insight into the strengths and weaknesses of their leadership styles. While some of these methods are flawed and do not rely on psychometrically valid instruments, many leaders have received useful information about their approaches through such instruments as the Myers-Briggs Type Indicator, the DiSC Assessment Tool, the Strength Deployment Instrument, the Thomas-Kilmann Conflict Mode Instrument, FIRO-B (Fundamental Interpersonal Relations Orientation), and other devices of this kind. Inventories that measure aspects of one's personality, interests, or communication style allow leaders to identify assets that they can take better advantage of and target areas where they may wish to seek further improvement and growth.

Another way of promoting reflective practice is systematic mentoring and coaching. Most effective department chairs believe that a significant part of their success was due to their having had a great mentor (Advisory Board, 2011). In addition, they identified these key elements of a successful mentoring relationship:

o Having a mentor who was genuinely invested in the protégé's success

o The protégé's sincere respect and admiration for the mentor

o Choosing a mentor whose skills align well with the protégé's needs

o A commitment by both parties to take the process seriously, maintain regular contact, and preserve a candid dialogue

As we saw in chapter 1, the Partners in Academic Leadership (PALs) initiative at Iowa State was created to enhance the opportunity for pairs of administrators to reflect on their experiences and assist each other with challenges as they arose. The result was something of an oxymoron: it created a formal structure that encouraged informal mentoring. But different types of structures may be better at different institutions. For example, a leadership development program that involves a large number of deans and chairs may discover that the two groups have very diverse needs when it comes to the type of mentoring that can help them the most. Department chairs are frequently faced with their first administrative challenges as academic leaders and may benefit from a mentor who can simply introduce them to fundamental principles of effective college administration. Deans usually come to their positions with significant leadership experience and may profit more from working with senior administrators who can help them perfect their skills and, if they choose, advance to the next administrative level. Alternatively, they could benefit from the services of professional executive coaches. Unfortunately, "in higher education, many deans and senior leaders are unaware of executive coaching; others believe the practice belongs in the corporate world or is solely for low performers" (Advisory Board, 2011). While working with an executive coach can have that type of negative connotation—people believe that administrators are working with a coach because they were told that they were unsuccessful on their own—the truth of the matter is that coaches are typically hired to help put promising leaders on the fast track, not to remediate those who are in trouble. (See, for example, Kauffman and Coutu, 2009. For more on reflective practice, see chapter 8.)

Leadership development is not simply about learning knowledge and developing skills. It is also an inner journey, often the most difficult part of professional growth. Self-knowledge, personal awareness, and corrective feedback should be integral parts of the leadership development system (Gmelch, 2002). Moral, ethical, and value-based dimensions, at times even spiritual dimensions, can also be of tremendous value to administrators as they proceed on their leadership journey. We discuss the role of this ethical and value dimension in greater detail in chapter 8. In the meantime, suffice it to say that the three delivery systems we just considered—conceptual understanding, skill development, and reflective practice—represent three different types of pedagogies, each contributing in its own way to the development of a fully rounded academic leader. In this way, they are themselves integral parts in a complex system: individual components that affect and are affected by one another in a significant way, as we will consider next.

Propositions for Developing Leadership Education Systems

One of the lessons that we have learned from working with many leadership development programs at many different institutions is that "it is not 'individuals' who should be developed, but members of a social system in which leadership is embedded" (Minzberg, 2004, 242). Universities and campuses can send their academic leaders to off-campus seminars to be "fixed" (if they view them as "broken") and informed or trained, but the results are likely to be disappointing. Some of these programs are of great value in that they can enlighten inexperienced administrators and provide them with a broader vision of the field of higher education. Nevertheless, as we have already noted, off-campus programs inevitably miss the institution-specific context that is critical for leaders to understand specific campus issues. These programs also do not build campus social systems or provide an opportunity for campus leaders to develop key relationships and support systems with colleagues from across campus. The benefit of creating support networks through in-house programs has been underscored at many of the campuses we have visited and seems to be nearly a prerequisite for making the ideas leaders bring back from workshops part of their daily procedures. In *Managers Not MBAs* (2004), Henry Minzberg discusses the state of MBA programs and makes recommendations about how they can be improved. If we adapt his eight propositions as a framework for how administrators can develop their academic leadership, we might suggest the following guidelines for how campus systems of leadership development can be made as effective as possible:

1. *Because of the unique organizational culture of colleges and universities, leadership development programs should remain focused primarily, perhaps even exclusively, on academic leadership.* In an effort to be all things to all people, some campus initiatives have sought to become clearinghouses for issues related to all kinds of leadership. By so doing, these projects tend to lose their focus or voice on critical issues. It is not that these programs do not have renowned international models for this broad approach. For example, Harvard's Management Development Program (MDP; see www.gse.harvard.edu/ppe/programs /higher-education/portfolio/management-development.html) combines athletic directors, deans, department chairs, and others, all of whom lead in very different institutional environments. Other programs combine graduate students, emerging faculty leaders, and current administrators into a single program. While we have seen the value in bringing together entire work teams, including those at different hierarchical levels, within the same program or activity, that value is lost when the participants work in different areas, at different institutional levels, and with different responsibilities and expectations. Leadership development works best when the learning wraps a context around the content. That is one of the reasons that Stanford's Graduate School of Business does not admit graduate students unless they have had a couple of years of experience in business organizations. Henry Mintzberg (2004) makes a strong case that "managers cannot be created in a classroom, but that existing managers can further develop there" (243).

2. *Take full advantage of the resources that a university has to offer.* We saw in chapter 3 that there is so much talent already existing at a college or university that you can staff most or all of your program without bringing in speakers or trainers from the outside. Something similar can be said about the other resources that a university has to offer: you have so much instructional technology available at your institution that you can provide an innovative program with little initial investment. Consider for a moment the access you have to distance learning classrooms and equipment. With them, you provide the benefits of your leadership development program to participants who are unable to be on-site for a workshop. In a

similar way, you can tap into speakers and programs being conducted at other universities as a way of expanding what your institution is able to offer by itself. You have talent and resources available to you for making video clips addressing various leadership challenges, recordings, and publications that can disseminate materials you develop and computer servers that can download materials. Participants in the program can use these resources to carry the benefits of the program back to their academic units at the same time that they add to the information and training materials that will be available to future generations of participants.

3. *A theoretical framework can help leaders make better sense of their experience.* In figure 1.1, we saw that the term *grounded theory* can be used to explain the part of leadership development where conceptual understanding and reflective practice overlap. A theoretical understanding that is grounded in reflection helps academic leaders make sense of the university and of their experience while leading it. We need both sound theories and grounded practice. In the familiar words of John W. Gardner (1995), "The society which scorns excellence in plumbing as a humble activity and tolerates shoddiness in philosophy because it is an exalted activity will have neither good plumbing nor good philosophy: neither its pipes nor its theories will hold water" (102). For most, if not all, of us in academic life, being a scholar is probably the most exalted role we can think of at a university. But scholarship and the understanding of the world that it brings can also add a dimension to what is, for many people, the most suspect and demeaned role at the university: the professional administrator. A provost who participated in our study commented that "any good academic can be a good dean as long as he or she is smart and knows how to analyze data." We don't agree. We think it is important for effective leaders also to understand something about leadership theory, organizational behavior, and the broader context of higher education in the twenty-first century. Academic leaders who are expected to act on behalf of their programs without the benefit of this theoretical framework are thus placed at a disadvantage that a leadership development initiative should seek to address.

4. *Thoughtful reflection on their experience can be an important prerequisite for leadership development.* Academic leaders need to stop and think, stepping back from their daily immersion in administrivia and reflecting systematically on their experiences and the context in which they work. As Donald Schön concluded in *The Reflective Practitioner* (1983), traditional managers seldom find time to reflect on their reflections. They pay scant attention to how the type of understanding

they need as leaders is both similar to and different from the kinds of knowledge represented in management books, scientific papers, and the opinions of external consultants. Even in higher education, there is rarely sufficient time to reflect on what it is we do, why we do it, and how we learned to do it. Competent chairs and deans know a good deal more than they realize, and they exhibit a kind of "knowing-in-practice," most of which is tacit, when they understand from experience what approach is most likely to be successful in a given situation. When practicing administrators build on this knowing-in-practice through reflection-in-action, they become researchers into more effective means of academic leadership. The goal, therefore should be for academic leaders to become reflective practitioners: professionals whose cycle of doing, learning from doing, and then doing better continually grows over time (figure 4.1).

5. *Sharing their experiences and describing their processes with others improves leaders' understanding of what they do.* As every teacher knows, you do not truly understand a subject until you try explaining it to others. The same principle holds true for leadership development. But there is also a greater urgency for administrators to engage in this practice now than there has been in the past. Along with the rise of the accountability culture in higher education and the dominant role played by accreditation agencies (Buller, 2012), the emphasis on assessable competencies has received a great deal of attention in the world of higher education. As we have seen, gaining the information needed to be a successful academic leader represents the first level of leadership development: conceptual understanding. But reflective practice, including the

---

**Figure 4.1 Reflection-in-Action
Cycle**

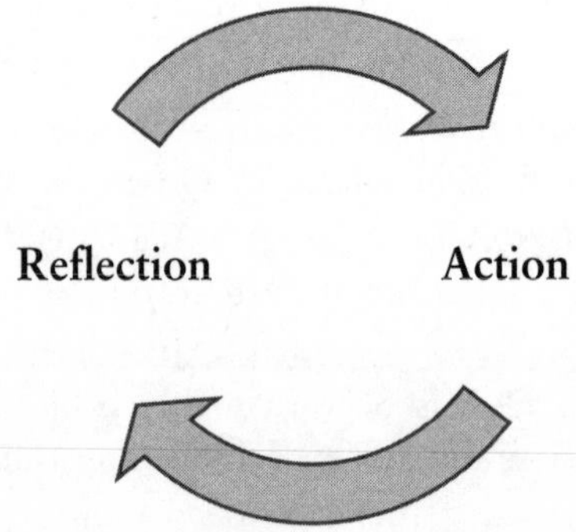

Reflection   Action

need to articulate one's reasoning to others, adds a focus on the how and why of administration to the mastery of the what that leaders receive at the level of conceptual understanding. As Mintzberg notes in *Managers Not MBAs* (2004), acquiring competencies does not necessarily result in competence. Skill training turns awareness of concepts or thoughts into action; you can learn about them in a classroom, but you truly learn them only when you put them into effect, reflect on what occurs, and try to convey a sense of that experience to others. New skills such as strategic thinking, executive execution, and facilitating change require a combination of knowledge and practical experience, and sharing what one has learned with others makes participants more aware of how their experience informs their understanding and vice versa.

6. *Treat the institution itself as a constantly evolving case study in how to develop leadership skills.* By selecting academic leaders from inside the institution, colleges and universities build more than just a strong sense of commitment from those administrators. They also put leaders in place whose institutional memory can serve them well. These administrators have a shorter learning curve than those hired in from the outside because not everything is new to them. Even more important, they are aware of many examples of what works and what does not work in that specific environment. In other words, they know their institution as an organic and constantly evolving case study. Leadership development programs can encourage participants to preserve that perspective throughout their leadership roles. Periodically they can pull back and try to interpret the situation as a paid consultant might. "If I were looking at this situation with fresh eyes," they might ask, "what would I conclude? How are those conclusions modified by what I do know about this institution, and does that perspective give me a clearer or more distorted view of what is going on?"

7. *Comprehensive academic leadership is the product of bringing all three components of leadership development—conceptual understanding, skill building, and reflective practice—together and seeing how they support one another.* As figure 1.1 makes clear, no single system of learning or leadership development can produce the type of academic leaders needed for the twenty-first century. Rather, all three activities have to be integrated into a single approach. We might say that in institutions of higher education, administrators "live in the territory" while faculty members can "provide the maps" through theories, concepts, and models. Both of those experiences are important: practice helps keep theory

grounded, and theory keeps practice from degenerating into a mere succession of unrelated experiences. Adding systematic reflection to this mix helps participants draw lessons of personal significance from this theory and practice, relating them to their own values, vision, and philosophy as academic leaders.

8. *Viewing academic leadership development as a system means that centers and programs are most effective when they engage in flexible facilitating rather than a rigid, preplanned design.* Ever since Robert Barr and John Tagg's landmark article on learning-based college education in 1995, the way in which college professors see their role has changed dramatically. The well-known shift of the teacher from "sage on the stage" to "guide on the side" means that instructors see themselves as not solely teaching what they know but meeting students where they currently are in their educational journeys. Nevertheless, academic leadership programs have not kept pace with this new paradigm. Where they exist at all, they usually consist of workshops on set topics that provide an old-fashioned type of instruction—a presenter talking while the participants passively listen and take notes—that we have long since outgrown in college classrooms. The successful paradigm of leadership development needs to change from the older teaching/training model to one that takes better account of everything we have learned about how adults master new material and skills. There will be less classroom instruction and more structured and supervised practice, fewer talking heads and more collaboration between instructor and participant, and less dependence on short-term workshops and more opportunity for long-term programs tailored to the individual needs of each participant.

Designing a More Flexible System

Whoever is in charge of the academic leadership initiative—whether it is a director, steering committee, or leadership team—will function as something of a designer or architect of a fairly complex system. The structure that is developed should be aligned to specific learning outcomes to advance each participant's leadership development in each of the three spheres outlined. As a result, the structure will need to be rather flexible. Whatever system architecture is developed should not result in just another rigid learning structure but should be capable of adapting as needs evolve. Those in charge of the program will have to be "designers of an ongoing social process as much as the conveyers of conceptual knowledge. And unlike most architects today, they [will] have to remain on site as much as the conveyers of conceptual knowledge" (Mintzberg, 2004, 271).

One important way in which flexibility can be demonstrated is in the variety of instructional platforms the initiative makes available. Lee S. Shulman (2005), who had a distinguished career as an educational psychologist at Stanford University, notes that each discipline tends to have its own signature pedagogy. For example, law schools rely on the case study method, medical schools tend to use problem-based learning, departments of biology and chemistry conduct experiments according to the scientific method, and the social science disciplines apply statistical tests to data based on human behavior. No one method is *the* correct method for understanding everything we need to know, and each discipline may learn from others by borrowing from and adapting approaches to knowledge used in other fields. In a similar way, we might say that the system we create for developing academic leadership can be improved by learning from signature pedagogies used in other fields. So in addition to the lecture or lecturette, higher education's traditional teaching method, we can imagine a highly innovative, flexible leadership development program that chooses the right tool from a large toolbox of instructional methods:

Toolbox of Instructional Methods

Expert facilitation	Case studies
Models	Simulations
Negotiations	Lecture-case-discussion
Web-based learning	Problem-based learning
Action learning	Service-learning
Mentorships	Support groups
Executive coaching	Self-appraisals
Evaluation and assessment instruments	Role playing
Instructional games	Shadowing current leaders
Feedback mechanisms	Personalized 360-degree evaluations
Learning needs assessment	Mental imaging
Focused writing assignments	Competency-based leadership training
Formal socialization processes	Teamwork exercises
Structured interactions	Outdoor initiatives (ropes courses, Outward Bound)
Videos, films, multimedia	Retreats
Personal growth and planning	Webinars
Directed self-study	Critiques

Each of these learning methods brings with it underlying assumptions about how students will learn and how they will apply each of the three spheres of leadership development that we discussed earlier. Conger and Benjamin (1999) concluded that multiple learning methods are essential to a well-designed leadership program. The use of different instructional techniques increases the chances that one or more of the methods will meet the needs of any particular student. Nevertheless,

> most action learning programs continue to be implemented with little understanding of the design elements that are needed to ensure learning actually takes place. Leadership programs of the future will have to do a better job of leveraging adult learning principles if they hope to accelerate and enhance strategic thinking and other critical complex capabilities. (Conger and Benjamin, 1999, 253–254)

Finally, to meet this challenge, the entire system of the leadership development program will have to be designed differently:

o   Programs will need to identify each goal more definitively.

o   Programs will need to take full advantage of new technologies so they no longer simply deliver information but also improve strategic thinking.

o   As universities become ever more competitive and technologically complex, they will need to develop strategic partnerships to acquire the expertise required to keep their leaders on the cutting edge. Alone, a campus leadership development program is not enough; tomorrow's university leaders will be required to reach out to other competitors and social and economic sectors of the world.

Conclusion

Leadership, by its very nature, entails a systems approach to fulfilling this mission of the unit or institution. Despite all the maxims about life being lonely at the top, no one ever leads alone. There is always a network of followers, competitors, societal expectations, institutional history, and institutional baggage that complicates the environment in which every leader works. The more effectively that academic development programs incorporate this type of systems thinking into their own planning and the content they provide, the more realistic and successful the experiences of their participants will be.

Clarifying the System

As you review the system that you have in place for your leadership development initiative, here are some questions you can use to determine whether your concept is clear enough to achieve the results you envision:

1. Is sufficient attention being paid to the specific system in which the participants will be working? In other words, is there consideration not just of academic leadership in general but also the unique environment of the institution and unit where the participant works?

2. Is sufficient attention being paid to theories that regard leadership not as a fixed set of traits or skills, but as a set of interrelations that occur within a highly dynamic organizational culture?

3. Are the activities of the program being offered through a variety of delivery systems so that each participant can learn in the way that best suits his or her individual needs and provides a balanced mix of content, skill building, and reflection?

4. Is the system that you designed flexible enough so that as changes in the institution or the participants' needs occur, they can still be addressed effectively by your initiative?

5. Is a plan in place for the participants to use their own institution and units as an evolving case study from which to learn?

6. Have you focused your initiative on academic leadership so that its value is not diluted in an effort to be all things to all people?

REFERENCES

Advisory Board. (2011). *Developing academic leaders: Cultivating the skills of chairs, deans, and other faculty administrators*. Washington, DC: Advisory Board.

Barr, R. B., & Tagg, J. (1995). From teaching to learning: A new paradigm for undergraduate education. *Change, 27*(6), 12–25.

Bennis, W. G. (1989). *On becoming a leader*. Reading, MA: Addison-Wesley.

Bess, J. L., & Dee, J. R. (2008). *Understanding college and university organization: Theories for effective policy and practice*. Sterling, VA: Stylus.

Birnbaum, R. (1992). *How academic leadership works: Understanding success and failure in the college presidency*. San Francisco, CA: Jossey-Bass.

Bolman, L. G., & Deal, T. E. (2013). *Reframing organizations: Artistry, choice, and leadership* (5th ed.). San Francisco, CA: Jossey-Bass, 2013.

Bolman, L. G., & Gallos, J. V. (2011). *Reframing academic leadership*. San Francisco, CA: Jossey-Bass.

Buller, J. L. (2012). *Best practices in faculty evaluation: A practical guide for academic leaders*. San Francisco, CA: Jossey-Bass.

Buller, J. L. (2013). *Positive academic leadership: How to stop putting out fires and start making a difference*. San Francisco, CA: Jossey-Bass.

Burns, J. M. (1978). *Leadership*. New York, NY: Harper.

Cashman, K. (2008). *Leadership from the inside out: Becoming a leader for life*. San Francisco, CA: Berrett-Koehler.

Conger, J. A. (1992). *Learning to lead: The art of transforming managers into leaders*. San Francisco, CA: Jossey-Bass.

Conger, J. A., & Benjamin, B. (1999). *Building leaders: How successful companies develop the next generation*. San Francisco, CA: Jossey-Bass.

Ericsson, K. A., & Smith, J. (1991). *Toward a general theory of expertise: Prospects and limits*. Cambridge: Cambridge University Press.

Fisher, R., Ury, W., & Patton, B. (1991). *Getting to yes: Negotiating agreement without giving in*. New York, NY: Penguin Books.

Gärdenfors, P., & Sahlin, N.-E. (1982). Unreliable probabilities, risk taking, and decision making. *Synthese, 53,* 361–386.

Gardner, J. W. (1995). *Excellence: Can we be equal and excellent too?* New York, NY: Norton.

Gladwell, M. (2008). *Outliers: The story of success*. New York, NY: Little, Brown.

Gmelch, W. H. (2002). *Deans' balancing acts: Education leaders and the challenges they face*. Washington, DC: American Association of Colleges for Teacher Education.

Harrison, R., & Lomi, A. (2012). *The garbage can model of organizational choice: Looking forward at forty*. Bingley, UK: Emerald Group.

Kauffman, C., & Coutu, D. (2009, January). *The realities of executive coaching*. Harvard Business Review Research Report. Retrieved from http://www.carolkauffman.com/images/pdfs/Kauffman_Coutu_HRB_survey_report.pdf

Lussier, R. N., & Achua, C. F. (2013). *Leadership: Theory, application and skill development* (5th ed.). Mason, OH: South-Western Cengage Learning.

March, J. G., Simon, H. A., & Guetzkow, H. S. (1993). *Organizations* (2nd ed.). Cambridge, MA: Blackwell.

Marion, R., & Gonzales, L. D. (2014). *Leadership in education: Organizational theory for the practitioner*. Long Grove, IL: Waveland Press.

Mintzberg, H. (2004). *Managers Not MBAs: A hard look at the soft practice of managing and management development*. San Francisco, CA: Berrett-Koehler.

Northouse, P. (2012). *Leadership: Theory and practice* (6th ed.). Thousand Oaks, CA: Sage.

Schön, D. A. (1983). *The reflective practitioner: How professionals think in action.* New York, NY: Basic Books.

Shulman, L. S. (2005). Signature pedagogies in the professions. *Daedalus, 134*(3), 52–59.

Westley, F. (1992). Vision worlds: Strategic visions as social instruction. *Advances in Strategic Management, 8,* 271–305.

Williams, C. (2013). *Effective management.* Mason, OH: South-Western.

5

STAFF

THROUGHOUT THIS BOOK, we have been using the term *staff* in at least five different senses. First, the staff of a leadership development initiative can be seen as consisting of a number of presenters and participants. In other words, many campus leadership programs, at least in their early phases, do not draw a clear line between the staff providing expertise on and insight into leadership and the staff receiving the benefit of the development effort. In fact, those two groups are often the same: the participants teach others about what they themselves know and receive help from others in those areas they would like to improve. That was the case for the Academic Leadership Forum (ALF) at Iowa State University that we explored in chapter 1. Second, the staff of a program might consist of people, both within and outside the institution, who lead sessions for the participants on various topics related to leadership. In this instance, the presenters and the participants are distinct (although perhaps partially overlapping) groups of mentors and protégés, teachers and students, or trainers and trainees. Third, the staff of a leadership development initiative might be a blend of the first two groups, with some expertise being contributed by the participants themselves and other expertise provided by on-campus administrators not otherwise involved in the program, former deans and chairs, and other people with special skills or leadership positions at the university. Fourth, the term *staff* may be used to refer to the administrative or clerical support staff for the program—the people who reserve the rooms, maintain the records, and set the schedule of activities. Fifth, for reasons of institutional history or mission, there may be a decision to staff a leadership development initiative in a wholly unique way.

Staffing Models

The various approaches to staffing fall along a continuum that ranges from programs so internally staffed that the participants and the presenters are identical, to those that are so externally staffed they rely entirely on outside consultants for their programming (figure 5.1). No single staffing model will meet the needs of all institutions. There are benefits and drawbacks to each of these approaches, and so we address them in some detail.

Staff as Support Group

Perhaps the most common staff structure for leadership initiatives that are either experimental or just getting under way is the form that we might describe as the mutual support group. Each member of the group contributes his or her expertise for the benefit of the other members and learns from them in turn. So, if a particular dean or department chair has had some success in building collegiality in a program, that administrator might conduct one or more sessions on professionalism and academic civility, while learning from his or her peers about such matters as effective budgeting, time management, faculty evaluations, fundraising, and the like. In this type of arrangement, the participants themselves are the experts, consultants, or content providers. This leadership development initiative is rather similar to the colleague-based support groups described in the online premium content in Buller (2012).

There are many excellent reasons for structuring a leadership development program as a mutual support group. First, it is quick to organize and inexpensive to run. All someone has to do is identify a group of six or eight individuals who share a common interest in improving their academic leadership, have each person select some aspect of administration with which he or she has had some experience, and find a time when the group can get together. Each presenter could organize the session in whatever manner best lends itself to the material. For example, we could

---

Figure 5.1 Academic Leadership Program Staffing Continuum

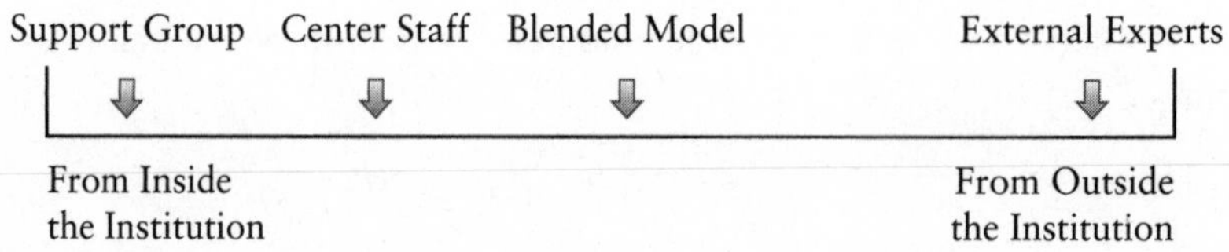

Support Group   Center Staff   Blended Model   External Experts

From Inside   From Outside
the Institution   the Institution

imagine the following schedule for a mutual support group in leadership development at a college or university:

Peer-to-Peer Leadership Development Group: Calendar of Activities

Group meetings occur on the first Friday of each month at 4:00 p.m.

Month	Topic	Leader	Format
September	Organizational culture	Dr. Able	Book discussion
October	Planning budgets	Dr. Baker	Guest lecture
November	Supervising budgets	Dr. Charlie	Simulation
December	Evaluating faculty	Dr. Dog	Lecture-case-discussion
January	Conflict resolution	Dr. Echo	Role play
February	Strategic planning	Dr. Fox	Case study analysis
March	Time management	Dr. George	Self-appraisal and discussion
April	Data-driven decision making	Dr. How	Video

In this hypothetical example, the eight participants in the program are also the eight presenters, trainers, or content experts. By selecting a topic of common interest with which he or she has some experience, the leader for that meeting shares knowledge with other participants while not being burdened by preparing a presentation on an unfamiliar topic. By varying the format of each session, the participants make the program more interesting for themselves and are able to select the most appropriate means for addressing each individual topic.

The great challenge of support group leadership programs is sustaining them. It is relatively easy for each of the participants to select a single topic of expertise or experience for the first year. But what happens in the second and subsequent years? Some participants may feel that they have already "used up" their one area of greatest knowledge and are at a loss over how to make an equivalent contribution later. In addition, the direct impact of such a program is relatively small. Although these eight academic leaders will probably benefit greatly from their sessions, the program will probably not do very much to improve the level of administrative efficiency throughout the entire institution. For this reason, the support group model tends to work best at rather small schools and at institutions that want to pilot a leadership development program to ascertain the level of interest that exists for a more substantial initiative. As was the case with Iowa State's ALF program, a small number of highly committed academic leaders can try out different topics and formats, which then can be used as the basis for a larger program later if one seems justified.

One successful example of the Staff-as-support-group model is the Academic Leadership Program (ALP) at the University of North Carolina at Chapel Hill. The initiative was begun by Ruel Tyson, a professor of religion at the university, who had attended a week-long leadership program offered by the Center for Creative Leadership and wanted to bring many of the benefits he gained from that experience back to his own campus. The ALP serves eight or nine faculty members a year who are selected to be fellows of the program. The fellows spend a week in residence at the Center for Creative Leadership and then participate in weekly three-hour seminars throughout the spring semester, as well as two overnight retreats. Beginning the following year, cohorts of fellows continue developing their leadership skills in a largely self-directed forum. Since the forum selects its own topics and the participants provide their own insights, the structure provides an ongoing support group of peers who can assist one another as new problems or opportunities arise. One interesting feature of the ALP is that it has its own selection committee; the university's administration has little involvement in the process except when they themselves happen to be program graduates. Since a number of people who entered the ALP without any administrative title or experience later became senior administrators, the ALP has developed a reputation for identifying and developing leadership potential through its support group structure.

In 2006 the Hyde Foundation provided the ALP with permanent support by means of an endowment and gave the university an opportunity to create a second leadership initiative, this one intended solely for department chairs. The additional project, known as the Chairs Leadership Program (CLP), is offered to new and reappointed chairs in the College of Arts and Science and, on a space available basis, chairs from the School of Dentistry and the Gillings School of Global Public Health. The latter two schools were included in the project since they are the only professional schools outside the medical school that have true department chairs. The CLP operates as a peer-mentoring group for first-year chairs. It has a largely open-ended agenda and serves about a dozen chairs each year. It is led by an experienced chair and a professional group facilitator who together engage the participants in discussions that are confidential and issue oriented. A common comment seen in the evaluation forms completed by participants is that the CLP serves as "therapy for chairs." That is one of the strengths of peer-based, support group staffing structures: participants find that they have a safe environment in which to share their concerns with others who are going through many of the same experiences. Since the composition of the group does not change (as it would in a program where each topic was presented by a different external expert), these programs tend to develop an esprit de corps that encourages frank and open reflection on specific problems within specific units. (For more on the ALP and CLP, see iah.unc.edu/programs/leadership-programs.)

Staff as Expert Consultants

The second model, the expert consultants approach, draws a clearer line between the content providers/presenters and the participants in the program. This approach can be found in initiatives like the leadership development program of the Center for University Learning at Kennesaw State University. The goal of this center is to provide professional, personal, and leadership development for members of the university faculty, staff, and administration. The services offered by the center cover a wide spectrum: workshops, extended programs, online courses, coaching sessions, a resource library, individual and group assessments, team-building and organization development services, tailor-made personal development plans, and social activities. The center also serves as a clearinghouse for additional types of training provided by other departments, such as safety, human resources, and information services. Featured courses are listed on the center's website (www.ksulearning.com), which is updated every six months and includes courses that are scheduled up to a year in advance so that potential participants can plan their schedules. The logistics necessary to run such a complex array of services are handled by a full-time director, an associate director, a project and communications coordinator, and an administrative assistant. Together with a student worker, this team handles purchasing, scheduling, registrations, classroom setup, communications, and general administrative duties. The director and associate director, who are both Development Dimensions International certified facilitators, provide some of the programming themselves, but they also rely heavily on expert consultants and trainers from both inside and outside the institution. Many of these additional facilitators became known to the center by completing an online form through which they submit their contact information, the courses or programs they wish to offer, the objectives and learning outcomes for each activity they propose, the fees to charge for materials and services, and additional information about the training activity. The center staff then plans annual activities based on the needs and interests of the university's stakeholders.

By scaffolding various workshops and minicourses so that each successive activity builds on the previous one, the center is able to offer various certificates to participants, which they can use to document their professional development. For example, here are the requirements established by the Center for University Learning for its Management Development Certificate.

Kennesaw State University Management Development Certificate

Complete all of the following foundational courses:

1. Essentials of Leadership
2. Setting Performance Expectations
3. Coaching for Peak Performance

Complete any three of the following electives:

- Managing Conflict Productively—Professionally and Personally
- Resolving Conflict in Teams
- Leading Change
- Leading High Performance Teams
- Delegating with Purpose
- Introduction to Project Management

Source: mlmdp.weebly.com/.

One distinctive aspect of the Kennesaw State initiative is how the programs are funded. Within the university itself, departments are charged for the cost of materials when they send employees for training. But other funding is derived from partner institutions within the University System of Georgia, which are permitted to send participants to the programs at a charge for facilitator costs and materials.

In all of its offerings, the Center for University Learning places a premium on experiential and service-learning. The directors feel that it is much better for program participants to learn a few discreet skills through experience and then be able to apply them immediately in their work than for them to receive a thick binder of articles, theoretical materials, and vague instructions that they are not likely to put to practical use.

One example of this practicality based training is the Excel Leadership Program, which is offered during the university's May term and gives members of the faculty and staff an opportunity to develop leadership skills and build relationships with and form networks among other colleagues at Kennesaw State. Participants receive practical exposure to the university's organizational structure, strategic goals, mission, relationship with the University System of Georgia and board of regents, and the way in which state government affects educational policies. In addition to sessions with senior leaders of the university and the state system, the participants complete a team-based service project as a hands-on exercise in leadership. Each Excel class consists of ten faculty members and ten members of the staff or administration, each of whom applies individually to the program in a competitive process. The result is not only an improvement in overall administrative effectiveness at the university but also, it is hoped, additional internal experts who can serve as facilitators for the center's other programs. (See www.ksulearning.com/excel-leadership-program.html.)

Staff as a Blended Group

The two examples that we have explored so far represent, in certain ways, the two extremes of the staffing spectrum: at one end, a leadership initiative that operates with no staff at all, and at the other end, a fairly comprehensive center that combines full-time administrative employees, expert consultants from within the institution, and external trainers, some of whom operate their own staff development businesses. Most institutions, at least after their early experimental stages, are likely to decide on a staffing model that falls somewhere between these two extremes. The blended group approach to staffing provides the advantage of having administrative support available to handle logistics, be on hand if questions arise, and preserve institutional memory as the program's participants change over time. As an added benefit, this approach allows costs to be kept low and the level of institution-specific training high by relying heavily on internal experts as presenters.

A good example of the blended or peer-to-peer approach to staffing is the University of Alaska Anchorage's Center for Advancing Faculty Excellence (CAFE), founded in 2000. In this initiative, leadership development programs are united with faculty development programs within a single center. Although there is a full-time staff—a director, associate director, and program coordinator—its responsibilities are largely organizational, with the content of the program provided by experienced in-house administrators. External speakers are occasionally brought in to deal with individual topics, such as team building or promoting collegiality, but the vast majority of programming is provided by the university's current and former chairs, deans, and directors. CAFE's programs take a variety of forms: traditional workshops, online resources, book discussion groups, faculty learning communities, discussion panels, retreats, and the like. In keeping with the center's mission, the topics covered in these programs combine leadership training with general faculty development issues. During a typical year, the seminars offered by the center might include such topics as these:

○ Advice to New Faculty
○ Faculty Collegiality at the University of Alaska Anchorage: Strategies for Faculty Members
○ Faculty Collegiality at the University of Alaska Anchorage: Strategies for Chairs
○ Introduction to Team-Based Learning
○ How to Write More Effective Multiple-Choice Questions
○ Negotiating the System at the University of Alaska Anchorage
○ What You Should Know before Submitting Faculty Development Grant Applications
○ What You Should Know before Submitting Sabbatical Leave Applications
○ Grant Proposal Basics at the University of Alaska Anchorage
○ Making Learning Visible
○ Promoting Student Success
○ Academic Freedom and Engaging Controversy in the Classroom

By combining faculty development and leadership issues, the center reinforces its identity as a clearinghouse for all types of professional development. Faculty members who are introduced to its offerings when they join the institution will thus feel comfortable with returning there for leadership training when they become chairs of committees, departments, or institution task forces.

Since the blended group approach tends to be particularly successful in providing leadership development in an institution-specific manner, that form of organization fits the unique needs of the University of Alaska Anchorage. For example, the programming offered by CAFE must take into account that roughly a quarter of the state's K–12 population consist of students from the indigenous Alaskan population, a constituency that is familiar with traditional ways of learning that an outside consultant or leadership expert may know little about. Moreover, the university has seven community campuses, some of them in rather remote areas. Experts from outside the institution may not be familiar with the leadership challenges that arise in a multicampus setting, particularly one that combines urban and rural settings, a multiethnic student population, and the ruggedness of the Alaskan climate and geography.

A very different program that also makes use of the blended staffing model is the Institute for Academic Leadership (IAL), which serves the State University System of Florida. The core of IAL's activities is a two-session series primarily for department chairs, although other administrators may attend. One session is held in the fall and the other in the summer, with each session having its own set of topics. The sessions serve about seventy participants, who are divided into groups of seven to nine individuals who work together over the course of each three-day session. Every group is assigned a facilitator who is an experienced chair and assists the group in its discussions and other activities. The program uses a blended model of staffing in that it always begins with a speaker, often an external expert, who introduces one of the topics of the workshop with a brief overview. Participants read materials relevant to that topic, break into discussion groups, and discuss the topic for about ninety minutes. The breakout groups then reassemble, and each group provides a summary of its perspectives on the topic.

IAL has been in continual operation since 1978 and traces its continued success to several factors. First, the support staff carefully screen all presenters and facilitators to make sure that participants are being exposed to only the most respected and experienced academic administrators in Florida. Second, the structure of small breakout groups provides many of the benefits of the support group model at the same time that it promotes networking with peers from across the state's university system. Third, the program draws on aspects of the expert consultant model by having both speakers and written materials that introduce new department chairs to the basic knowledge and skills they will need during their time in office. The following is an example of typical topics that would be covered during a two-session program:

Summer Program Topics	Fall Program Topics
Fundamentals of Academic Leadership	Faculty Evaluation
Maintaining Morale	Performance Counseling
Financial Management	Legal Implications of Being a Chair
Departmental Goals and Assessment	Delegation and Using Committees
Promoting Effective Teaching	Taking Full Advantage of Chair Evaluations

Staff as Administrative and Clerical Support

Even in cases where the content of a program is provided completely by in-house experts, someone needs to reserve rooms, make sure that equipment essential to a session is on hand, handle expenditures (if any), take care of communications, and perform a plethora of other clerical functions. In the smallest support group structures, the volunteers in the program will probably take care of these activities themselves. But once a program grows beyond this initial form, the sheer complexity of day-to-day operations will require at least some administrative or clerical support. In these cases, the staff of the program may consist of a single administrative assistant or even a student worker who takes care of these logistical matters. In very small programs or those that are still in an experimental phase, this administrative or clerical support may be just one of many other duties assigned to a member of the staff. For instance, deans who start leadership programs for their chairs may assign organizational duties to their own program assistants, or an initiative begun at the provost level may have technical details managed by a staff member in that office.

This approach has the advantage of making it relatively quick and easy to get a leadership development program under way: no additional personnel need to be hired; content can be provided by either in-house or external experts as was the case for several of the models already outlined; and the new duties are absorbed by someone already on the payroll. The problem is that this approach probably limits the size and effectiveness of the leadership development initiative. Most clerical staff members at colleges and universities are overworked as it is. Taking on additional responsibilities means that the time they have available for new tasks will be limited. For this reason, although several of the programs we examined in this chapter began with only a part-time clerical staff person, the demand for their services and the success of their endeavors soon made it necessary for them to explore other staffing models.

When leadership development activities preserve the staff-as-clerical-support model, they tend to remain small or highly focused programs. In order for them to grow, they usually need to develop a decentralized approach where administrative duties are distributed among a number of clerical workers from different units or institutions. A successful example of this approach is the Schwab Institute for Academic Leadership, a systemwide program that involves thirteen community colleges, four state universities, and an online institute (Charter Oak State College) in Connecticut. Beginning in 2004 as an opportunity for college presidents, the institute has evolved so that each year it focuses on a different stakeholder group, such as deans, department chairs, faculty members, or upper administrators. The distinctive feature of the Schwab Institute is that its primary activity is a single one-day program that takes place each spring. Because the program is so focused, it seeks to condense many different types of leadership development activities into the day-long event: an expert consultant presents an interactive program in the morning related to the theme chosen for the year; for about the last hour before lunch, there is usually a case study analysis conducted first in breakout groups and then in a plenary session; over lunch, more breakout discussions are held among the participants at each table; the afternoon is spent in a panel discussion and question-and-answer session in which both the expert consultant and peers from the state take part. The goal is to make the program as experiential as possible, tying the issues that are discussed to local concerns and emphasizing practical concerns over more theoretical analyses of leadership in general.

The annual budget for the Schwab Institute is extremely small: ten thousand dollars is allocated at the system level, primarily to cover the honorarium and travel expenses of the external consultant, release time for the coordinator and others as necessary, supplies, and the cost for the venue. Participants or their home institutions fund their travel to the program. As a result, the clerical work needed to make the institute a success has been decentralized. Each institution has a teaching and learning consultant who serves as a liaison to the institute. A program coordinator and two committee members are selected from among these consultants to handle such logistical details as the topic for the year, the speaker who will be invited, and changes made to future programs based on the evaluations that were completed by the participants. Since the institute retains no full-time staff of its own, clerical work usually becomes the responsibility of an administrative assistant at the coordinator's home institution. Because the initiative is only a one-day program, this staffing approach is adequate to cover its needs, but it is likely to become severely strained if there is ever a desire for the program to expand or take on more ambitious goals.

Innovative Approaches to Staffing

The fifth major approach to staffing is when an institution decides to adopt a wholly unique model for reasons related to the school's history, mission, or leadership needs. For example, the staff of Cornell University's Leadership Development Academy consist of three trainer/consultants with business or organizational development backgrounds and improvisational actors drawn from the Cornell Interactive Theatre Ensemble (CITE) who assist with various role plays and scenarios that are part of the academy's leadership programs. A five-day leadership immersion program might be structured as follows:

> Day 1: *Self-Awareness*: Participants complete the Myers-Briggs Temperament Indicator and other instruments to gain insights into their personalities, leadership styles, and priorities.
>
> Day 2: *Case Study*: Participants are presented with a hypothetical case involving how to merge two departments and are asked to consider what issues might arise and how they might deal with the resulting group dynamics.
>
> Day 3: *Simulation*: CITE actors portray faculty members from the case study considered on day 2, and the participants interact with them and attempt to address their issues and concerns.
>
> Day 4: *360-Degree Analysis*: Participants engage in a 360-degree feedback exercise (an activity in which they receive insights from their supervisors, peers, and those who report to them) that continues after the five-day intensive program is complete.
>
> Day 5: *System-Level Change*: Participants address how to prepare a system (such as a college or department) for change through strategic planning, program review, or similar processes.

In addition, CITE actors are sometimes used in individualized training sessions for administrators who are facing a specific challenge. A chair might have a faculty member, for instance, with whom he or she has ongoing problems because the faculty member regularly uses certain terms or engages in certain behaviors that provoke an unconstructive response from the chair. Meeting with a consultant/trainer from the Leadership Development Academy, a clinician who is experienced in dealing with such issues, and an actor who will portray the faculty member in question, the chair learns to develop a more constructive approach and then practices it in realistic exchanges with the actor until the provocation no longer triggers the undesired response.

The academy's staff background in management and organizational development led them to adopt this innovative approach due to their belief that short workshops, focused more on conveying information than providing opportunities for practice, tend to have relatively little effect on what faculty members and administrators actually do once they leave the program. By offering an immersion experience that requires the participants to engage in realistic scenarios, the academy has found that it has a much greater impact on how participants approach various leadership challenges. Moreover, there is extended follow-up to the immersion experiences. In many cases, the 360-degree analysis that is planned and initiated on day 4 of the program is launched with the participant's chosen reviewers about two weeks after the workshop is over. Those results are then gathered and discussed with each participant about six weeks after the workshop. Then the participant receives two additional coaching sessions to ensure that the lessons learned from the program have become a regular part of his or her leadership activities. None of that immersion and follow-up would be possible, however, if it were not for the unique way in which Cornell staffs its academy. (See www.hr .cornell.edu/life/career/academic_org_develop.html and www.hr.cornell .edu/life/career/cite.html for more information.)

Training the Trainers

Since so many staffing models use in-house experts for at least part of their programming, it can be beneficial for these experts to receive training in how best to develop leadership in others. Although many of these presenters have academic backgrounds, leadership development training has certain differences from classroom teaching. For one thing, the dynamic is different. Even in the most egalitarian college classroom, there is a distinct gap between the professor and the students in terms of power, authority, and expertise. That gap is far narrower in leadership development programs. It may even be reversed in cases where, for example, a chair is an expert on assessment and thus is leading a program in which the president and provost are participants. The result is that the trainer's relationship to the participants must always be much more that of a peer and colleague than that of a superior and authority. Second, despite the volumes that have been written on leadership skills and strategies, academic leadership remains amorphous: the way in which it is manifested by one person in one environment can be utterly different from how it is best demonstrated by a different person in a different environment. For this reason, even though the trainer may teach participants certain concepts or recommended approaches, his or her primary duty is often to serve as a catalyst for discussion. Participants in leadership development activities frequently learn more by being encouraged to articulate ideas they have long had, although perhaps only subconsciously, and to consider the reasons that some of the approaches they have taken in the past were successful while others were not.

For this reason, an important element of staffing a leadership development initiative is often designing a training-the-trainers program that can help presenters be as effective as possible in the sessions they conduct. The following topics are among those that could form the basis of such a program:

o Similarities and Differences between Teaching and Training
o Assessing the Needs of Participants
o Structuring Effective Training Modules or Sessions
o Creating Effective Training Materials
o Use of Technology in Training
o Developing Your Own Training Style
o Promoting Participant Interaction
o Promoting Active Learning
o The Use of Case Studies, Role Plays, and Simulations
o Common Problems That Arise in Training
o Assessing Participants' Progress
o Assessing Your Own Effectiveness as a Trainer

Many excellent resources are available to help universities prepare training-the-trainer programs. Among the best are Harold Stolovitch and Erica Keeps's *Telling Ain't Training* (2002), Cy Charney and Kathy Conway's *The Trainer's Tool Kit* (2005), Mary Jo Dolasinski, Anna Graf Williams, and Karen Hall's *Training the Trainer* (2004), Lou Russell's *Leadership Training* (2006), and Melvin Silberman and Carol Auerbach's *Active Training* (2006).

Highly complex training programs may even wish to consider having their trainers certified by a group like Development Dimensions International (a consultant firm that specializes in talent management), as was the case at Kennesaw State University, or (more commonly) the

American Society for Training and Development (ASTD). ASTD certification is widely recognized and provides an almost universally accepted
endorsement that the trainer has reached a high level of competence.
(See www.astd.org.) Certain university systems that have their own
unique needs, like the Saudi Academic Leadership Center (ALC) that
we mentioned in chapter 2, have even developed their own certification
system. ALC certification is based on achievements in four areas.

1. *Content and preparation*: How well prepared was the trainer?

2. *Materials*: Were the materials created by the trainer effective?

3. *Delivery*: Was the trainer's oral delivery effective?

4. *Interaction with participants*: Was active learning used?

Although many of the criteria in these four areas are unique to the
ALC's individual needs (e.g., the trainer's command of the English language), others are useful as guides for how programs may wish to evaluate
their trainers and presenters. The sections of the ALC's scoring rubric for
the areas of content and participation and interaction with participants
are in table 5.1. In all, fifteen criteria are spread over the four categories.
Since each criterion is scored on a range that extends from a low of 1 to
a high of 4, the participant's total score will range from 1 to 60, with 48
generally considered the minimum acceptable level for certification.

Budgeting for Staff

Because there are so many models for staffing a leadership development
initiative, there can be no single formula for funding these projects. Leadership development budgets can range all the way from nothing at all
for support group approaches to very substantial amounts that provide
staff salaries, honoraria for guest experts, stipends for participants, travel,
food, lodging, and other expenses. Moreover, the sources of those budgets
can different greatly. As we saw, the Schwab Institute in Connecticut has a
small budget provided by the central system, with participants' own institutions covering the costs of their travel to and from the institute. Cornell
University's Leadership Development Academy has its own budget that is
supplemented by charging units a set fee for each participant it has in the
program; participants from institutions other than Cornell are charged a
higher fee.

A number of leadership development programs begin with seed
grants and are ultimately continued by their own system or institution.
For example, Florida's Institute for Academic Leadership began with a
$500,000 grant from the Kellogg Foundation. When the grant expired,

Table 5.1. ALC Scoring Rubric for Content and Participation and for Interaction with Participants

	1	2	3	4	Total Points
Content and preparation: How well prepared was the trainer?					
Organization	Participants cannot understand presentation because there is no sequence of information.	Participants have difficulty following presentation because trainer is disorganized.	Trainer presents information in a logical sequence that participants can follow.	Trainer presents information in a logical, interesting sequence that the participants can follow.	
Subject Knowledge	Trainer does not have grasp of information; trainer cannot answer questions about subject.	Trainer is uncomfortable with information and is able to answer only rudimentary questions.	Trainer is at ease with expected answers to all questions but fails to elaborate.	Trainer demonstrates full knowledge (more than required) by answering all questions with explanations and elaboration.	
Interaction with participants: Was active learning used?					
Engagement	Trainer makes no effort to include all participants.	Trainer fails to include three or more tables of participants.	Trainer fails to include one or two tables of participants.	Trainer effectively includes all participants.	
Evaluation	Trainer gives participants no feedback on how well they're doing.	Trainer gives participants little feedback on how well they're doing.	Trainer gives participants some feedback on how well they're doing.	Trainer gives participants good feedback on how well they're doing.	
Facilitation	Trainer uses no active learning techniques (role play, case study, and the like).	Trainer uses few active learning techniques (role play, case study, and the like).	Trainer uses several active learning techniques (role play, case study, and the like).	Trainer uses many active learning techniques (role play, case study, and the like).	

the state university system picked up the program's funding. As might be expected for an activity that serves more than 150 academic leaders a year, those costs can be substantial (table 5.2). The table shows that the cost breaks down to slightly less than $1,000 a participant. While the cost will vary, of course, according to how ambitious the program's goals are and how comprehensive the services are that it provides, for most initial programs, a budget of approximately $1,000 per participant (in 2014 dollars) is sufficient to meet its needs.

Clarifying Staffing Issues

As you consider the type of staff to put in place for your leadership initiative, here are some guiding questions that can help you make the right choices to suit your institution's individual needs:

1. Where are you in the process of developing your leadership initiative? Are you still in the experimental and planning stage, which is best addressed through a pilot program staffed largely with volunteers? Are you fairly far along in your leadership development activity, which would indicate that you are in a position to take best advantage of a dedicated, full-time staff? Or are you somewhere between these two points, which suggests that a hybrid or blended approach to staffing might best suit your needs?

2. Who will handle each of the following responsibilities?
   - Choosing topics
   - Choosing presenters
   - Choosing participants
   - Choosing the venue
   - Advertising or promoting the program
   - Scheduling program sessions
   - Reserving rooms for sessions
   - Reserving equipment for sessions
   - Preparing and duplicating materials
   - Making travel arrangements
   - Securing refreshments
   - Cleaning and reorganizing facilities after sessions
   - Communicating with participants between sessions

Table 5.2. Institute for Academic Leadership Budget, 2012–2013 and 2013–2014

Year	Number of Participants	Travel Expenses (Presenters and Participants)	Copying, Books, Materials	Hotel and Meals (Presenters and Participants Only)	Honorarium (Presenters Only)	Total
2012–2013	162	$25,291	$2,055	$120,897	$3,000	$151,243
2013–2014	174	$27,000	$2,200	$135,024	$1,500	$165,724

3. Whom will you be paying in your program?
   - No one at all (i.e., people are freely donating their time or the activities are incorporated into existing loads and job descriptions)?
   - External experts?
   - In-house experts?
   - Clerical staff?
   - Participants?
4. Whose expenses will be covered? Just external presenters? External and internal presenters? Participants?
5. Will you need to fund buyouts of time for the organizers, presenters, or participants?
6. Will you be providing training for your presenters or facilitators, or both?
7. Will you charge participants for the program? If so, will participants from outside your institution or system be charged at a higher rate?

REFERENCES

Buller, J. L. (2012). *The essential department chair: A comprehensive desk reference*. San Francisco, CA: Jossey-Bass.

Charney, C., & Conway, K. (2005). *The trainer's tool kit* (2nd ed.). New York, NY: AMACOM.

Dolasinski, M. J., Williams, A. G., & Hall, K. J. (2004). *Training the trainer: Performance-based training for today's workplace*. Upper Saddle River, NJ: Prentice Hall.

Russell, L. (2006). *Leadership training*. Oxford: Pergamon Flexible Learning.

Silberman, M. L., & Auerbach, C. (2006). *Active training: A handbook of techniques, designs, case examples, and tips*. San Francisco, CA: Jossey-Bass/Pfeiffer.

Stolovitch, H. D., & Keeps, E. J. (2002). *Telling ain't training*. Alexandria, VA: American Society for Training and Development.

6

SKILLS

WE OFTEN HEAR PEOPLE describe someone as "a natural leader." Usually the person in question is someone who seems to know, intuitively and without any formal instruction, the right approach to take in every situation. In reality, however, born leaders are extremely rare. Most college administrators need instruction, experience, nurturing, and time to develop the skills they need. But those opportunities are not always available. Deans, chairs, and other administrators quickly realize that the expertise and behaviors they need in order to be successful leaders must be acquired—for the most part—piecemeal, while they are on the job. Moreover, the skills they learned in their former positions are not always applicable to their new responsibilities. What makes someone an effective chair does not always translate well when that person becomes an associate dean. And what makes a person succeed as an associate dean is not always the same skill set required when that person becomes a dean. It seems ironic that so many of the people that colleges and universities rely on for leadership are essentially self-taught. Their skills develop gradually and often haphazardly, the result of arbitrary training, inadequate feedback, and random mentoring. There has to be a solution to this problem, and an institutionally based leadership development initiative can often be a key component of this solution.

At the heart of any leadership development initiative is the question: What does it take to be an academic leader? The relatively high turnover rates of deans and department chairs suggest that institutions of higher education do not groom their leaders in ways that promote longevity, success, and effectiveness. For this reason alone, your institution cannot afford to overlook the value of preparing, advancing, and transitioning department chairs and deans. As we saw in chapter 1, today as never before, colleges and universities must answer the call to develop their leaders. As should now be very clear, the leadership development of deans, chairs, and faculty members is a process that extends over many years—in fact, through all the seasons of their professional lives. Moreover, as we have noted earlier, our research suggests that there are three spheres essential to developing academic leaders:

1. *Habits of mind*: Developing the conceptual understanding of how academic leadership requires unique roles, concepts, and areas of knowledge

2. *Habits of practice*: Perfecting the skills needed to achieve desired results through work with faculty, staff, students, other administrators, and external constituents

3. *Habits of heart*: Engaging in reflection to learn from experience and continue making progress in the art of leading

In this chapter, we build on this framework by highlighting the strategies academic leaders can use to develop their skills through effective habits of practice. We then consider a number of specific practices leaders can use to continue their leadership development.

Strategies for Skill Development

One way to visualize the three habits that we have been discussing in this book is to see each of them as having what we might call three levels of intervention: the personal, the institutional, and the professional.

At the personal level, people can improve their leadership skills through formal assessments and inventories, feedback from colleagues and mentors, advice from trusted confidants, books and journals devoted to various aspects of academic leadership, and reflection on what has worked and not worked in their own experience. They can benefit from engaging in networking, seeking out opportunities to be mentored or coached (and, later, seeking opportunities to mentor or coach others), practicing reflective writing, and building an active library of books, journals, and other resources related to academic leadership.

An effective personal development plan often starts with an assessment of the types of skills a person brings to his or her position and the specific needs of the institution. All too often, academic leaders have been expected to develop their skills on their own with little or no formalized training. As a result, many administrators who are starting out rely on books written about general approaches to management or leadership, often for contexts very different from that of higher education, or what they can glean from colleagues in similar positions. Even with these resources, the tasks that veteran campus leaders take for granted often stymie inexperienced leaders. Lacking well-developed skills, they may resort to problem solving through trial and error, an approach that can frustrate faculty members in their area who want their leaders to be decisive and have ready solutions.

Certainly there is no shortage of commercial purveyors of management seminars, instruments that measure current performance, and advice on how to manage conflict or build efficient teams. Not so abundant are skill development programs tailor-made for academic leaders and the types of issues they will actually face. It is here that a well-conceived leadership development initiative can be of great help. Mentors can work one-on-one with new chairs, deans, and other administrators to design a personal development plan that puts them in contact with resources tailored to helping those working in the setting of higher education, choosing the appropriate conferences and workshops that can provide the most benefit, and offering the services of a mentor or coach who provides advice based on the person's individual needs.

In-house mentorships are particularly valuable in terms of what they can contribute to skill development. New administrators benefit greatly from having access to someone who can listen to their concerns and help with decisions. Unfortunately, experienced vice presidents, deans, and chairs who could best mentor novice leaders are often the very people who are too busy to do so. Even when they are available, new administrators may be reluctant to ask their more experienced colleagues for help. They may worry that admitting they do not know how to do things will be perceived as a weakness. To counter this common occurrence, leadership initiatives can assume the task of pairing seasoned leaders with those who are new to their positions in a safe and supportive environment. More formally, internships, shadowing experiences, and partnerships with colleagues at other institutions can help shorten the new administrator's learning curve and speed his or her acquisition of important skills.

At the institutional level, colleges and universities can learn from the example of many of the programs we outlined in chapters 5 and 6 and create their own structured approaches for selecting, orienting, socializing, and developing their academic leaders. They can provide current and prospective leaders with opportunities for continual professional development through in-house retreats, personalized professional development plans, and periodic reviews and renewals (such as administrative sabbaticals or study leaves). They can also create their own academic leadership center or program, with a structure, staffing, and style that best suits their individual needs.

At the professional level, organizations such as the American Council on Education (ACE), the Council for the Advancement and Support of Education (CASE), the Association of American Colleges and Universities (AACU), the American Association of State Colleges and Universities (AACSU), the Council of Colleges or Arts and Sciences (CCAS), the Institute of Electrical and Electronics Engineers (IEEE), the American Conference of Academic Deans (ACAD), the American Association of Colleges of Teacher Education (AACTE), and many other disciplinary organizations can supplement campus leadership programs through forums, conferences, and literature that expose academic leaders to strategic issues in higher education. These groups, as well as the conferences and resources mentioned in chapter 1, give academic leaders a national perspective, an advantage that even the best campus-based centers cannot provide by themselves. In table 6.1, these and other strategies are outlined to provide the basis for developing a set of strategies that best serve the needs of academic leaders at a particular college or university.

If institutions lack their own center for academic leadership and professional development, they can provide workshops and training opportunities through the provost's office or division of human resources. Even highly developed campus programs have limits, however. It is simply not possible for a single academic leadership development initiative to cover every aspect of administrative work. As we have seen, most programs are designed for chairs and deans. They primarily address issues of policy and procedure, such as personnel practices, legal matters, and budget development. It is the very rare program that deals with such concerns as ethical dilemmas and preparing for executive-level positions. The philosophy is that leadership development programs exist to prepare someone to do his or her current job, not to prepare for a possible future job, particularly if that would take the person away from the institution. As a result, administrative skills typically are ignored in leadership training. It can thus be a very innovative approach to combine typical training workshops with sessions that probe complex challenges of ethics and integrity, executive internships or exchanges across units, and opportunities to shadow a senior administrator for an extended period of time. It would also be innovative to introduce a system of minisabbaticals when the administrator's duties would be covered by a well-respected faculty member for a period between one week and one semester. Not only would such a system help prepare new academic leaders who could eventually step into an administrative role full time, but it also solves the problem of how to free up busy administrators for extended training programs. Many administrators claim that they

Table 6.1. Strategies for Academic Leadership Development

Leadership Development Component

Levels of Intervention	Habits of Mind: Conceptual Understanding	Habits of Practice: Skill Development	Habits of Heart: Reflective Practice
Personal	Higher education courses Leadership conferences Books and journals Assessments and inventories Exposure to new mental models	External seminars (such as offered by ACE and CASE) Assessments and inventories related to skills Support groups Short commercial seminars Executive MBA/MPA programs	Journaling Reflective practice Facilitated peer mentoring Executive coaching Values clarification Faith or other spiritual practices Consultations with mentors or confidants
Institutional	Orientation processes Seamless socialization Executive development Administrative sabbaticals Team-building activities Professional stipends	Campus leadership seminars Internships and shadowing Mentorships Consultations with campus administrators Consultations with colleagues off campus Professional development projects	Annual reviews Leadership councils Chair/dean or dean/provost one-on-one sessions Campus support groups Leader "therapy sessions" Campus-based mentor programs
Professional	Higher education organizations (such as ACAD, AACU, and AACSU) New Leaders Council Institute (newleaderscouncil.org) Higher education leadership organizations (such as the UK's Leadership Foundation for Higher Education and Australia's LH Martin Institute for Tertiary Education) Personal networks Former chairs, deans, and provosts	Leadership and management books Organizations designed for certain levels of administration (e.g., deans' organization, conferences for chairs) Conference workshops Skill-based training Professional organizations Disciplinary organizations	Internet and intranet networks Consortia Regional, state, national networks National cohort programs

cannot afford the time to take advantage of leadership development opportunities when they arise because their primary responsibilities are so time-consuming. A minisabbatical avoids this problem and provides an opportunity to engage in skill development, the very type of leadership training that is least likely to come from reading a book or attending a short workshop.

On the professional level, programs devoted largely to skill development are uncommon. Developing skills requires sustained effort and guidance, but few professional programs provide any kind of ongoing evaluation or systematic follow-up. Part of this gap may be filled by ongoing webinar series and multipart training programs, such as Magna Publication's 20-Minute Mentors (www.magnapubs.com/online/mentors) and the Wiley Learning Institute's online programs (wileylearninginstitute.com/). Another part can be filled by attending annual meetings of higher educa- tion associations or accrediting bodies, keeping abreast of publications like *Change* magazine, *Academe*, and the *Chronicle of Higher Education* and building professional networks, from which many administrators pick up the language and discover current thinking in higher education (Green and McDade, 1994). In general, however, administrators who maintain active memberships in broad-based professional organizations concerned with higher education reap the benefit of learning more generalized approaches to academic leadership than they probably receive from their specialized discipline-centered professional organizations (Wolverton and Gmelch, 2002). Although many administrators we interviewed still expressed concern about keeping up with the literature in their discipline, they also felt a strong need to hone their leadership skills. A valuable resource that leadership development programs can provide therefore is funding for administrators to attend meetings and subscribe to webinar series, so that skill development activities have as much continuity as possible.

The Importance of Developing a Broad Base of Skills

Because many leaders at colleges and universities have received extensive training only in their academic disciplines, they rarely know more than the fundamentals about management and leadership when they enter their administrative positions (Hecht, Higgerson, Gmelch, and Tucker, 1999; Wolverton and Gmelch, 2002). But, somewhat surprisingly, there is a par- allel phenomenon in corporate cultures as well. Many businesses recruit people and then, for as long as those people are employed, reward them for doing a specific and often narrowly defined job. When a managerial post opens up, they look around in frustration and ask, "Where are all the statesmen?" As John Gardner (1987) points out, no one consciously intended to restrict those employees from taking a broader view of the industry, but the rewards system of their organizational culture produced that result all the same. We create the same situation in higher education, socializing and rewarding our new PhDs to become internationally renowned experts in rather narrow fields, and then complain that no one is willing or has the skills to serve in any leadership capacity that requires the ability to see the big picture. For many academics, the terminal degree is all too worthy of its name: from the time they receive it, they lose interest in branching into other areas, including those that deal with leadership, management, and interpersonal relations.

Where the similarity between the academic and corporate worlds breaks down is that in business, those targeted for leadership roles typically begin amassing supervisory experience early in their careers. That experience is then compounded with ongoing, formal support and feedback designed to assist them in developing as managers (Advisory Board, 2011). To compound the problem in higher education, even where administrative training programs do exist, too many remain focused on administrivia, imparting information about policies and procedures rather than developing the core leadership skills academic leaders need to succeed. Typical chair training devotes about 95 percent of its time to policies and procedures and only 5 percent of its time to skill development (Advisory Board, 2011). The likelihood that academic administrators are going to improve their skills any faster than if the training opportunities did not exist at all is remote. In addition, there is very little chance that participants in these programs will develop the increasingly larger perspective that, for instance, the chair of the department of chemistry needs when he or she becomes the dean of the college of science, then provost, and then president.

Developing a broad base of administrative skills is important for a unit's succession planning. If the provost, dean, or chair leaves the institution to take another job, his or her responsibilities will need to be covered, at least on a temporary basis, even if there will be a national search for a permanent successor. In fact, one of the reasons that so many colleges and universities feel compelled to devote so much time and expense to national searches for administrators is that they have not taken steps to prepare anyone in-house for the duties of these positions. Even with the best external candidate, there is always a steep learning curve while the person learns policies and traditions, the specific people in charge of various administrative and academic offices, and historical or cultural factors that may make the school very different from his or her previous institution. By developing its own academic leaders from within, colleges and universities can promote individuals who understand institutional history, already know the key players in various programs, and can tackle ongoing challenges without an extended learning process. In addition, it is always possible that a school will need broadly prepared academic leaders because an administrator is away due to illness, a well-deserved vacation, or a family emergency. If administrators are trained so narrowly that they are "indispensable," institutions can never really afford to let them leave, no matter whether they have to because of their health or want to because a better opportunity has been offered to them.

If we are going to counter the trend of overspecialized training with a well-designed program of broad skill development in academic leadership, we need to be able to answer three key questions:

1. What is it that administrators do?
2. What skills are most important for their success?
3. In what areas do administrators most need training?

What Do Administrators Do?

In an extended study of what it takes for managers to succeed, Henry Mintzberg (2004) concluded that the skills they require fall into four major categories: personal competencies, interpersonal competencies, informational competencies, and actionable competencies (table 6.2).

That is one way of answering the question of what administrators do: they manage their priorities and time so that they can lead others in the areas they supervise. They analyze the information they receive, draw conclusions from it, and communicate those ideas to others. They schedule, administer, design, and mobilize. Presented in this way, Mintzberg's list of managerial skills certainly describes some of the things that college administrators do. But it also misses a great deal. A similar outline of administrative tasks created by the Advisory Board specifically for department chairs and deans complements this framework a bit (table 6.3).

The Advisory Board notes that college administrators also promote teamwork, negotiate among their various stakeholders, deal with difficult people, develop and align long-term goals, make decisions based on data, and manage change. That comes a little closer to capturing the tasks regularly assigned to academic leaders, but it still fails to embrace everything that makes college administration such a complex and challenging profession.

Table 6.2. Managerial Competencies

PERSONAL COMPETENCIES

o Managing self, internally (reflection, strategic thinking)
o Managing self, externally (time, information, stress, career)

INTERPERSONAL COMPETENCIES

o Leading individuals (selecting, mentoring, inspiring)
o Leading groups (team building, resolving conflict, facilitation)
o Leading organization or unit (organizing, managing change, building culture)
o Leading organization or unit (networking, representing, collaborating)

INFORMATIONAL COMPETENCIES

o Communicating verbally (listening, interviewing, speaking, writing, information gathering and dissemination)
o Communicating nonverbally (seeing, sensing)
o Analyzing (data processing, modeling, measuring, evaluating)

ACTIONABLE COMPETENCIES

o Scheduling (prioritizing, agenda setting, juggling, timing)
o Administering (resource allocating, delegating, authorizing, systematizing, goal setting, performance appraising)
o Designing (planning, crafting, visioning)
o Mobilizing (firefighting, project managing)

Source: *Mintzberg (2004, 261).*

Table 6.3. High-Level Skills Required of College Administrators

Managing and working with people	Managing faculty and staff performance
	Cultivating self-awareness
	Facilitating effective teamwork
	Negotiation
	Dealing with difficult people
	Managing organizational conflict
	Aligning unit and institutional goals
Advancing unit-level and institutional goals	Advancing long-term objectives
	Managing change and transition
	Data-driven leadership
	Improving financial decision making

Source: *Advisory Board (2011).*

A different way of answering the question about what academic administrators do might be to say that regardless of their specific duties, all academic leaders must master skills related to the four major frames of leadership described by Bolman and Deal (2013): structural frame, human resource frame, political frame, and symbolic frame. In other words, they have to know how their institution works, what agendas motivate the different stakeholders at the institution, which alliances and conflicts will affect their work, and how organizational culture and traditions shape the way in which decisions are made and visions are developed. Moreover, as an academic leader rises in the hierarchy, the significance of these different frames will change somewhat. For example, deans often deal in the political and symbolic frames of leadership and require excellent skills in diplomacy, building networks of support, and long-term planning. Department chairs, who devote much of their time dealing with issues related to the structural and human resource frames, often find the transition to a deanship very difficult because the skills they then need are not just the ones they have "writ large" but an entirely new set of proficiencies (Gmelch, Reason, Schuh, and Shelley, 2002). For this reason, skill development as part of an academic leadership program needs to take account of two dimensions simultaneously: the skills administrators need in order to do their current jobs more effectively and the skills they may eventually need if they want or need to take a higher administrative role. It also means that we were initially asking the wrong question. The real question should be not, "What do administrators do?" but, "What do department chairs do?" (or faculty leaders or deans or provosts or college presidents). Asked in this way, the question brings us a good deal closer to a sense of the skills a well-designed leadership initiative might foster.

What Do Department Chairs Do?

Many books on academic leadership try to outline the various tasks, duties, roles, and responsibilities of administrators. If we focus just on the responsibilities of department chairs for a moment, we discover that the content of those lists vary widely. A research team at the University of Nebraska listed ninety-seven activities that department chairs performed (Creswell, Wheeler, Seagren, Egly, and Beyer, 1990), while a study of Australian heads of department (Moses and Roe, 1990) listed only forty. Other studies list even different numbers for the major functions of chairs (Gmelch and Miskin, 2011; Seagren, Creswell, and Wheeler, 1993; Smart and Montgomery, 1976). In addition, faculty manuals at colleges and universities often provide lists of chairs' activities and responsibilities usually including the all-encompassing "and other duties as assigned." In order for us to have one consistent list of responsibilities to consider, let's explore the results of one national study of sixteen hundred department chairs (Gmelch and Miskin, 2004). Of thirty-five duties commonly assigned to chairs, the following were identified as the most important by at least three-quarters of the respondents. In priority order:

1. Recruit and select faculty   93 percent
2. Represent the department to the   92 percent
    administration and discipline
3. Evaluate faculty performance   90 percent
4. Encourage faculty research and publication   89 percent
5. Reduce conflict among the faculty   88 percent
6. Manage departmental resources   85 percent
7. Encourage professional development of the   85 percent
    faculty
8. Develop and initiate long-range   83 percent
    departmental goals
9. Remain current within the academic   78 percent
    discipline
10. Provide informal faculty leadership   75 percent

One way of developing a program to improve or develop the academic leadership skills of chairs would be to identify the specific skills most commonly associated with each of these tasks and build the curriculum around them. Another way would be to ask the chairs directly what skills they regarded as most essential for success at their jobs. In a six-year study conducted by Robert Cipriano and Richard Riccardi (2013), there was a surprising degree of agreement among chairs regarding the type of skills people in their positions needed most:

1. The ability to communicate effectively   98.9 percent
2. Interpersonal skills   98.6 percent
3. The ability to make decisions effectively   98.4 percent
4. The ability to solve problems effectively   98.4 percent
5. The ability to act with integrity   98.1 percent

On this basis, it would appear that the most important workshops for a leadership initiative for chairs would be sessions like Written Communication Skills for Chairs, Oral Communication Skills for Chairs, Improving Interpersonal Relations, Decision Making for Chairs, Problem Solving for

Chairs, Leading the Department with Integrity, and the like. Ironically, if you review the offerings of most campus leadership programs, only sessions on decision making and problem solving appear with any regularity. The other topics tend to be all but ignored.

Both of the approaches we have just considered provide answers to the second question raised above: What skills are most important for a chair's success? There will, of course, be a certain amount of variation among institutions, depending on their mission and organizational structure. For instance, a private university that is governed by a collective bargaining agreement may have department chairs who do not select and evaluate their faculty. A highly productive research university may regard remaining current within the academic discipline as such a given that the chair never needs to provide leadership in this area. For this reason, if an academic leadership program is going to serve the needs of its chairs, it must first decide not simply what chairs do, but what chairs do at this particular institution.

Yet when we move to the third question, it must then decide where the greatest training needs are within that framework. In other words, there may be a duty that is critically important for all of the school's chairs to do, but it is also so familiar to the chairs that providing skill development in this area would be a waste of time. The same national study of department chairs that produced the list of chair responsibilities outlined above also identified the following training needs cited by a majority of department chairs (Gmelch and Miskin, 2004):

1. Evaluating faculty performance
2. Reducing conflict among the faculty
3. Obtaining and managing external funds
4. Preparing and proposing budgets
5. Developing and initiating long-range departmental goals
6. Managing departmental resources
7. Encouraging professional development activities of the faculty
8. Managing nonacademic staff
9. Planning and evaluating curriculum development
10. Providing informal faculty leadership

It is interesting to note how little the two lists line up. In other words, just because chairs feel that a large portion of their time is devoted to a certain activity, it does not mean that they want training in that area. In fact, the opposite may be true: duties they perform repeatedly may become easier to them by being routine; it may be the functions they perform only rarely that cause them to feel they need training to help them become more proficient. It is for these reasons that institution-based leadership development programs are so valuable. These programs can be tailored to the duties and needs of chairs at that particular college or university. Skill development can be made far more relevant by engaging participants in case studies and simulations that directly relate to university policies, as well as the trajectory set by the school's strategic plan and vision for the future.

In order to determine these needs, it is often useful to conduct a local survey of what current chairs regard as the most important skills for their success and the most important skills in which they feel inadequately prepared. That type of inventory will tell you far more than will the list of duties outlined in the university policy manual or faculty handbook. While all campuses are different, what you are likely to discover from this survey is how ill equipped most chairs feel about responsibilities that they are expected to undertake nearly every day.

What Do Deans Do?

The roles of deans have changed significantly over time. When we see the first references to deans at American universities during the nineteenth century, scholar-deans were expected to provide little more than emotional support to students (McGrath, 1999). But over time, deans began to assume more and more responsibilities, eventually becoming full-time administrators and midlevel academic supervisors.

There are several approaches we can take in order to get a sense of what it is that deans do. The first is to examine their responsibilities presented by the policy manuals and administrative handbooks of various institutions. If we do that, we often encounter lists like the following summary of assignments for deans at the University of Texas–Pan American, which notes that each dean is responsible for:

1. Leading college strategic planning and assessment efforts
2. Maintaining an environment of collegiality and shared governance
3. Promoting the welfare of the university in concert with university vision and strategic goals
4. Leading college fund-raising and out-reach efforts to community, industry, and government
5. Coordinating the assessment and development of academic programs within the academic unit

6. Preparing and revising as necessary academic program plans for the academic unit

7. Promoting and serving as a model for teaching or librarian effectiveness, professional achievement and professional service

8. Overseeing all personnel matters involving academic and non-academic employees including recruiting, appointment, reappointment; termination and dismissal; faculty evaluation, tenure promotion and merit

9. Maintaining good working relationships with faculty and administration in all academic and non-academic areas

10. Communicating effectively with relevant constituencies within the University, surrounding community and state regarding the academic unit

11. Maintaining effective communication among students, faculty and chairpersons within the academic unit and with other academic unit personnel

12. Serving as a liaison to relevant professional associations and state and national regulatory and accrediting agencies

13. Articulating University policy and procedures to members of the academic unit

14. Insuring that the academic unit's policies and practices are consistent with those of the University

15. Articulating and advocating for the budgetary needs of the academic unit and overseeing the allocation and expenditure of resources

16. Coordinating the use of facilities assigned to the academic unit

17. Overseeing the preparation of class schedules and complying with institutional reporting requirements

18. Working with chairs to encourage grant applications by faculty members for outside funding of special projects

19. Additional responsibilities as assigned by the Provost/Vice President for Academic Affairs or President. (www.utpa.edu/hop/policies/?6.5.2)

While each college or university will, of course, describe these various duties in ways that best align with its mission and operating procedures, several commonalities do emerge. First, there is almost always a juxtaposition of activities that call for rather high levels of academic leadership (such as guiding strategic planning efforts and coordinating the development of academic programs) and those that require more routine skills of management, scheduling, and proofreading (such as coordinating the use of facilities and overseeing the preparation of class schedules). Second, these lists provide evidence that deans often act as buffers or conduits between upper administration and the faculty. For example, in the list we just examined, we saw that deans are expected to advocate for the budgetary needs of the academic unit (carrying a message from the department up to the upper administration) and articulate the institution's policies and procedures to members of the academic unit (carrying a message from the upper administration down to the department). Third, there is a recognition that no list, no matter how detailed it is, can ever capture everything that a dean does (hence the "and other duties as assigned" clause). These campus lists are thus useful for general information, but they tend to provide only a limited picture of what a dean actually does.

A second approach is to examine a comprehensive guide written for deans at all types of institutions, like *The Resource Handbook for Academic Deans* (Behling, 2014) and *The Essential Academic Dean* (Buller, 2007). Both of these books are commonly used in campus-based leadership programs for deans. *The Resource Handbook* divides its topic into five parts:

1. Becoming a dean
2. Roles and responsibilities of being a dean
3. What a dean does
4. Fostering teamwork across the institution
5. Developing faculty excellence and achieving student success

The Essential Academic Dean breaks up its topics a bit differently, with sections on:

1. The dean's role
2. The dean's constituents
3. The dean's staff
4. The dean's budget
5. The dean's documents
6. The dean's leadership
7. The dean's challenges
8. The dean's unique opportunities
9. The dean's next step

Some of these sections tell us immediately about many of the tasks that have to be handled at the dean's level. Budgeting and the management of personnel must be done. There are also responsibilities related to upper-level supervision (leadership, challenges, opportunities) and duties related to more routine functions (documents such as personnel evaluations, position requests, policy revisions, and program reviews). Moreover, if we delve a little deeper into the sections devoted to the dean's role, challenges, and opportunities, we discover that deans are expected to articulate a vision for their areas, lead initiatives and reforms, interview candidates for jobs, deal with the media, promote diversity, and resolve intellectual property disputes. That is an extremely broad mix of activities, and leadership programs could fill their entire schedules for a year by devoting a single workshop to each activity.

A third method of identifying the tasks commonly assigned to deans would be to ask the deans themselves. A 2002 study of more than thirteen hundred academic deans at 360 universities in the United States found that deans regard the following six responsibilities, listed in order of importance, as encompassing most of what they do (Wolverton and Gmelch, 2002):

1. Promoting internal productivity
2. Managing academic personnel
3. Maintaining good external and political relations
4. Providing leadership to their colleges
5. Managing resources
6. Remaining active in personal scholarship

Three of these responsibilities (academic personnel management, internal productivity, and fiscal resource management) fall generally into the category of management as opposed to visionary leadership, while the three others (leadership, external and political relations, and scholarship) have a more external focus by dealing with the community, the discipline as a whole, or the relationship of the college to the institution and the larger academic world.

Clearly the challenges facing deans are varied and complex, ranging from the most rudimentary administrative or clerical tasks (making sure that requisitions are completed in a timely fashion) to the most creative and consequential activities (charting the entire future direction of a discipline). As a result, the programs that seek to develop these skills in current or prospective deans need to be similarly varied and complex as well. It is not enough merely to provide opportunities to practice budgeting through simulations or faculty evaluation through case studies. The type of skill training that most deans need is greatly enhanced by the type of long-term development that comes from work with a mentor, support group, or executive coach. For this reason, it is important that leadership development programs for deans include more than just periodic workshops. Deans need opportunities to practice the skills they acquire, try out different approaches to various challenges, and learn from their own inevitable mistakes. As we will see in the model programs we examine later in this chapter, there are creative ways of providing this type of leadership development in a manner that can still be accommodated within a dean's busy schedule.

What Do Other Academic Leaders Do?

So many campus leadership programs focus their attention on department chairs and deans that it sometimes appears as though they are the only type of academic leader who can benefit from formal leadership initiatives. That is hardly the case. Presidents, vice presidents, board members, directors, faculty members, committee chairs, and a host of other academic positions all offer their own leadership challenges, many of which the people occupying these positions are not well prepared for. In fact, there are so many levels of a college or university at which leadership development is beneficial that we cannot devote an entire section to each of them. Instead, we make some general comments about what tasks are required of these positions and how that should affect the type of leadership training offered:

o *At the vice-presidential level, duties are so varied that interinstitutional programs for different types of vice president work best.* Although the duties of deans and department chairs vary somewhat from institution to institution, that variation is usually minor when compared to the different responsibilities of vice presidents even at the same college or university. The vice president for student affairs has a very different assignment from colleagues in academic affairs, business affairs, communication and public relations, strategic planning, and however else the specific divisions of the institution have been established. For example, when the Academic Leadership Center in the Kingdom of Saudi Arabia (see chapter 2) was planning its first training workshop for vice rectors (the equivalent of vice presidents), the assumption was that all vice rectors shared at least some responsibilities regardless of their area or institution. But it became clear from the first session in 2010 that this assumption was

severely flawed. In order to find topics that applied to everyone in attendance, the program relied on the approach of finding the least common
denominator. The result was a program that was so broad and introductory that relatively few of the participants found it valuable. As a result,
the training program for vice rectors almost ended before it was given a
fair chance to succeed. In subsequent years, the organizers of the program
learned to run multiple tracks simultaneously so that no matter what the
specific job responsibilities of the participants were, they would always
find a panel that was directly relevant to the skills they needed.

   ○ *Leaders in support positions, such as assistant department chairs
and associate deans, require a special set of skills that are often overlooked in leadership development initiatives.* A significant proportion
of what gets accomplished at any college or university is done by administrators in supporting roles. In many ways, these jobs are the most challenging at the university. They often have huge responsibilities but very
little authority. If an assistant department chair cannot get his or her work
done, courses may be omitted from the schedule, reimbursements may
not be processed, essential equipment may not be ordered, and deadlines
may be missed. But assistant chairs hold very few carrots and virtually
no sticks. Since they do not evaluate anyone or set anyone's salary, they
are not in a position to impose sanctions when a faculty member does
not provide key information. At best, they can run and tattle to the chair,
but by themselves there is little that they can do. In a similar way, deans
are heavily reliant on their associate deans to achieve the goals they have
set for the college, but the associate deans have little power of their own
with which to reward anyone for a good job or to punish them for failing
to fulfill their responsibilities. Special sessions on the skills needed to be
effective in these auxiliary positions can be a valuable contribution of any
leadership development initiative. A good place to begin is with Tammy
Stone and Amy Coussons-Read's *Leading from the Middle* (2011), which
uses a case study approach to give associate deans practice in the skills
that are most needed for the role they play at the institution. Building outward from that approach, the leadership program can then develop its
own set of case studies based on the skills support staff need at that particular college or university. The training sessions can also be an excellent
source of mutual assistance as the different participants learn from one
another the practical skills that will help them to carry out their responsibilities effectively.

   ○ *Skill development for academic administrators should not be limited
to managerial skills.* The study conducted by the Advisory Board (2011)

that we mentioned previously concluded that basic management skills are no longer enough for administrators at universities today. The skills most critical to administrative success fell, according to the Advisory Board, into two broad categories: (1) managing and working with people and (2) advancing unit-level and institutional goals. (See table 6.3.) In short, the current environment in higher education requires academic leaders to develop leadership skills that extend far beyond Bolman and Deal's (2013) human resource frame, which involves such skills as communication and conflict management, to the symbolic and political frames. In other words, the tasks academic leaders perform include setting a vision for the future, thinking strategically, executing plans, and evaluating results. Rather than maintaining the status quo (encompassed within Bolman and Deal's structural frame), academic leaders also need to strategically allocate scarce resources and direct complex change. As a result, while fundamental skills like time management and conducting effective performance appraisals are important, the reality of administrative work today includes a large number of vital high-end tasks that a well-developed leadership program should also address.

    ○ *It is important to remember that not all academic leaders have a specific title.* Many current and potential leaders at any institution do not hold a job that people automatically associate with vision and leadership. Nearly every faculty assembly has its opinion leaders. People often confer with certain members of the staff whose views are valued because of their gravitas, longevity at the institution, or sheer common sense. And others may be those who should eventually become chairs, deans, or provosts but are not ready yet. So although it is a sound practice to structure skill training so that it accurately reflects the needs each person has in his or her current job, it is equally important to provide opportunities for emerging leaders and those without any formal administrative positions at all. As the title of Mark Sanborn's 2006 guide to leadership suggests, *You Don't Need a Title to Be a Leader.* If leadership initiatives focus only on people's current responsibilities, they fail to prepare them for what they might possibly become in the future. If they focus only on those in clear administrative positions, they overlook the leaders who exist outside the administration. For this reason, in addition to reflecting on the specific skills that deans, directors, and chairs need in order to succeed at your institution, it is important to reflect on the skills that any type of leader needs in order to succeed at your institution.

Best Practices in Developing Leadership Skills

Since leadership skills are best developed in programs that do not assume all administrators are engaged in the same tasks, a great deal can be learned from programs at institutions where training opportunities are tailored to the specific needs of the participants. Two very different schools, Indian River State College (IRSC) in Florida and the University of North Carolina at Chapel Hill (UNC-Chapel Hill), provide useful models for how to accomplish this leadership development goal.

IRSC provides what it calls targeted offerings to make sure that specific employee groups get the exact type of training they need without having their time wasted with programming that is irrelevant to the work they actually do. Some of the targeted offerings in their employee development program are:

- *Effectiveness Series*: A program that is open to all employees and focuses on broad-ranging topics to help them become more effective at their jobs and in their personal and professional lives. Specific topics for the program are drawn from employee recommendations and often include issues related to technology, customer relations, stress relief, and time management.

- *Professional Enhancement Day*: An annual full-day event when the college closes for business and focuses on employee development. Typical workshops address instructional techniques, customer service, leadership, communication, and technology. There are also departmental planning sessions that set goals and objectives for the coming year.

- *Update IRSC*: A series that highlights departments, campuses, and programs that have achieved noted successes. The series features both formal presentations and tours of buildings as a way of keeping employees informed of new developments on campus as well as opportunities to learn best practices from other areas.

- *Institute for Academic Excellence*: A program run by the Kight Center for Emerging Technologies that offers advanced training in technology. Workshops feature specific applications or hardware as well as more general sessions exploring how technology can be used to address different learning styles, develop critical thinking, and promote student engagement.

- *Anne R. Snyder Department Chair Leadership Academy*: Development opportunities that help department chairs become more effective in their positions. Topics include effective leadership, delegation skills, state curriculum issues, finance and budgeting, and student issue management.

○ *Great Managers*: A training program tailored to the needs of non-administrative supervisors. Offerings include delegation skills, time management, coaching and feedback skills, legal issues information, hiring processes, customer service, and communication skills.

○ *Enlightened Leaders*: A series that includes both applied and theoretical training for college administrators in leadership, coaching, mentoring, vision setting, and communication.

Similarly, at UNC-Chapel Hill, the Leadership Coordinator Center for Faculty Excellence conducts seven programs, each designed to help prepare leaders who play different roles or have different needs at the university:

○ *The Academic Leadership Program,* which began in 2001 to provide senior lecturers (fixed-term faculty members with ten years or more of experience at the university) with a multifaceted program of study in the nature of academic leadership

○ *The Chairs Leadership Program,* designed to help new department chairs get off to a good start during their first year in these exceptionally challenging leadership roles

○ *The Faculty Learning Community on Strategic Leadership*, which anyone may apply to, although it primarily serves deans, department chairs, and center directors in developing innovative leadership approaches and helping them align their goals with those of the university as a whole

○ *The Faculty Administrator Development Program,* a pilot program intended to prepare faculty members to step into such roles as program directors, associate deans, department chairs, and center directors

○ *The Faculty Leadership Development Series,* which helps expose faculty members to resources available on various leadership issues and to learn about accepted best practices in such areas as conducting effective meetings, setting goals, handling conflicts, and managing change

○ *The Faculty Entrepreneurship Development Program,* for as many as thirty faculty members a year from across the UNC system to spend four intense days learning entrepreneurial skills that, it is hoped, they will apply to improving their academic programs

o *Leader and Organizational Consulting Services,* which work one-on-one with members of the faculty and administration to improve their skills in such areas as assessment, planning, and making important career decisions

To understand more completely the advantages of this segmented approach, let's explore several of these programs in more detail, beginning with the Chairs Leadership Program, which provides a voluntary year of supportive and confidential discussions about the role of department chairs and the types of problems they face. In order to promote as much interaction as possible, the program is limited to a dozen participants each year. Participants are selected in the spring and given a copy of C. K. Gunsalus's *The College Administrator's Survival Guide* (2006) to read over the summer.

When the program begins the following September, the new chairs come to the discussions with an understanding of what some of the challenges facing them will be and a few initial ideas about how to address them. Throughout the program, the chairs are given articles on various topics and use the Stylus series Effective Practices for Academic Leaders as a guide to current issues in academic leadership. The sessions are held once a month at a dinner meeting lasting from 5:30 until 8:00 p.m. Topics addressed include the skills chairs need in a number of areas:

o Recruiting, mentoring, and evaluating new faculty
o Developing incentives and rewards for faculty productivity
o Allocating merit increases
o Practicing strategic leadership
o Setting departmental goals
o Conducting faculty retreats
o Dealing with difficult situations
o Managing the instructional budget
o Conducting posttenure reviews; creating joint appointments
o Negotiating with candidates for positions
o Interacting effectively with deans and other administrators
o Securing additional resources
o Improving the quality of teaching
o Encouraging a collegial climate

Because of the sheer number and importance of these topics, sessions are grouped thematically and carefully sequenced so that the appropriate skills are developed before the new chairs have to take action on that particular issue. For example, early in the program, the participants discuss ways of assigning merit increases. A bit later they address effective ways to conduct faculty searches. In the spring, they work on issues related to budget proposals, recruiting a new class of graduate students, negotiating a job offer with a candidate, evaluating tenure-track faculty members, and managing graduation ceremonies.

The university's Faculty Learning Community on Strategic Leadership (FLC) seeks to develop a different type of skill set in administrators. Rather than concentrating on the day-to-day skills chairs need to manage a program, it deals more with bringing creative vision into an area and helping to bring about transformational change. Participants read two works by Jim Collins, *Good to Great* (2001) and *Good to Great and the Social Sectors* (2005). The FLC has also produced a video series, *Good to Great at Carolina,* that shows how various leaders at Carolina have applied Collins's principles to their own areas. Holden Thorp and Buck Goldstein's *Engines of Innovation* (2010), Michael Porter's *What Is Strategy?* (1996), and Peter Brews's article, "Great Expectations: Strategy as Creative Fiction" (2005) serve as additional texts in the program. The participants also make use of a framework for strategic leadership in research universities developed by UNC-Chapel Hill former chancellor James Moeser.

The basic idea of FLC, imported from the entrepreneurship boot camp run by Buck Goldstein, is that the participants develop final presentations to make in a public session before the chancellor, provost, and other senior leaders at the university. The goal is to make the program as much of a high-stakes operation as possible so as to encourage serious reflection on issues and the development of truly innovative solutions. The program thus provides senior leaders with the support they need to identify and resolve the major strategic issues facing their areas, with systematic analysis of how to assess each issue, formulate a plan, and create a persuasive presentation of that plan that makes the case for the resources and support needed to address the issue. The number of substantial results produced by the FLC is truly impressive:

○ The dean of UNC-Chapel Hill's graduate school used the program to develop a plan to provide better support to the 60 percent of PhDs who were unlikely to receive academic positions after they graduate.

o The vice chancellor for research developed a plan for diversifying the university's research funding, which had relied heavily on the National Institutes of Health in the past.

o The associate dean of the medical school developed a new approach for retaining minority faculty members.

o The vice chancellor for enrollment sought a way to endow the university's famous Carolina Covenant, which provides grant support for low-income students.

o The dean of the School of Dentistry prepared a case statement arguing that the dental school needed to hire 20 percent more faculty.

o The dean of the School of Education explored ways of solving the problems of schools in impoverished areas.

o The chair of the department of chemistry worked on ways of building a culture of team science in that program.

By structuring the program in this way, UNC-Chapel Hill has tried not only to develop transferable skills that administrators can use across a broad range of leadership challenges but also to address specific needs that the institution has. With hands-on skill development, the program provides the same sort of experiential education that higher education has found is so important for the success of students at all levels.

Clarifying Skill Development

As we have seen, skill development can assume a wide variety of forms according to the mission and focus of that specific leadership program. As you plan your own initiative, some questions can guide you in matching the skills your program develops to the specific needs of your participants:

1. What are the specific tasks performed by the different types of academic leaders who will be served by your initiative? Don't focus merely on formal job descriptions. Rather, investigate what these administrators actually do in order to fulfill the responsibilities assigned them.

2. Which skills would best help the participants in your program complete those tasks? In other words, do they require skills that are largely managerial (making the best use of limited resources, delegating effectively, supervising personnel, and the like), directed toward larger tasks of leadership (developing a new vision, promoting transformative change, working diplomatically with other units or institutions, and the like), or some combination of the two?

3. What type of programming will best serve to develop these skills in your program's participants? What type of exercises will most effectively reinforce those skills?

4. Within the resources you have available, how much segmenting of skill development (i.e., different programing for chairs, directors, associate deans, deans, and vice presidents) is it reasonable for you to provide?

5. How could you complement the opportunities that you provide within your own institution with those that are available by professional organizations at the state or national level?

In the next chapter, we encounter one additional approach to skill development: aligning essential skills with the leader's personal style. (See especially figure 7.3.) In order to create that type of alignment, however, we must first examine the concept of personal and programmatic style from a broader perspective, a matter that we take up at the beginning of chapter 7.

REFERENCES

Advisory Board. (2011). *Developing academic leaders: Cultivating the skills of chairs, deans, and other faculty administrators.* Washington, DC: Advisory Board.

Behling, L. L. (2014). *The resource handbook for academic deans* (3rd ed.). San Francisco, CA: Jossey-Bass.

Bolman, L. G., & Deal, T. E. (2013). *Reframing organizations: Artistry, choice, and leadership* (5th ed.). San Francisco, CA: Jossey-Bass.

Brews, P. (2005). Great expectations: Strategy as creative fiction. *Business Strategy Review, 16*(3), 4–10.

Buller, J. L. (2007). *The essential academic dean: A practical guide to college leadership.* San Francisco, CA: Jossey-Bass.

Cipriano, R. E., & Riccardi, R. L. (2013). A continuing analysis of the unique department chair. *Department Chair, 23*(4), 20–23.

Collins, J. C. (2001). *Good to great: Why some companies make the leap—and others don't.* New York, NY: HarperBusiness.

Collins, J. C. (2005). *Good to great and the social sectors: Why business thinking is not the answer: A monograph to accompany* Good to Great. Boulder, CO: J. Collins.

Creswell, J. W., Wheeler, D. W., Seagren, A. T., Egly, N. J., & Beyer, K. D. (1990). *The academic chairperson's handbook.* Lincoln: University of Nebraska Press.

Gardner, J. W. (1987). *Leadership development.* Washington, DC: Independent Sector.

Gmelch, W. H., & Miskin, V. D. (2004). *Chairing the academic department.* Madison, WI: Atwood.

Gmelch, W. H., & Miskin, V. D. (2011). *Department chair leadership skills.* Madison, WI: Atwood.

Gmelch, W. H., Reason, R. D., Schuh, J. H., & Shelley, M. C. (2002). *The call for academic leaders: The Academic Leadership Forum.* Ames: Iowa State University, Center for Academic Leadership.

Green, M. F., & McDade, S. A. (1994). *Investing in higher education: A handbook of leadership development.* Phoenix, AZ: Oryx Press.

Gunsalus, C. K. (2006). *The college administrator's survival guide.* Cambridge, MA: Harvard University Press.

Hecht, I.W.D., Higgerson, M. L., Gmelch, W. H., & Tucker, A. (1999). *The department chair as academic leader.* Phoenix, AZ: Oryx Press.

McGrath, J. E. (1999). The dean. *Journal of Higher Education, 70*(5), 599–605.

Mintzberg, H. (2004). *Managers not MBAs: A hard look at the soft practice of managing and management development.* San Francisco, CA: Berrett-Koehler.

Moses, I., & Roe, E. (1990). *Heads and chairs: Managing academic departments.* Queensland, Australia: University of Queensland Press.

Porter, M. E. (1996). *What is strategy?* Boston, MA: Harvard Business School Press.

Sanborn, M. (2006). *You don't need a title to be a leader: How anyone, anywhere, can make a positive difference.* New York, NY: Currency Doubleday.

Seagren, A. T., Creswell, J. W., & Wheeler, D. W. (1993). *The department chair: New roles, responsibilities, and challenges.* Washington DC: ASHE-ERIC.

Smart, J. C., & Montgomery, J. R. (1976). *Examining departmental management.* San Francisco, CA: Jossey-Bass.

Stone, T., & Coussons-Read, M. E. (2011). *Leading from the middle: A case-study approach to academic leadership for associate deans.* Lanham, MD: Rowman & Littlefield.

Thorp, H. H., & Goldstein, B. (2010). *Engines of innovation: The entrepreneurial university in the twenty-first century.* Chapel Hill, NC: University of North Carolina Press.

Wolverton, M., & Gmelch, W. H. (2002). *College deans: Leading from within.* Phoenix, AZ: Oryx Press.

7

STYLE

STYLE IS PERHAPS THE most elusive of the 7 S's to define. It consists of such different factors as these:

○ The mission and vision of the institution where the leadership development program takes place

○ The specific focus (if any) that the program has

○ Modes in which it is anticipated that the participants will interact

○ The favored activities of the program's organizers or presenters

○ The specific outcomes expected of the program

○ The style of individual culture of the institution

There is no such thing as a right or wrong style for a leadership development initiative. The only criterion is that it suits the needs of its stakeholders.

In this chapter, we examine some of the ways in which a leadership program's style can evolve to suit those various needs. Because it is sometimes easier to trace how those programs evolve through regular faculty discussions and votes rather than the initiative of a small group of administrators, we broaden our focus slightly throughout this discussion. In addition to leadership development programs intended for the faculty and administration, we consider a few credit-bearing programs designed primarily for students because these often capture an institution's mission and style in a particularly clear way. (Besides, those who design programs for administrators can often learn a great deal from how we teach our students to be leaders.) For this reason, we are going to examine several programs that enroll working adults and professionals along with traditional-aged college students and are intended to provide exposure not simply to leadership but to leadership with a focus or characteristic dimension. With that background in mind, let's examine some of the ways in which these distinctive and successful leadership programs develop a style of their own.

Mission and Vision

One of the greatest strengths of higher education is its sheer diversity. Students looking for advanced education can choose from public and private institutions, two-year and four-year schools, professional universities and liberal arts colleges, secular and religious institutions, plus a host of other schools, each distinctive in its own ways. Many of these differences are important to us in chapter 8 when we discuss shared values, but for now we focus solely on the way in which the specific mission and vision of an institution can affect the style, tone, and tenor of its leadership development activities.

An institution with a strong affiliation to a specific religious tradition will thus often reflect those values in the way it approaches leadership development. For example, Naropa University describes itself as "a Buddhist-inspired, student-centered liberal arts university in Boulder, Colorado. A recognized leader in contemplative education, Naropa's undergraduate and graduate programs emphasize professional and personal growth, intellectual development, and contemplative practice" (www.naropa.edu/about-naropa/index.php). Because of its mission, leadership development programs at this university have a style that is much different from what one might find only a short distance away at the University of Colorado at Boulder. Its Authentic Leadership Program borrows from "the disciplines of neuroscience, Buddhism, complexity science, organizational learning, and leadership, . . . [offering] proven methods and practices that help leaders cultivate self-awareness and creativity, strengthen and enhance their relationships with others, and effectively lead the changes they want to see in their organizations and in the world" (www.naropa.edu/academics/extended-studies /certificate-programs/authentic-leadership-certificate-program/). As a result, the program engages participants in mindfulness exercises including meditation, emphasizes collaboration and teamwork over top-down leadership strategies, and promotes the ideals of authentic leadership (see chapter 2). In much the same way, many other colleges and universities that are closely associated with a particular faith tradition will develop leadership initiatives with a style rooted in the mission and values of that tradition.

Mission and vision can influence the style of leadership activities even at the unit level. The Christine E. Lynn College of Nursing at Florida Atlantic University has structured its entire curriculum, pedagogical approach, research focus, and service mission around what it terms the concept of caring. Here is how that concept is described on the college's website:

> It is caring that informs how we study nursing, how we practice our profession and how we interact with others throughout our lives. At the Christine E. Lynn College of Nursing, we study caring as lived in the ordinariness of life and as a central domain of our profession. We recognize each individual as caring and uniquely connected with others and the environment. We also believe that every interaction we have with others is an opportunity to demonstrate and live this caring philosophy ... Dean, faculty, students, provost, president, etc. are each [in their roles in order] to offer their special and unique contributions. These roles exist so that we can provide the highest quality educational programming for the needs of the healthcare profession, now and in the future. Our focus is on the person(s) nursed and the special contributions of nursing to nurturing the wholeness of persons and environment through caring. (nursing.fau.edu/index.php?main=1&nav=302)

With this philosophy as a conceptual framework, it is no wonder that when the college established its own Nursing Leadership Institute (NLI) in 2002, the concept of caring informed the style by which future leaders would be prepared. The institute seeks to make sure that leaders in nursing, no matter whether they are in an academic or a hospital setting, are prepared in six key competencies:

- o Systems thinking
- o Personal mastery
- o Financial management
- o Human resource management
- o Interpersonal communication
- o Caring

In many ways, it is the final competency, caring, that affects the entire way in which the other five competencies are taught.

The NLI defines *caring* as compassion and understanding that is directed toward staff, patients, and self. Among the behaviors it cites as integral to this competency, the NLI notes that the effective leader in

nursing (nursing.fau.edu/uploads/docs/358/nursing_leadership_model2
.pdf):

- Recognizes the importance of building a sense of community in the
  work environment
- Takes time to learn about the families of staff
- Demonstrates a commitment to personal wellness and work-life
  balance
- Promotes celebrations and activities to build a cohesive unit
- Models effective personal stress management
- Maintains a sensitivity about staff reluctance to change and works
  with staff

The result is a very different training style from what one might
encounter in a school of business or military science. Not only is the
content of the program itself focused on the need for nurses to care for
others, but the leadership development activities are themselves presented
with a style that illustrates compassion for the program participants and
embodies the college's distinctive mission and vision.

Specific Focus

Leadership development programs can also develop their own style if they
focus on a certain leadership approach or problem. For example, the
University of Alaska Anchorage's Center for Advancing Faculty Excellence (CAFE), which we encountered in chapter 5, seeks to integrate principles from the Ford Foundation's Difficult Dialogues Initiative across
the entire program (www.difficultdialoguesuaa.org). This initiative tries
to prepare faculty members and administrators to deal effectively and
professionally with issues that are regarded as controversial, sensitive, or
unpleasant. In many cases, these topics are challenging because they deal
with race, ethnicity, religious beliefs, political points of view, or other subjects that tend to polarize people. This specific focus led to the blended
staffing structure that we saw earlier: helping people deal with difficult
issues in their classes is best handled peer-to-peer, but it can also benefit
from the advice of professionals who have been trained to work through
challenging issues with others. It also affects the style of the program.
A great deal of emphasis is placed on teamwork, open discussion, balancing safety and risk in addressing important issues, promoting civil
discourse, learning from actual cases, and improving collegiality. Much

of the center's programming is conducted through faculty learning communities, book discussions, and other activities that reflect the center's informal style of mutual support and open discussion.

Other activities conducted as part of CAFE's programming also reflect this style. For example, some of the exercises that participants are exposed to through the center's *Start Speaking* handbook (www.uaa.alaska.edu/cafe/difficultdialogues/handbook.cfm) are the "cocktail party" (participants mingle in an ever-changing set of small groups while addressing various sensitive issues), the "code of conduct" (subgroups develop a list of desirable and undesirable behaviors for the discussion of a sensitive issue, come together as a large group to reach consensus on a set of operating principles, and then adhere to those principles throughout their discussion of the issue), and "role play" (participants enact a scenario in which they have to respond to a challenge posed by one or more of the other participants). (On these activities, see Landis, 2008.) The role plays, for example, might unfold in this way in a Difficult Dialogues workshop:

> Say, for instance, you're a science professor. You're teaching your class, covering your content, talking about evolution or the physical age of the earth or the vastnesses of space and time. Suddenly one of your students erupts. In response to the scientific content of your class, the student stands up, calls you "the devil's own messenger" and begins witnessing about religion. How do you handle this? What do you do? (Landis, 2008, 124)

That type of activity, combined with the presence of a trained professional staff, lends itself particularly well to CAFE's faculty-centric style of operation. Since there is no definitive right or wrong answer to the role-playing scenarios, a broad range of suggestions is encouraged from the participants so that there are multiple perspectives to consider. There is also active involvement of senior or former administrators and trained staff members who can guide the conversation toward productive approaches based on their own experience.

Modes of Interaction

The way in which the participants in a leadership program interact with one another also affects its style. We saw in chapter 1 that the style of the Academic Leadership Forum (ALF) program at Iowa State University was "business casual." Without formal policies, bylaws, or minutes, the program was characterized by a very informal style. Participants had the freedom to try out new ideas about what the program should be because there was a sense that they were all just feeling their way, inventing how the initiative should function as they went along. That resulted in a very different style from, for instance, the Academic Leadership Center (ALC) of the Saudi Ministry of Higher Education, which has a formal, structured style. The ALC adheres to a hierarchical structure with a general supervisor, director, national and international boards of advisors, staff, and campus liaisons at each Saudi university. Every workshop or conference has a formal structure: each day consists of four ninety-minute sessions, punctuated by fifteen-minute breaks and a one-hour lunch period. That more formal style tends to suit the ALC since the university system in Saudi Arabia is expanding so rapidly that programs need to be exceptionally rich in content to make sure that all participants keep up to date with evolving trends in international higher education.

A highly informal style of interaction tends to be typical of newer or more experimental leadership development programs. They are still in the process of determining what works best in their particular contexts and are constantly trying out new ideas as they develop. Frequently these programs have a fairly flat administrative structure. Either decisions are made by a committee of the whole, with no one person even nominally in charge, or different participants are tasked with different responsibilities, each according to his or her individual expertise or interest. This informal mode of interaction thus suits the support group and blended group staffing models (see chapter 5) particularly well. More fully developed leadership programs tend to have more formal modes of interaction.

As programs grow beyond an initial circle of eager volunteers, their needs change with respect to the challenges of scheduling, setting priorities, and the specific type of programming that is needed. They have learned from experience what works and what does not work. There may begin to be a stratification between the old guard (the people who began the project) and the new guard (more recently hired administrators or those who became involved with the initiative later). In order to avoid chaos when decisions need to be made, these initiatives thus start interacting more formally with rules and procedures, an officially designated chair or steering committee, and a more fixed calendar of activities. Whereas informally organized initiatives may be open to anyone who wants to attend—often without even the need to RSVP—programs with a more formal style of interaction often develop application procedures, committees to select participants, titles to distinguish different roles in the program, and perhaps even certificates of completion for those who fulfill stated requirements.

Most leadership development programs fall somewhere along the spectrum between being as highly informal as ALF and as highly formal as the ALC. For example, we have already seen that the Schwab Institute in Connecticut combines both structured and unstructured activities throughout its day-long program: the interactive session conducted by the guest expert and the plenary discussion tended to be formal; the breakout discussions, lunch conversation, and panel discussion tended to be informal. That same combination was seen in their staffing model, which relied primarily on administrative or clerical support to handle the logistics, with more decentralized responsibilities falling to the teaching and learning consultant at each institution. That blended style affects the entire spirit of the program. Interaction among members often feels more like a reunion of colleagues than a formal professional meeting, but a number of more structured aspects—formal registration, evaluation forms, minutes, and annual reports—also exist. As a result, participants interact with one another with a mixture of formality and informality according to how the program involves them at that point.

Distinctive Program Activities

In much the same way, activities that are unique to a leadership development program can have a significant effect on its style. In chapter 5, for example, we saw that the use of improvisational actors from the Cornell Interactive Theatre Ensemble made Cornell University's Leadership Development Academy quite different from most other leadership initiatives. Its style is both hands-on and intense. While role plays in other programs usually preserve a certain air of artificiality since participants are always aware that the other participants are simply enacting a part, those activities become highly realistic at Cornell. There is such a degree of immersion in the role that participants sometimes forget that the activity is merely an exercise and react with genuine flashes of anger or indignation. That degree of realism is particularly useful in sessions where academic leaders are learning about the triggers that cause them to react in inappropriate or unconstructive ways. They cannot become fully desensitized to these behavioral triggers unless the reenactment is so realistic that they almost forget they are conducting an exercise. In this way, the style of the Leadership Development Academy can be described as a highly intense, full-immersion experience, very different from programs that rely almost exclusively on oral presentations with little participant response.

The Leadership and Employee Enrichment Program (LEEP) at California State University East Bay incorporates a distinctive focus on the integration of personal well-being and professional development throughout its programs. The program's concept is that such issues as health, work-life balance, and personal growth are inseparable from the professional and leadership growth of the university's employees. For this reason, in addition to workshops on using technology and interpersonal relationships, LEEP's schedule is filled with sessions on stress management, caring for elderly parents, personal nutrition, and positive self-image. Midday meditation periods occur every Tuesday, and the program's resource page includes links to centers that promote such qualities as empathy, forgiveness, gratitude, happiness, and mindfulness (www20.csueastbay.edu/af/departments/leep/resources.html). The result is that this theme of caring for the individual permeates the program's style and everything it does. While still seeking to offer the opportunities that administrators and faculty members need in order to do their jobs better, it embodies the philosophy that employees are more than just their jobs alone. For this reason, even its workshops on technical topics are imbued with a sense that skills are to be used to make the community better, not simply for career enhancement or to become more efficient at work.

The distinctive style of the Regional Education for Achievement in Leadership (REAL) program—a joint venture of the California State University campuses in Bakersfield, Fresno, and Northridge—arises from a philosophy that genuine leadership requires candid self-awareness. Although understanding one's own values and goals is an element of many campus leadership initiatives, it serves as a true centerpiece of the REAL program. It uses self-assessment tools to help individual leaders chart a unique path that works best for them and their programs. A typical year-long schedule consists of six sessions that might look like the following:

1. Developing the Leader Within
2. University Leadership: Perspectives from the Inside
3. Leading and Motivating Teams
4. Thinking Holistically: Shaping Effective Challenges to Campus Solutions
5. Effective Leadership Communication and Presentation Skills
6. Managing Power, Conflict, and Organizational Politics

Each year, ten participants are selected from each of the three participating campuses. Nominees tend to be supervisors, managers, assistant or associate deans, and those with similar positions. Throughout the program, they review case studies, engage in skill-building exercises, meet with senior university leaders, and complete a project designed to improve their institutions in some way. Since its activities begin with assessments and inventories that seek to identify each participant's personal leadership style and philosophy, the entire program preserves the sense that it is an extended journey of self-discovery. But the REAL program also has a more explicitly business management orientation than do other leadership programs, particularly the LEEP initiative. Those two characteristic elements, self-discovery and a management focus, combine to give REAL its own style. In addition, its culmination in a project that contains concrete recommendations gives participants a sense that the training is practical and goal oriented. They are given a sense that they are learning how their own values and perspectives drive them, not simply because this insight is interesting but also because this insight is useful in solving problems and taking best advantage of opportunities (www.fresnostate.edu /adminserv/hr/learning/documents/Real%20Flyer%202013_14.pdf, www.calstate.edu/hr/success-jul13.pdf, and www.calstate.edu/hr /documents/SuccessStories.pdf).

Desired Program Outcomes

A practical, goal-oriented philosophy can also affect the intended outcomes of a leadership development initiative, and those outcomes also can define a program's style. At Florida International University, the Leadership Development Institute (LDI) has precisely this type of results-driven mission. Housed in the division of human resources (as opposed to the office of the president or provost, where many institutions locate their leadership programs), LDI establishes outcomes based on what it terms its four pillars of leadership:

- o Institutional knowledge
- o Effective communication
- o Operational excellence
- o Performance management

As might be expected, setting outcomes in these areas gives the institute a very different style from, for example, Naropa University's Authentic Leadership Program or the Nursing Leadership Institute at nearby Florida Atlantic University. The Leadership Education Advancement

Program (LEAP), LDI's signature offering, has a fixed curriculum that focuses on developing key competencies that fall under each of the four pillars (hr.fiu.edu/ldi/leap.php):

Pillar 1: Institutional Knowledge

Module 1: The FIU Pillars of Management

Module 2: Avoiding Legal Landmines

Pillar 2: Effective Communication

Module 3: The Power of Communication for Managers

Module 4: Managing Conflict and Disagreements Constructively

Pillar 3: Operational Excellence

Module 5: Decision Making and Delegation

Module 6: Managing Change and Transitions in a Fast-Paced Environment

Pillar 4: Performance Management

Module 7: Performance Management

Module 8: Fostering Teamwork and Collaboration

Final Session: Overview and Wrap-Up

Each pillar is the subject of a full-day session, with one module taking place in the morning and the other occupying the afternoon. Two cohorts of up to twenty-five participants take the program simultaneously, with each cohort assigned its own day of the week. Since LEAP is offered in the fall, spring, and summer terms, it has the capacity to have a significant effect on the university's leadership within a very short period of time.

The desired outcomes for LDI and LEAP establish a clear tone: while the word *leadership* appears in the program's title, the terms *management*, *managers*, and *managing* permeate the four pillars and the eight sessions. The program's style is not one of a leisurely voyage of self-discovery; it is a task-focused, results-oriented program. Those who enroll in the program know that there will be clear results when they complete their training. Unlike other leadership centers that continually vary their programming, LEAP has a set curriculum and structure. Entering it feels much more like registering for a class than merely joining a support group of peers. But that style best addresses the university's needs and helps it to accomplish its administrative objectives.

Style and Local Culture

Perhaps the most difficult aspect of style to define is that which results from an institution's individual culture. If you visit enough different colleges and universities, you soon realize that cultures vary widely across institutions of higher education. Some are more formal, others extremely casual. On some campuses everyone who passes you offers some form of greeting, while on others, passersby never even look one another in the eye. These aspects of culture develop gradually over time and are the function of the school's history, the personalities of the people who work or have worked there, and all the other factors we have examined in this chapter. Effective leadership development initiatives tend to suit the culture of the institutions that sponsor them. So if you are setting out to launch a new program or center of this kind, it pays to reflect on what the culture of your school is and how that might affect the style of the leadership development opportunity you create.

There are a number of ways to characterize local culture, but we focus on two that seem particularly productive. The first is based on the Global Leadership and Organizational Behavior Effectiveness (GLOBE) study. GLOBE was a project led by Robert J. House of the Wharton School of Business at the University of Pennsylvania. House and a team of researchers (House, Hanges, Javidan, Dorfman, and Gupta, 2004) built on earlier work by the Dutch social psychologist Geert Hofstede (2001) and sought to characterize national cultures in terms of nine major competencies:

1. *Assertiveness*: The degree to which individuals tend to be confrontational or aggressive in social relationships

2. *Future orientation*: The degree to which individuals plan, invest in long-term strategies, and delay personal gratification

3. *Gender egalitarianism*: The degree to which distinctive gender roles are equalized and regarded as of equivalent value

4. *Humane orientation*: The importance to which individuals attribute to the act of being fair, altruistic, friendly, generous, and caring to others

5. *Institutional collectivism (collectivism I)*: The degree to which institutions and the units within them encourage and reward the equitable distribution of resources

6. *In-group collectivism (collectivism II)*: The degree to which individuals express pride in and loyalty toward the units and organizations to which they belong

7. *Performance orientation*: The degree to which leaders reward and recognize successful performance or improvements in performance

8. *Power distance*: The degree to which power increases as one moves up the hierarchy

9. *Uncertainty avoidance*: The degree to which individuals avoid change and risk relying on established practices, norms, traditions, and bureaucratic structures

Although these nine competencies were developed to characterize national cultures, they are also useful in assessing institutional cultures. For example, a leadership initiative for chairs is likely to be very different in a culture where this position is rotated and chairs are viewed largely as facilitators than where the chair is a full-time administrative position for which the "power distance" from the faculty is perceived to be great. Similarly, an institution or unit in which people have the reputation for being brusque and bottom-line-oriented may respond completely differently to a leadership initiative that suits a less assertive area in which extensive small talk and social conversation always precede getting down to business.

The GLOBE project also identified six dimensions of leadership that, although recognized as important in the vast majority of cultures, could each serve as a continuum along which its self-perceived progress toward its aspirations could be charted (House et al., 2004; www.grovewell .com/pub-GLOBE-intro.html):

1. *Charismatic/value-based dimension*: How well does the culture meet its ideal of having leadership that is visionary, self-sacrificing, and characterized by integrity?

2. *Team-oriented dimension*: How well does the culture meet its ideal of having leadership that is collaborative, benevolent, and diplomatic?

3. *Participative dimension*: How well does the culture meet its ideal of avoiding leadership that is autocratic and averse to consultation?

4. *Humane-oriented dimension*: How well does the culture meet its ideal of having leadership that is modest and interested in the welfare of others?

5. *Autonomous dimension*: How well does the culture strike a balance between leadership that is neither too dependent on direction from the hierarchy above it nor too alienated from the viewpoints of those in the hierarchy below it?

6. *Self-protective dimension*: How well does the culture meet its ideal of avoiding leadership that is self-centered, status conscious, and the cause of conflict?

You can form a good initial impression of the local culture of an institution, division, or unit in higher education by reflecting on how well the leadership meets these aspirations and characterizing it in terms of GLOBE's nine competencies. This exercise provides guidance not merely into what style of leadership initiative is likely to best suit the needs of your stakeholders, but also what some of the program's content should be. For instance, are sessions in ethical decision making likely to be valuable in the program, or does the local culture suggest that participants will probably regard this topic as redundant?

We might also want to expand on GLOBE's cultural framework by considering how our institutions fall on the following scales:

Primarily Interested in Process: How Do We Do Things?	Primarily Interested in Results: What Do We Get Done?
Primarily motivated internally: I will be proud if I succeed and feel guilty or disappointed if I fail.	*Primarily motivated externally: I will be recognized and praised if I succeed and feel shame or lose face if I fail.*
Ethnicity blind: People are people.	Ethnicity aware: Our diversity is our strength.
Secular in mission: We may study spiritually, but we do not inculcate it.	*Spiritual in mission: We promote and encourage faith-based values.*
Critical of authority: We respect you because of what you do, not who you are.	Respectful of authority: We may not respect the person, but we respect the office he or she holds.
Group oriented: The achievement of the team is paramount.	*Individual oriented: The achievement of the person is paramount.*
Emotionally demonstrative: You always know how we feel.	Emotionally reserved: The workplace must preserve a certain level of decorum.
Pawns of destiny: Our good intentions are often stifled by forces we do not control.	*Captains of destiny: We are in control of our future.*

These factors too can help define the most appropriate style for a leadership development initiative. What one university or department might find "cozy," another university or department might find "stifling." Incentives that reward success by the team may be quite effective at one school yet have little impact at another. Studying the culture of your institution can thus be a critical element of getting the style of your leadership development program right. If the style seems wrong, participants will soon become detached and drift away.

While the GLOBE approach to local culture and the additions we have suggested are useful ways of helping you match your program's style to your stakeholders' needs, there is also a second major way of looking at this issue: the high-context/low-context continuum first suggested by the anthropologist Edward T. Hall in his book *Beyond Culture* (1976). High-context cultures are those in which communication can be effective even though very little is spelled out. There is sufficient continuity and conformity in the group that most members understand the context of a communication even if it may seem vague or excessively general to an outsider. Low-context cultures are those in which miscommunication occurs unless statements contain a great deal of information. Frequently that type of environment occurs where there is high turnover, with the result that stakeholders do not have the same degree of institutional memory that people in high-context cultures often have.

Think of your own institution, and imagine a situation in which a colleague asks you about how to get a classroom changed. If your response is likely to be, "Call Diane" (or whatever the name of the person authorized to change classrooms happen to be), you are probably operating in a low-context culture. But if your response is, "Call the registrar's office," or even, "Call the associate registrar for space utilization in the registrar's office," you are probably operating in a high-context culture. As Hall noted, however, few cultures are consistently at one of these extremes or the other. There is a full range of intermediate responses, like, "Call Diane Robertson in the registrar's office," that fall somewhere along the high-context/low-context continuum. As you examine the culture in which your leadership development initiative will occur, here are a few factors to consider in order to determine the most appropriate style for your program (Hall, 1959, 1966, 1976, 1983):

High-Context Culture	Low-Context Culture
Relationships tend to be friendships that develop gradually over time.	Relationships tend to be acquaintances that are often in flux.
People readily call the institution a family or community.	*People regard their workplace as something different from their family or community.*

People tend to know immediately and intuitively whether they do or do not belong to a certain subgroup.
How things get done depends largely on relationships.

Self-image is defined by the groups one belongs to (department, institution, family, church, job).
Interaction often occurs on a first-name basis. (Jim, Sheila)

Context is more important than content in communication. (How you say it matters more than what you say.)
Verbal communication tends to be indirect and social.
Disagreement is personal. (If you insult my work or opinion, you insult me.)
Conflict must be solved before work can advance.
Learning occurs by observation.
Quality is valued over speed. (It is better to get it done right than to meet a deadline.)

People may be uncertain, tentative, or hesitant as to whether they do or do not belong to a certain subgroup.
How things get done depends largely on titles and job descriptions.
Self-image is defined by what one has achieved (the length of a CV, academic rank, awards received).
Interaction usually occurs on a title plus last-name basis. (Dr. Jones, Dean Cunningham)
Content is more important than context in communication. (Say what you mean and mean what you say.)
Verbal communication tends to be direct and to the point.
Disagreement is impersonal. (If you insult my work or opinion, it is no reflection on me.)
Conflict is irrelevant to the pace of work.
Learning occurs by instruction.
Efficiency is viewed as an intersection of speed and accuracy. (The first word in deadline *is* dead.*)*

Identifying style in this way helps you define what your participants will need. Should you spend more time with them explaining the organization chart or simply introducing them to other people? Will you need to devote a great deal of time to icebreakers and other activities that help people get to know one another, or would those activities come across as a waste of time? Is conflict management going to be regarded as a critical topic, perhaps worthy of several entire workshops, or will people feel that valuable work can be done despite—or even because of—a great deal of conflict? Without understanding what the style of your program should be because of how your local culture has developed, it can be very difficult to meet these needs effectively. And if you are not meeting the needs of your stakeholders, then your leadership development initiative has very little reason to continue.

Competing Values Framework

In the early 1980s, Robert E. Quinn, who would later serve as the Margaret Elliott Tracy Collegiate Professor in Business Administration at the University of Michigan, published an influential model for classifying organizations known as the competing values framework (CVF; Quinn and Rohrbaugh, 1983; Quinn, 1984). At its most basic level, CVF plots the culture of an organization along two axes:

1. A vertical scale ranging from highly flexible and adaptable cultures at one end to highly stable and controlled cultures at the other end
2. A horizontal scale ranging from cultures that focus exclusively on internal processes at one end to cultures that focus exclusively on their relationships with external constituents at the other end

Subsequently the CVF (now also sometimes called the Quinn model) also began being applied to the leadership styles of executives and managers. The idea was that a leader's style should harmonize with (or at least not be in opposition to) that of the organization. In this way, both the leaders themselves and the organizations they led could be characterized as falling into one of four quadrants (see figure 7.1; competingvalues.com; Quinn, 1988; Cameron and Quinn, 2011):

1. *Collaborate*: People and organizations that maintain high flexibility with an internal focus. Those who fell within this quadrant tended to emphasize adherence to core values, sharing the same beliefs, building community, and promoting teamwork. They placed a premium on human relations. Leaders whose style fell within this quadrant saw themselves as facilitators and mentors, while organizations that fell within this quadrant possessed the nurturing atmosphere of a clan.
2. *Create*: People and organizations that maintain high flexibility with an external focus. Those who fell within this quadrant tended to emphasize vision, innovation, optimism, and the importance of launching new ventures. They placed a premium on open systems. Leaders whose style fell within this quadrant saw themselves as

Figure 7.1 The Four Quadrants of the Competing Values Framework

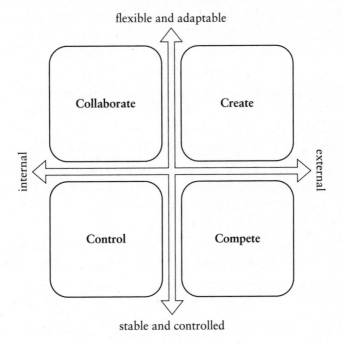

flexible and adaptable

internal

external

| Collaborate | Create |

| Control | Compete |

stable and controlled

innovators and brokers, while organizations that fell within this quadrant possessed the highly dynamic atmosphere of an adhocracy (a group that constantly adapts its structure to its current needs).

3. *Compete*: People and organizations that maintain high stability with an external focus. Those who fell within this quadrant tended to emphasize speed, decisiveness, systematic strategies for achieving objectives, and the importance of maximizing profits. They placed a premium on rational goals. Leaders whose style fell within this quadrant saw themselves as producers and directors, while organizations that fell within this quadrant possessed the results-oriented atmosphere of a market.

4. *Control*: People and organizations that maintain high stability with an internal focus. Those who fell within this quadrant tended to emphasize efficiency, practicality, the pursuit of high quality, and adherence to established budgets. They placed a premium on internal processes. Leaders whose style fell within this quadrant saw themselves as coordinators and monitors, while organizations that fell

within this quadrant possessed the chain-of-command atmosphere of a hierarchy.

Leadership styles stemming from the Quinn model can be organized as four pairs of opposites (figure 7.2):

1. Facilitators emphasize team building and managing conflict, while producers emphasize completing tasks and achieving results.
2. Mentors are helpful and caring for those in their charge, while directors make it a priority to complete tasks and achieve results.
3. Innovators take calculated risks in order to bring about change, while coordinators work within existing systems to manage projects.
4. Monitors track performance and see their role as dealing with paperwork and established procedures, while brokers focus on building coalitions, determining power relations, and serving external constituencies.

Elaborations of the Quinn model subdivided these eight leadership styles into twelve leadership skills (three characteristic skills per quadrant; see below) and proposed strategies for incorporating features of seemingly contradictory leadership styles into a more integrated and balanced

---

Figure 7.2 The Leadership Styles of the Competing Values Framework

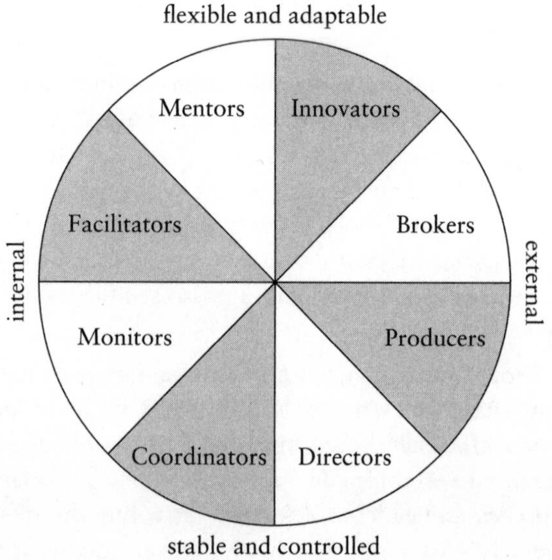

approach (Belasen, 2000; Quinn, 2004). Nevertheless, for our purposes, the four original quadrants of the CVF and the eight major leadership styles provide a useful taxonomy to use in academic leadership training (Cameron and Quinn, 2011):

COLLABORATE (STYLE OF A CLAN), ESSENTIAL SKILLS

o Managing teams

o Managing interpersonal relationships

o Managing the development of others

CREATE (STYLE OF AN ADHOCRACY), ESSENTIAL SKILLS

o Managing innovation

o Managing the future

o Managing continuous improvement

COMPETE (STYLE OF A MARKET), ESSENTIAL SKILLS

o Managing competitiveness

o Energizing employees

o Managing customer service

CONTROL (STYLE OF A HIERARCHY), ESSENTIAL SKILLS

o Managing acculturation

o Managing the control system

o Managing coordination

For example, we can use the Quinn model to help identify the default decision-making and problem-solving styles of participants in our programs. A number of instruments can be used to assess an administrator's leadership style and make that person more aware of why he or she tends to respond to challenges in a particular way. Chief among these instruments are the Octogram (www.octogram.net) and the Management Skills Assessment Inventory (www.josseybass.com/go/cameron). By using instruments of this kind, complemented perhaps with other approaches like the GLOBE taxonomy and the high-context/low-context continuum, leadership development programs can analyze the leadership styles of their participants from a number of important perspectives. In addition, they can convey the message that these styles serve as an additional set of tools in their leadership toolbox, offering them guidance in how to adopt alternative approaches when their default style does not appear to be working.

Clarifying the Style

Style means many different things when it comes to a leadership development program. The style you adopt is a direct result of what you are trying to do, how you are trying to do it, and why you are trying to do it. To help you focus on some of the most important aspects of your initiative's style, here are a few questions to consider:

1. *How does the mission of your institution or program distinguish you from your peers?* Don't think merely of the mission statement. Mission statements, formal documents created for external audiences, often do not adequately capture the unique nature and flavor of the institution or program they describe. Think about what you do better than or different from anyone else. When a student is deciding between your institution or program and another, what would you say to make that choice easier? What needs would be underserved if your institution or program did not exist?

   - Where does your institution fall on the spectrum between being entirely associated with the traditions, beliefs, and values of a specific religious group and being completely secular? How does that identity inform what you do as an institution?

   - Where does your institution fall on the spectrum between providing maximum access (allowing anyone to enroll who wishes to do so, regardless of past performance) and maintaining maximum selectivity (admitting only students with the best academic records and test scores)? How does that degree of access or selectivity inform what you do as an institution?

   - How comprehensive is your institution? Does it provide preparation in specific areas (such as a seminary, conservatory, or culinary institute), or does it offer a broader range of degrees? How does that degree of focus or comprehensiveness inform what you do as an institution?

   - What is the balance of research to teaching at your institution? How does that balance affect how faculty members are evaluated?

   - What is the level of prestige that your institution has? How does that status affect its identity and mission?

2. *What is the vision of your institution or program?* Again don't merely consider formal vision statements. Like mission statements, these documents are usually created for external audiences and may not contain an accurate portrait of where most people believe they are headed.

What do you personally regard as the likely trajectory of your institution or program? Would most of your colleagues agree? How does that vision affect the type of leadership development that people at your institution will need to have? How might it affect the urgency of your program to make an immediate difference?

3. *Is your leadership development initiative likely to have a specific focus,* such as servant leadership, positive leadership, and the other approaches discussed in chapters 2 or 8? How might that focus impart a particular style or flavor to your program?

4. *How do people tend to interact at your institution?* Is the atmosphere more formal or casual? Do most people prefer to receive their information electronically or in meetings? How might the way in which people are used to interacting shape the type of leadership development experiences you are providing?

5. *Are there particular program activities for which you or your colleagues in this initiative have had special training?* For example, have you had training as mediators, discussion leaders, case study designers, actors, or curriculum designers? Should you bring anyone else into the effort to compensate for backgrounds that your stakeholders will need but that you and your colleagues do not have? How might broadening your initiative beyond your original concept improve or hinder your efforts and affect the style of the program?

6. *What assessable outcomes have you set for your initiative?* What do those outcomes suggest in terms of how your program should be designed and the style it should adopt?

7. *Most important, what is your local culture, and which style of development activity suits it best?* As you review the culture of your institution and program in terms of GLOBE's nine cultural competencies and six dimensions of leadership, the expansion of that framework that we provided in this chapter, and Edward T. Hall's concept of high-context versus low-context cultures, what do you conclude about the needs and expectations of your prospective participants? What sort of style will strike them as most relevant to the culture with which they are familiar?

REFERENCES

Belasen, A. T. (2000). *Leading the learning organization: Communication and competencies for managing change.* Albany: State University of New York Press.

Cameron, K. S., & Quinn, R. E. (2011). *Diagnosing and changing organizational culture: Based on the competing values framework* (3rd ed.). San Francisco, CA: Jossey-Bass.

Hall, E. T. (1959). *The silent language.* Garden City, NY: Doubleday.

Hall, E. T. (1966). *The hidden dimension.* Garden City, NY: Doubleday.

Hall, E. T. (1976). *Beyond culture.* Garden City, NY: Anchor Press.

Hall, E. T. (1983). *The dance of life.* Garden City, NY: Anchor Press/Doubleday.

Hofstede, G. H. (2001). *Culture's consequences: Comparing values, behaviors, institutions, and organizations across nations.* Thousand Oaks, CA: Sage.

House, R. J., Hanges, P. J., Javidan, M., Dorfman, P. W., & Gupta, V. (2004). *Culture, leadership, and organizations: The GLOBE study of 62 societies.* Thousand Oaks, CA: Sage.

Landis, K. (Ed.). (2008). *Start talking: A handbook for engaging in difficult dialogues in higher education.* Anchorage: University of Alaska Anchorage.

Quinn, R. E. (1984). Applying the competing values approach to leadership: Toward an integrative framework. In J. G. Hunt, D. M. Hosking, C. A. Schriesheim, & R. Stewart (Eds.), *Leaders and managers: International perspectives on managerial behavior and leadership* (pp. 10–27). New York: Pergamon Press.

Quinn, R. E. (1988). *Beyond rational management: Mastering the paradoxes and competing demands of high performance.* San Francisco, CA: Jossey-Bass.

Quinn, R. E. (2004). *Building the bridge as you walk on it: A guide for leading change.* San Francisco, CA: Jossey-Bass.

Quinn, R. E., & Rohrbaugh, J. (1983). A spatial model of effectiveness criteria: Towards a competing values approach to organizational analysis. *Management Science. 29,* 363–377.

RESOURCES

Al-Omari, A. A. (2005). *Leadership styles and style adaptability of deans and department chairs at three public research universities.* Unpublished doctoral dissertation, Washington State University, Pullman.

Bremer, M. (2012). *Organizational culture change: Unleash your organizations potential in circles of 10.* Zwolle, Netherlands: Kikker Groep.

Driskill, G. W., & Brenton, A. L. (2011). *Organizational culture in action: A cultural analysis workbook.* Thousand Oaks, CA: Sage.

Glanz, J. (2002). *Finding your leadership style: A guide for educators.* Alexandria, VA: Association for Supervision and Curriculum Development.

JB Intercultural Consultants. (2003). Culture at work. www.culture-at-work.com/highlow.html.

Rath, T., & Conchie, B. (2009). *Strengths based leadership: Great leaders, teams, and why people follow*. New York, NY: Gallup Press.

Schein, E. H. (1985). *Organizational culture and leadership*. San Francisco, CA: Jossey-Bass.

Scott, G., Coates, H., & Anderson, M. (2008). *Learning leaders in times of change: Academic leadership capabilities for Australian higher education*. Melbourne, Australia: ACER.

8

SHARED VALUES

AS WE SAW IN chapters 2 and 7, gaining the knowledge and mastering the skills of academic leadership, although vital, are not sufficient by themselves to make administrators effective and successful. For many administrators, leadership development is an inner journey, and aligning their knowledge and skills with their core values is often the most difficult part of their professional growth. Self-knowledge, personal awareness, and reflective critique are all part of becoming more mature as an academic leader. We call development in this key area an exploration of the habits of heart. When a group of Australian administrators was asked what skill they most needed in order to be effective, the head of the engineering department responded, "Know thyself—I have to know myself before I can lead my team and faculty" (Gmelch, Hopkins, and Damico, 2011, 77). Leadership development is very much about finding one's voice (Kouzes and Posner, 1987).

Many academic leaders have found that credibility and authenticity lie at the heart of leadership, and so they must examine and identify their core beliefs and assumptions as they grow in their positions. That process can occur at the same three levels of intervention that we examined with regard to skill development in chapter 7: the personal, institutional, and professional:

- ○ *Personal level.* In chapter 1, we encountered Donald Schön's (1983) concept of reflection-in-action. While many managers in all kinds of organizations engage in this type of reflection, it is relatively rare for them to carry this process to its next step: the type of meta-analysis we might call *reflection-on-reflection*: "To what extent am I using this process merely to justify my decisions to myself? When I review my performance, am I being too easy on myself? Too hard on myself? Do I engage in this activity intending to impose a predetermined interpretation on the facts, or am I truly being open to seeing myself as others see me without either false modesty or self-flattery?" Without this type of meta-analysis, it is very hard to improve one's abilities to reflect-in-action. The person tends to draw the same conclusions over and over—"There I go again, so typical of me"—without bringing about any genuine improvement. In higher education, this lack of reflection on reflection, common to most managers, is frequently coupled with a second major omission: discussing these contemplations with peers. As a result, many academic leaders feel alone and falsely believe that they are the only people who struggle with certain challenges. Many administrators seem afflicted with the imposter syndrome—the type of self-doubt that causes people to believe they are in over their heads and that it is only a matter of time before everyone discovers what phonies they are. By engaging in reflective practices like journaling or systematic self-analysis, and then articulating to colleagues some of the conclusions arising from this practice, administrators become more aware of their core values, thought processes, and genuine (not merely imagined) areas of strength and weakness.

○ *Institutional level.* Leadership development does not take place within a vacuum. It is a process that works best when it is shared with a group of trusted colleagues who are mentors, partners, and coaches to each other. Many institutions have formal structures in place like leadership councils, academic partnerships, and annual reviews that provide campus leaders with systematic access to formative evaluation and feedback. Many have also developed an informal support system in which colleagues meet, sometimes without their supervisor being present, in a "safe" environment such as over coffee or a meal, so they can discuss and explore common issues and needs. Academic leaders often find that these opportunities become sessions in which they can vent about frustrations and discover that they are far from alone in being challenged by certain situations or problems. One-on-one meetings with the administrator's supervisor also provide times for discussion of a variety of topics from campus issues to the meaning of life. Although these supervisors will vary widely in how easy they are to open up to and how supportive they are of personal reflection, in the best of these relationships the opportunity to have a boss who is interested in one's personal development and willing to act as a mentor can be the most satisfying leadership development opportunity of all. It can also be useful to have a confidant outside the department, college, or institution who can provide a supportive bonding experience to explore ethical and moral dilemmas.

o *Professional level*. Professional organizations can help administrators establish networks they can use to reflect on and clarify their shared values. By attending national conferences and professional development programs, academic leaders connect with colleagues, form personal relationships with other like-minded people, and develop expanded networks of confidants. By helping academic leaders from many different institutions explore what it is they really do, how they do it, why they do it, and what differences they make in their activities, these extramural opportunities can be a valuable component of a comprehensive leadership initiative. The campus leadership program or center can provide a useful service by informing administrators about professional groups they may not be aware of, reminding them of upcoming conventions, and handling the logistics of registration and securing funds to attend.

Shared Institutional Values

In the corporate world, it is not uncommon to find well-established programs devoted to training employees in the institutional culture and what Terence Deal and Allan Kennedy (2000) call "the way we do things around here" (4). Many corporations develop a "brand" of institutional values and philosophies, including such famous corporate cultures as Disney ("Creating Magic"; Cockerell, 2008), Hewlett-Packer ("The HP Way"; Packard, Kirby, and Lewis, 1995), Marriott ("The Spirit to Serve"; Marriott and Brown, 1997), IBM (simply referred to as "IBM's Values"; Watson, 2003), and Google ("Don't Be Evil"; Vise and Malseed, 2005). This practice is far less common at colleges and universities. Some try to fill this gap with mission statements, vision statements, and catalogues of institutional values. But frequently those documents are generated more to impress external audiences, such as donors and potential students, than to provide guidance to internal stakeholders. While they can provide insight into the values that a college or university aspires to, they may not be very informative about "the way we do things around here."

To identify those ideas, it may help to reflect on what type of institution the academic leader is working for. How, in other words, would the values, practices, and priorities be different for the following categories of schools?

o Land grant universities
o Faith-based colleges

○ Comprehensive master's degree institutions

○ Liberal arts colleges

○ Research universities

○ Historically black colleges and universities and Hispanic-serving institutions

○ Community colleges

○ Conservatories or schools of art and design

○ Flagship universities

○ Regional state-supported universities (i.e., schools with one or more "compass points" in their names, like Southwest Missouri State University and the University of Northern Iowa)

○ Elite and highly selective private universities

○ Single-sex institutions

○ Technical schools

Although these categories are not always mutually exclusive, certain values tend to be associated with certain types of schools. For example, community colleges place a priority on providing access; elite, highly selective universities emphasize rigor, lofty expectations, and maintaining strong academic standards. An administrator who is a perfect fit for one type of institution may not find it easy at all to work at a different kind of school. So a good way to begin identifying the unspoken shared values at your college or university is to ask:

○ What assumptions can I make about our institutional priorities based on the type of school we are and the sorts of students we admit?

○ In order to be highly successful as an administrator in that type of environment, what sort of outlook and expectations would I probably bring to the job?

○ How well aligned are my own values and core beliefs to that outlook and those expectations?

If institutions desire to become more intentional about instilling their values into those who work and study in them, there are many mechanisms they can use to do so. These mechanisms can be incorporated into a leadership development program as a way of encouraging administrators to reflect not merely on their own values, but on the relationship of their values to the institution as a whole:

○ *Develop mission statements that are genuine, not designed for marketing purposes.* As we have seen, the mission statements of many colleges and universities are really designed to communicate a message to external stakeholders, not to inform and guide internal stakeholders. But as corporations have already found, mission statements don't have an impact simply because they have been eloquently worded. They have an impact when they resonate with people and when leaders take personal interest in promoting that mission (Lowney, 2003). It can therefore be useful for institutions to create a document that is a bit more reflective than the traditional mission statement that exists primarily for the public. This type of candid self-analysis would include a summary of institutional values that are meaningful to internal constituents and would be used during the orientation and training of those who are new to the campus community.

○ *Use a variety of media to reinforce these shared values.* Even the best mission statement is of little use in communicating shared values if it is relegated to the college catalogue, web page, or accreditation report. Some schools find it useful to place a framed statement of institutional values in every classroom or hallway. Others have quotations from it painted on walls of the administration building or other facilities that commonly receive a great deal of traffic. Doing so is easier, of course, if there are passages of the mission statement that are concise and immediate in impact, like, "We make dreams come true," "We are committed to the success of each student who walks through our doors," or "Creative thought matters." If there is already a mission statement in place and the institution does not wish to modify it, it may be possible to capture its intent through mottos or slogans like, "If you want to see what tomorrow's leaders look like, just look around you," or, "Meeting you where you are and taking you where you need to go."

○ *Schedule programs that reinforce the notion that the institution takes its mission seriously.* Even if people see the mission and the values of the school every day when they open their web browser or walk around campus, they may not realize how it affects them personally and what the school's expectations are in terms of how they should represent these shared values. To achieve this goal, a liberal arts college might organize faculty learning communities around a theme of "The Significance of

Liberal Arts Education in the Twenty-First Century"; the president might structure public addresses so that statements beginning with, "As a liberal arts college, we value ..."; and deans might follow a parallel approach in their meetings with department chairs. In a similar way, a research university might underscore the importance of inquiry and original discovery by incorporating these processes into everything it does. Like the "flipped classroom" in which students acquire knowledge of facts and formulas outside class and then use class time to process, challenge, and apply this knowledge, this research university might structure meetings of academic leaders so that reports and recommendations are all distributed to be read in advance, with the meeting itself devoted entirely to questioning, modifying, approving, or rejecting the proposals contained in those reports.

○ *Make sure that as many forms of communication as possible embed and reinforce the institution's values.* When we asked an executive from the accounting firm of Ernst and Young how corporate values were instilled in its leadership, he responded, "Every single memo from our CEO reinforced our corporate values." It may be unrealistic to expect that specific reference to these values would appear in all the e-mails, memos, and reports that an academic leader writes, but this goal is worth establishing as an ideal. One way of beginning this process is to ask yourself whether your communications are likely to convey your institution's core principles to someone who does not know you. Find a few memos and e-mails from the past and review what values they seem to convey. For instance, if you say that one of your most important values is treating all people as individuals and one of your institution's core principles is that student success is its highest priority, do the words you use, decisions you make, and tone you adopt reflect or undermine these values? Alternatively, you might take a few moments before leaving the office at the end of the workday to ask, "How did my words and actions today reflect my commitment to the treatment of all people as individuals and my school's emphasis on student success? If I'm not satisfied with what I discover, how can I do better tomorrow?"

Probably the most effective way to reinforce shared values is through telling stories. A statement commonly attributed to Patrick Kelly, the founder of Physician Sales and Services, is, "We've never had a policy manual. The way we pass along our values is to sit around the campfire and tell stories" (Kouzes and Posner, 1999, 103). Stories embody values in the way that mission statements and inspirational posters never can. They are particularly valuable when introducing someone new to the institution during the period of their orientation.

Leaders' Socialization Strategies

Perhaps the most important way that institutions have of developing shared values among academic leaders are the strategies they use to socialize or bring into the fold new members of their ranks. The technical term for this orientation process is *organizational socialization* or *onboarding*, and it includes passing on not merely new knowledge and skills but also new attitudes and expected behavior (Van Maanen and Schein, 1979). In Zen training, teachers often speak of taking robes off so that we know when we put robes on (Sorensen, 2000). The idea is that when the initiate moves into the temple (in the case of higher education, when the faculty member moves into the administrator's office), a change of appearance signifies to them and others that they have changed roles. When the monk leaves the temple, the robe is removed as a reminder that there are valuable roles to play in life outside the temple. In many cases, an almost identical process occurs with academic leaders: people in administrative positions tend to dress more formally than they did as faculty members, although they are likely to revert to more casual dress when they leave their positions. But more important, there are certain attitudes and behaviors people adopt when assuming positions of academic leadership. They are expected to take a more global view of matters when they make decisions, keep certain matters more confidential, find a different balance between speaking their mind and being diplomatic, and align their personal values more completely with those of the institution. New academic leaders sometimes do not understand that transition. They continue to think like an organic chemist rather than as a dean of the college of science or as someone who is interested only in his or her own priorities rather than the priorities of the school as a whole.

In the study of organizational behavior, the methods used to provide this socialization can be visualized as points falling at specific points on six scales of attitudes or behaviors (figure 8.1; Van Maanen and Schein, 1979; Gmelch, 2000; Kramer, 2010).

LEARNING THE CONTEXT OF CAMPUS LEADERSHIP

○ *Individual versus collective approaches.* In individual socialization, the academic leader is brought on board individually, usually receiving guidance from a mentor or supervisor. In collective socialization, this type of preparation is provided through group orientation sessions, workshops, or programs. Several decades ago, a study of new department chairs found that all of them were given their orientation individually as opposed to being part of a larger group

Figure 8.1 Socialization Strategies Used to Prepare New Academic Leaders

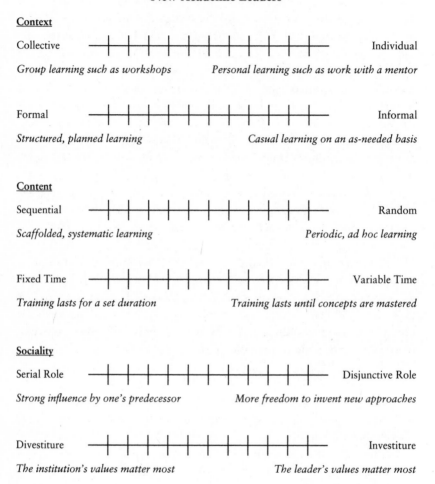

Context

Collective ———————————————————— Individual

Group learning such as workshops   Personal learning such as work with a mentor

Formal ———————————————————— Informal

Structured, planned learning   Casual learning on an as-needed basis

Content

Sequential ———————————————————— Random

Scaffolded, systematic learning   Periodic, ad hoc learning

Fixed Time ———————————————————— Variable Time

Training lasts for a set duration   Training lasts until concepts are mastered

Sociality

Serial Role ———————————————————— Disjunctive Role

Strong influence by one's predecessor   More freedom to invent new approaches

Divestiture ———————————————————— Investiture

The institution's values matter most   The leader's values matter most

of new employees (Staton-Spicer and Spicer, 1987). But even as recently as 2011, only 30 percent of pharmacy chairs said that they had received any formal orientation to prepare them for the job before assuming their administrative duties. About half of those who were trained (roughly 15 percent of the entire group of chairs) had received five or fewer hours of orientation. The remaining 71 percent of chairs had no formal orientation whatsoever and learned solely on the job (Schwinghammer et al., 2012).

o *Formal versus informal approaches.* Formal approaches are used when the new leader is provided a structure or planned set of learning experiences. Informal approaches adopt a far more casual style. The newcomer is given some general guidance and perhaps told to call the supervisor if a question arises. Formal leadership training is usually provided by the types of programs and centers described throughout this book. Informal training tends to be done by a supervisor or mentor who relies on personal and practical experience to guide the new leader in making appropriate decisions.

UNDERSTANDING THE CONTENT OF CAMPUS LEADERSHIP

o *Sequential versus random approaches.* School principals go through a specific sequence of discrete and identifiable steps that results in their administrative certification or doctoral preparation. By contrast, except for academic leaders with a degree in higher education administration, few, if any, university administrators go through this type of highly sequential process. That is one of the reasons that they may seem less well versed in core institutional values than their counterparts in primary and secondary education. As a result, their socialization in shared values may long remain incomplete, and they may find themselves periodically torn between what they themselves regard as best and what "the institution" regards as best.

o *Fixed-time versus variable-time approaches.* In fixed-time orientation, it is made clear to all participants what sort of time commitment is involved. The training starts on a specified date and time, lasts a certain number of hours or days, and concludes on a specified date and time. Variable-time orientation is far more flexible. Participants complete the program whenever they have mastered the material; it is expected that some people will take longer than others.

UNDERSTANDING ONE'S ROLE IN THE ORGANIZATIONAL STRUCTURE

o *Serial versus disjunctive approaches.* When academic leaders follow in someone else's footsteps and a strong role model exists, they experience serial socialization. This means that their predecessor is available for advice, consultation, and institutional history. The presence of this predecessor can be a positive or negative factor in the new leader's success, depending on the chemistry between them and their expectations of each other. If the new leader feels stifled by the previous dean or chair who seems to want everything done the way he or she did it, the result can be destructive. But if the person's predecessor acts more as a mentor, providing help when needed and fading into the background at other times, the experience can be positive for both of them. In a disjunctive approach, the new leader has no guidance from anyone who once occupied his or her role. Disjunctive socialization allows the academic leader to be more creative and innovative, but it can also cause the person to reinvent the wheel and waste a great deal of time.

o *Investiture versus divestiture approaches.* Divestiture approaches seek to "deny and strip away certain personal characteristics of a recruit" (Van Maanen and Schein, 1979, 250). In other words, they require newcomers to immerse themselves almost entirely in the values of the institution, even when their personal values may be in conflict with what they are required to say publicly. In contrast, university leaders could experience investiture processes that celebrate their unique contributions to the university. In some cases, investiture or divestiture occurs quite literally: leaders are told that they now have to dress in a particular way; men may be asked to shave their beards or moustaches; women may be asked to wear suits instead of casual clothing. At other times, this process occurs much more informally. The newcomer sees the way in which peers and supervisors dress, act, and express their opinions and soon learning to model these behaviors.

These six scales provide a useful way in which to determine how colleges and universities socialize their new leaders. Viewed from a different perspective, the same scales can be used to chart the shared values the academic leader acquires from the process of socialization (figure 8.2).

In other words, how much are leaders at that institution encouraged to think about their own needs and careers versus the good of the school as a whole? Is the environment one where faculty members tend to be on a first-name basis with their supervisors, or are formal titles the rule? (In fact, it can be interesting to see at what point in the hierarchy a more casual interpersonal style ends and greater formality begins. At some schools, a faculty member may feel perfectly comfortable addressing a college, the chair, or the dean by first name, but would never consider doing so with the provost or president.) Does the institution tend to be rigid in its approach to time ("You have to make an appointment if you want to discuss that") or more flexible ("Walk with me to my next meeting, and let's talk about it")? Is it expected that faculty meetings and other scheduled events will end at a particular time, or are they allowed to go as long as necessary to get through the entire agenda? Do people tend to

Figure 8.2 Shared Values at Colleges or Universities

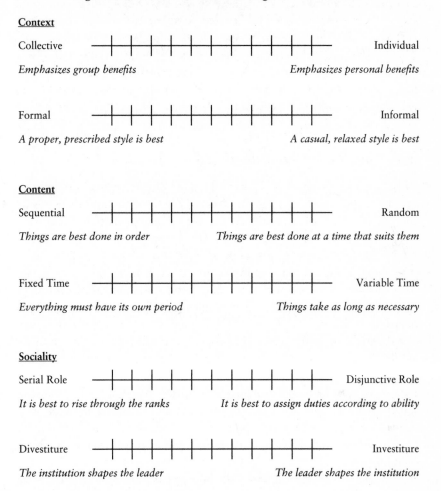

Context

Collective ——————————————————— Individual

Emphasizes group benefits   *Emphasizes personal benefits*

Formal ——————————————————— Informal

A proper, prescribed style is best   *A casual, relaxed style is best*

Content

Sequential ——————————————————— Random

Things are best done in order   *Things are best done at a time that suits them*

Fixed Time ——————————————————— Variable Time

Everything must have its own period   *Things take as long as necessary*

Sociality

Serial Role ——————————————————— Disjunctive Role

It is best to rise through the ranks   *It is best to assign duties according to ability*

Divestiture ——————————————————— Investiture

The institution shapes the leader   *The leader shapes the institution*

rise through the ranks, or could a wunderkind jump from chair to provost if he or she possessed the right set of skills? Which is the greater expectation: that the leader will toe the company line or give voice to objections and alternative views as often as necessary?

In most cases, the way the socialization strategy of a particular school or unit of that school can be plotted on figure 8.1 tells you a great deal about the shared values it is trying to promote on figure 8.2. Formal orientation processes are usually found at institutions that favor a more formal administrative style. Highly scheduled and regimented programs tend to occur at schools that expect all courses, meetings, and academic programs to be of a set duration, and so on. The interesting situations arise where there is a disconnect between these two scales. For instance, a school might claim to value individuality and complete freedom of speech and yet expect all administrators to speak with a single voice on every issue. The questions that then need to be asked are, "What is the origin of this schism between action and expectation? Is the institution being hypocritical in advocating certain values? Is the leader able to work effectively in an environment where the administration claims to believe one thing but acts as though it believes another?"

Two Case Studies in Promoting Shared Values

There are also many other ways in which the distinctive institutional values of a college or university can affect the way in which it develops its campus leaders. For example, we saw in chapter 5 that the University of Alaska Anchorage's Center for Advancing Faculty Excellence (CAFE) integrates aspects of the Ford Foundation's Difficult Dialogues Initiative into many of the programs it offers. But there is also a conscious effort to make sure those efforts reflect the distinctive cultural traditions of the region in which the university is located. Many of the students who enroll at the University of Alaska Anchorage belong to one of the indigenous Alaskan peoples, such as the Inupiaq, Unungan, and Haida cultures. While there are clear differences among all these cultures, as a group they often approach learning and interpersonal communication in ways that are different from what many of the university's European American faculty members might expect. For this reason, CAFE offers week-long intensive programs that help prepare administrators and faculty members to work more effectively as leaders within this distinctive cultural environment.

Whereas Western cultures attribute great importance to being assertive, goal oriented, and individualistic, native Alaskan cultures tend to emphasize being cooperative, putting the needs of the group ahead of personal concerns, and being process oriented (Merculieff and Landis, 2013). Here's an example of how CAFE used direct experience to teach the participants in its week-long program about an important aspect of communication in many Alaskan cultures:

> Indigenous cultures value silence. Too much talking interferes with observing, listening, sensing, experiencing, deciding wisely, and acting effectively. You have to be still in order to observe clearly and sense the connections between yourself, others, and the natural world. Silence creates the space for deepening that understanding and connection

and for getting a more accurate picture of the whole ... [To reinforce this concept, an activity in one of the university's development programs] invited people to prepare a personal story from their own lives that they could share without using any words. This afternoon, the bravest among us gave it a try. One flapped her wings to show how she came to Alaska. Another danced to show how she met her husband in Polynesia. A third used his daughter's stuffed lions and tigers to demonstrate field research in Africa. They were all pretty funny, and we laughed some more ... For several hours, we just hung out together, moving, mingling, connecting with one another and with the natural world around us. This is hardly a typical faculty development experience, but it was probably the most important few hours of the whole week. (Merculieff and Landis, 2013, 22, 116)

At the University of San Francisco (USF), institutional values are conveyed to members of the faculty and administration in a very different way, but with the same conviction that values should inform and guide everything done at the institution. USF is a Roman Catholic university in the Jesuit tradition. It outlines its values explicitly in its statements of mission, vision, and core values:

○

Vision

The University of San Francisco will be internationally recognized as a premier Jesuit Catholic, urban University with a global perspective that educates leaders who will fashion a more humane and just world.

Mission

The core mission of the University is to promote learning in the Jesuit Catholic tradition. The University offers undergraduate, graduate and professional students the knowledge and skills needed to succeed as persons and professionals, and the values and sensitivity necessary to be men and women for others.

The University will distinguish itself as a diverse, socially responsible learning community of high quality scholarship and academic rigor sustained by a faith that does justice. The University will draw from the cultural, intellectual and economic resources of the San Francisco Bay Area and its location on the Pacific Rim to enrich and strengthen its educational programs.

Core Values

The University's core values include a belief in and a commitment to advancing:

○ The Jesuit Catholic tradition that views faith and reason as complementary resources in the search for truth and authentic human development, and that welcomes persons of all faiths or no religious beliefs as fully contributing partners to the University

○ The freedom and the responsibility to pursue truth and follow evidence to its conclusion

○ Learning as a humanizing, social activity rather than a competitive exercise

○ A common good that transcends the interests of particular individuals or groups; and reasoned discourse rather than coercion as the norm for decision making

○ Diversity of perspectives, experiences and traditions as essential components of a quality education in our global context

○ Excellence as the standard for teaching, scholarship, creative expression and service to the University community

○ Social responsibility in fulfilling the University's mission to create, communicate and apply knowledge to a world shared by all people and held in trust for future generations

○ The moral dimension of every significant human choice: taking seriously how and who we choose to be in the world

○ The full, integral development of each person and all persons, with the belief that no individual or group may rightfully prosper at the expense of others

○ A culture of service that respects and promotes the dignity of every person

Source: www.usfca.edu/about/values/.

○

In order to reinforce these values throughout the institution, the university conducts a monthly program of readings and discussions with the president, vice president, and deans on what it means to be a Jesuit university. Deans are expected to hold similar discussions on shared values with their department chairs. Grants are available for faculty members who wish to explore ways of incorporating these values into their teaching and research. The Office of University Ministry offers leadership development programs that can help people better understand the Jesuit mission and how to embody their own spiritual values into their leadership activities. It also offers retreats and immersion programs in economically marginalized communities in order to provide current and prospective leaders first-hand experience in the importance of reflection, social responsibility, and service (www.usfca.edu/Provost/Teaching_and_Learning_Support/ and www.usfca.edu/University_Ministry/Faculty_Staff_Programs/).

Incorporating Personal Values into Leadership

In addition to reflecting the institution's values in their leadership, administrators must find a way to identify and represent their own values when making decisions or setting policy. According to Chris Lowney (2003), a one-time seminarian who went on to serve as a managing director of J.P. Morgan, effective leadership does not consist of dipping into a bag of tricks but of discovering a way to make appropriate decisions on the basis of one's personal life strategies and values. Or as John W. Gardner (1990) puts it, "The leaders whom we admire the most help to revitalize our shared beliefs and values. They have always spent a portion of their time teaching the value framework" (14).

In chapter 1, we noted that no one has ever transformed an institution by adopting a clever technique; instead leaders transform institutions by embodying worthy values. But which values should leadership programs be promoting? Is there any principle that, more than any other, is important for academic leaders to share? The answer is yes. In their research, James Kouzes and Barry Posner (2011) found that the most important value people expect in their leaders is credibility. Authentic leaders—those who say what they mean and mean what they say, whose values really inform their actions and are not merely put on for show, and in whom people have confidence that they are not merely being manipulated—tend to be admired regardless of whether they are in the corporate or academic world, represent any particular political view, or have a specific leadership style. Effective leaders tend to be those who are candid about what they intend to do and why. While they may need to be diplomatic in order to spare the feelings of people and preserve the confidentiality of those who have entrusted private information to them, they should never intentionally be deceptive. Trust, once lost, is extraordinarily difficult to regain. For this reason, we might consider the cluster of values closely related to credibility—such qualities as honesty, candor, and honoring one's commitments—as the sine qua non of academic leadership.

How is this credibility demonstrated on a daily basis? In a survey of department chairs from both the United States and Australia, respondents said that they found their deans to be most credible and easiest to work with when they (Gmelch and Sarros, 1996):

○ Are encouraging

○ Are accessible

○ Are trustworthy

○ Promote a positive relationship

○ Show confidence in the chairs and their departments

○ Encourage strategic decisions

○ Have a clear sense of direction and communicate it to others

○ Demonstrate all the other qualities we commonly associate with leadership

By having a clear set of core beliefs that are nonnegotiable, leaders can adapt more easily to changing situations since they know intuitively where they are able to give some ground and where they need to hold firm (Lowney, 2003).

In their study of credibility, Kouzes and Posner (1993) propose six practices that can help leaders develop this quality within themselves. Translating these practices into terms most appropriate for the work of higher education, we might describe these activities as:

1. *Discovering yourself* (reflecting on your values and core beliefs, developing a philosophy of leadership, assessing your commitment to others)

2. *Appreciating your faculty and colleagues* (finding value in their diversity, understanding their values and how they may differ from yours, promoting constructive controversy)

3. *Affirming shared values and interests* (publicly reinforcing those principles that your department, college, or university embraces as a community)

4. *Developing organizational capacity* (liberating the leader in everyone, empowering others, and helping people achieve their personal and professional goals)

5. *Serving the purpose* (seeing the role of the leader as service, placing the good of the whole before personal desires)

6. *Sustaining the hope* (finding optimism in adversity, engaging in positive academic leadership, celebrating achievements along the way)

In sum, growing as an academic leader has much to do with learning
the metaphors (mastering the terms and concepts needed to be competent
in the job), using the metaphors (applying this knowledge effectively and
consistently), and changing the metaphor (serving as a catalyst for needed
innovation and improvement). In the words of John Gardner (1990), ultimately "history will judge leaders on—among other things—how well
they understand the traditional framework of values, and how they renew
the tradition by adapting it to contemporary dilemmas" (191). Any social
organization that strives to be more than a "crowd of strangers" shares
a certain set of beliefs, aspirations, and operating principles. A leadership development program can serve as an appropriate place in which
these values are explored, challenged, and passed on to others. It can also
provide an effective framework for each current and prospective leader to
reflect on how his or her individual values relate to those of the institution
and whether these values are providing effective guidance on a daily basis.

Clarifying Shared Values

1. What opportunities does your program or center provide for leaders
   to reflect on their personal values, develop a philosophy of leadership,
   and understand the relationship between their values and those of the
   institution as a whole?

2. What institutional values exist at your college or university because of
   its type (such as research university versus liberal arts college) and heritage (such as public institution versus faith-based institution)? How
   are those values conveyed to members of the community? How do
   they inform daily actions and decisions?

3. What type of organizational socialization or onboarding can you provide to new leaders that not only exposes them to the knowledge they
   are expected to have but also conveys to them the principles they are
   expected to represent?

4. As you plot the values of your institution on figure 8.2, what are the
   areas where your institution is likely to differ the most from others in
   its peer group?

5. Since credibility is almost universally recognized as the most important
   value for leaders to have, what would most people at your institution
   describe as the second most important value?

REFERENCES

Cockerell, L. (2008). *Creating magic: Ten common sense leadership strategies from a life at Disney*. New York, NY: Currency Doubleday.

Deal, T. E., & Kennedy, A. A. (2000). *Corporate cultures: The rites and rituals of corporate life* (2nd ed.). Cambridge, MA: Perseus.

Gardner, J. W. (1990). *On leadership*. New York, NY: Free Press.

Gmelch, W. H. (2000). Leadership succession: How new deans take charge and learn. *Journal of Leadership Studies*, 7(3), 68–87.

Gmelch, W. H., Hopkins, D., & Damico, S. B. (2011). *Seasons of a dean's life: Understanding the role and building leadership capacity*. Sterling, VA: Stylus.

Gmelch, W. H., & Sarros, J. (1996). How to work with your dean: Voices of American and Australia department chairs. *Department Chair*, 6(4), 19–20.

Kouzes, J. M., & Posner, B. Z. (1987). *The leadership challenge: How to get extraordinary things done in organizations*. San Francisco, CA: Jossey-Bass.

Kouzes, J. M., & Posner, B. Z. (1999). *Encouraging the heart: A leader's guide to rewarding and recognizing others*. San Francisco, CA: Jossey-Bass.

Kouzes, J. M., & Posner, B. Z. (2011). Credibility: How leaders gain and lose it, why people demand it (2nd ed.). San Francisco, CA: Jossey-Bass.

Kramer, M. W. (2010). *Organizational socialization: Joining and leaving organizations*. Cambridge, UK: Polity.

Landis, K. (Ed.). (2008). *Start talking: A handbook for engaging in difficult dialogues in higher education*. Anchorage: University of Alaska Anchorage.

Lowney, C. (2003). *Heroic leadership*. Chicago, IL: Loyola Press.

Marriott, J. W., & Brown, K. A. (1997). *The spirit to serve: Marriott's way*. New York, NY: HarperBusiness.

Merculieff, I., & Landis, K. (Eds.). (2013). *Stop talking: Indigenous ways of teaching and learning and difficult dialogues in higher education*. Anchorage: University of Alaska Anchorage.

Packard, D., Kirby, D., & Lewis, K. R. (1995). *The HP way: How Bill Hewlett and I built our company*. New York, NY: HarperBusiness.

Schön, D. A. (1983). *The reflective practitioner: How professionals think in action*. New York, NY: Basic Books.

Schwinghammer, T. L., Rodriquez, T. E., Weinstein, G., Sorofman, B. A., Bosso, J. A., Kerr, R. A., & Haden, N. K. (2012). AACP strategy for addressing the professional development needs of department chairs. *American Journal of Pharmaceutical Education*, 76(6), 1–8.

Sorenson, G. J. (2000). Taking robes off: When leaders step down. In B. Kellerman & L. R. Matusak (Eds.), *Cutting edge: Leadership 2000*. College Park, MD: Center for the Advanced Study of Leadership.

Staton-Spicer, A. Q., & Spicer, H. H. (1987). Socialization of the academic chairperson: A typology of communication dimensions. *Educational Administration Quarterly*, 23(1), 41–64.

Van Maanen, J., & Schein, E. H. (1979). Toward a theory of organization socialization. In B. Straw (Ed.), *Research in organizational behavior* (vol. 1, pp. 209–264). Greenwich, CT: JAI.

Vise, D. A., & Malseed, M. (2005). *The Google story*. New York, NY: Delacorte.

Watson, T. J. (2003). *A business and its beliefs*. Maidenhead, UK: McGraw-Hill.

RESOURCES

Russell, J. F. (2008). Enthusiastic educational leadership. *Florida Journal of Educational Administration and Policy*, 1(2), 79–97.

Spiller, D. (2010). Language and academic leadership: Exploring and evaluating the narratives. *Higher Education Research and Development*, 29(6), 679–692.

Ward, D. (2007). Academic values, institutional management and public policies. *Higher Education Management and Policy*, 19(2), 1–12.

9

PUTTING IT ALL TOGETHER

COMPREHENSIVE ACADEMIC LEADERSHIP

WE HAVE SEEN THAT leadership development for academic leaders requires understanding basic information and concepts (habits of mind), developing essential skills (habits of practice), and engaging in ongoing reflection and values clarification (habits of heart). We have seen too that the 7-S Model (strategy, structure, system, skills, staff, style, and shared values) proposed by Thomas J. Peters and Robert H. Waterman (1982) and further developed by Mark Stevens (2001) offers the best framework for planning, implementing, and assessing a leadership development programs.

In this final chapter, we pull all of these concepts together and consider how they can be integrated into an approach that we call comprehensive academic leadership (CAL). The risk that even the best academic leadership programs run is that their numerous workshops and other resources can seem like isolated efforts. It can feel as though participants are asked to talk about strategic planning one month, faculty evaluation the next month, conflict management the month after that, with none of these experiences appearing at all related to any other. In a similar way, programs might give the impression that their offerings related to the habits of mind have nothing at all to do with habits of practice or habits of heart. But actual academic leadership does not fall into silos like that. The more we learn about effective leadership helps guide our reflection, and reflecting on our strengths and weaknesses can inform us how we can better apply what we have learned.

Providing academic leaders with a fully integrated program is often accomplished by following three critical steps:

1. Determine whether you have all the components you need for a well-integrated leadership development program.

2. Identify points of overlap or connection among those components.

3. Use those connections to give your program or center a distinct identity.

Let's explore each of these steps in turn.

Do You Have the Components You Need?

At the end of each chapter in this book is a section titled "Clarifying the Strategy," "Clarifying the Structure," and so on. These sections are designed to help you make a systematic analysis of whether you have all the key components of an effective leadership program in place and structured in such a way as to meet the needs of your stakeholders. Over time, however, needs change and programs change. The institution may become more complex. People who were once in leadership roles may be replaced by others. And new issues may emerge that affect everything we do in higher education. For this reason, it helps to take a periodic inventory of your program or center to make sure that the components are still meeting the institution's needs. We recommend using the Developing Academic Leadership Comprehensive Academic Leadership Inventory. Many of its questions are based on best practices in leadership development advocated by the Advisory Board (2011) and Green and McDade (1994). Other questions are based on principles we have explored in this book. It can be useful to complete this inventory about once a year, preferably during a period when you have adequate time to reflect and before you are asked to submit budget and staffing proposals for the following year.

Developing Academic Leadership Comprehensive Academic Leadership Inventory

	Yes	No
Does your institution provide any sort of leadership training for administrators?	□	□
Is leadership training available to those who do not have clearly assigned administrative responsibilities?	□	□
Is the program affordable for all potential participants?	□	□
Are the program's offerings aligned with your institution's mission and strategic plan?	□	□

	Yes	No
Has your institution named an individual whose job description makes it clear that he or she is charged with administrative development?	☐	☐
Does the person in charge of administrative development receive ongoing training/continuing education so that his or her own knowledge and skills remain up to date?	☐	☐
Is the CEO or someone at the vice-presidential level of your institution a vocal champion of this program?	☐	☐
Does your institution make it clear that administrative leadership development is important?	☐	☐
Is there a well-defined procedure for determining who is eligible to participate in your leadership development program?	☐	☐
Does your program make an effort to include participants from traditionally underrepresented groups (e.g., women and faculty of color)?	☐	☐
Does your institution offer new administrators a comprehensive orientation program?	☐	☐
If your institution offers new administrators a comprehensive orientation program, does it last longer than a day?	☐	☐
Does the program help participants understand institutional policies and procedures?	☐	☐
Does your program expose participants to major theories of leadership (traits theory, situational theory, path-goal theory, and the like)?	☐	☐
Does your program expose participants to major approaches to leadership (servant leadership, authentic leadership, positive leadership, and the like)?	☐	☐
Does your program help participants understand how leadership in higher education is different from leadership in other organizational cultures?	☐	☐

	Yes	No
Does your program expose participants to the core values of your institution?	☐	☐
Does your program offer administrators an opportunity to develop specific skills (such as time management, decision making, effective communication, and the like)?	☐	☐
Does your program make an effort to provide skill development related to the actual tasks performed by administrators at your institution (as opposed to skills in general)?	☐	☐
Are the offerings of the program sufficiently tailored so that chairs are exposed to the topics most appropriate for them, deans are exposed to those topics most appropriate for them, and so on?	☐	☐
Does your campus provide any kind of handbook or "survival guide" for academic administrators?	☐	☐
Is leadership training at your institution continuous, involving at least one day a month throughout the academic year?	☐	☐
Do administrators work with mentors at your institution?	☐	☐
Does your program provide opportunities for academic leaders to discuss issues informally with their peers?	☐	☐
Does your program provide opportunities for systematic reflection?	☐	☐
Is one-on-one coaching available to all academic leaders?	☐	☐
Does your program have a clear policy regarding which discussions are confidential and which are not?	☐	☐
Does your program provide participants with information and resources on career development?	☐	☐
Does your institution have a sabbatical leave policy that applies to administrators?	☐	☐
Does your program offer incentives for participation?	☐	☐

	Yes	No
If your program offers incentives, are those incentives sufficient?	☐	☐
Does your institution offer leadership development modules online?	☐	☐
Does your leadership development initiative have sufficient staff to meet the logistical needs of your program (e.g., communication, scheduling, record keeping)?	☐	☐
Does your leadership development initiative have its own budget?	☐	☐
If the program has a budget, has that budget been sufficient to meet the program's needs (as opposed to your long-term hopes and dreams for the program)?	☐	☐
Is your leadership development program cohort based?	☐	☐
If your program is cohort based, is the size of the cohort no more than twenty-five academic administrators?	☐	☐
Does your leadership program make use of experts who work at your institution?	☐	☐
If outside speakers or trainers are used by your program, do they receive information about your institution's specific vision, mission, and values?	☐	☐
Does your program provide participants with information about programs and resources beyond your campus that can support their development?	☐	☐
Does your institution provide support for academic leaders to attend regional and national leadership development programs?	☐	☐
Is the leadership development program sustainable over time?	☐	☐
Are administrators at your institution evaluated every year?	☐	☐
If administrators at your institution are evaluated every year, does any part of that evaluation relate to that person's annual goals and the institution's strategic initiatives?	☐	☐

	Yes	No
If administrators at your institution are evaluated every year, do those evaluations have a formative role?	☐	☐
If administrative evaluations have a formative role, does the information gained from them guide your program's offerings and opportunities?	☐	☐
If administrators at your institution are evaluated every year, do those evaluations have a summative role?	☐	☐
If administrative evaluations have a summative role, are administrators ever required to participate in leadership development based on those results?	☐	☐
Is the satisfaction of the participants in the program assessed regularly?	☐	☐
Is the impact the program has on leadership at your institution assessed regularly?	☐	☐

Completing the Comprehensive Academic Leadership Inventory can help you identify any gaps that may have developed in your program and what the next steps in its development should be. For example, you may have discovered that the president or vice president who championed your program when it was developed has now retired or moved on to other responsibilities; in this case, you might make it a goal to reiterate the significance of the initiative to your school's upper administration so that you continue receiving strong support for your programming. Or you may discover that an administrative sabbatical program, which had not been a priority when your program began a number of years ago, now has a good chance of being approved and an opportunity to address a genuine need. Moreover, the inventory may alert you to opportunities and services that you choose not to provide through your program. For example, you may have elected to create a leadership development center that focuses only on practical, real-world problems, not leadership theory or approaches to leadership like servant leadership and authentic leadership.

The point of the inventory is not to suggest that every program must offer every opportunity addressed on the inventory. Rather it is intended to make you consciously aware of what you are offering and what you are not. In that way, if you have overlooked an element that you believe should be present in your center or program, you will know precisely where to begin.

Are There Points of Overlap or Connection among Those Components?

As you review your results from the Comprehensive Academic Leadership Inventory, try to find a few areas where you can build meaningful connections among these components. In chapter 1, we saw that the Academic Leadership Forum (ALF) at Iowa State University had an explicit goal of finding connections among the knowledge, skills, and values addressed in the program. The model this program used is as follows.

1. *Application = Conceptual understanding + skill development*: Finding ways to take the concepts and skills covered during workshop sessions and apply them to real situations that the participants were facing
2. *Practice = Skill development + reflective practice*: Using systematic reflection to discover ways in which the skills addressed by the program could be applied to improve daily performance
3. *Grounded theory = Conceptual understanding + reflective practice*: Using systematic reflection to discover ways in which the concepts discussed throughout the program relate to each participant's actual experience

In a similar way, other programs might use the information gleaned from the Comprehensive Academic Leadership Inventory to make connections like these:

o Suppose you discover that the goals of your leadership development program are not well aligned with your institution's strategic plan and that you have not been able to provide as much practical skill development as you would like. One of the activities participants could engage in for the year is to advise you on developing a new proposal for what services your program could offer, how that new plan could best be communicated to the community, and how the program's improved alignment with the strategic plan could be measured. In this way, you would be providing opportunities for the participants to apply their skills in planning, communication, and assessment in a practical manner.

o Suppose you discover that your leadership development program has not been successful in exposing participants to common theories and approaches to leadership and that it has been difficult to come up with ideas for programs during each month of the academic year. You could design each month's programming around a particular leadership theory or approach—September is Situational Theory

Month, October is Servant Leadership Month, and so on—with all workshops and other activities connected in some way with that theme.

○ Suppose you discover that you are not providing any type of handbook or "survival guide" to administrators and that outside speakers in your program are not being adequately briefed in the specific vision, mission, and values of your institution. You could design a single publication that serves both of these audiences simultaneously, providing a concise background on how and why your institution functions as it does.

○ Suppose you discover that the goals of your leadership development program are not well aligned with your institution's strategic plan and that you have not been able to provide as much practical skill development as you would like. One of the activities participants could engage in for the year is to advise you on developing a new proposal for what services your program could offer, how that new plan could best be communicated to the community, and how the program's improved alignment with the strategic plan could be measured. In this way, you would be providing opportunities for the participants to apply their skills in planning, communication, and assessment in a practical manner.

The point is that the components of a well-designed leadership program should not stand in isolation. To return to the 7-S model, the strategy should shape the structure, the structure should shape the system, the system should shape the staff, and so on. If that type of alignment does not occur, the participants will end up feeling that they are being exposed to many different techniques or ideas that never really come together to form a unified whole, the concept that we are calling comprehensive academic leadership.

What Do These Connections Suggest about the Program's Identity?

Examining which connections among program components seem most important—because they represent critical needs or reflect singular successes—can provide insight into precisely what comprehensive academic leadership means for your leadership initiative. At times, you may find that the identity of your program is best reflected by some aspect of style such as those we explored in chapter 7. At other times, you may discover that it is best reflected in some of the shared values that we examined in chapter 8. At still other times, you may feel that what makes your program truly distinctive is something more intangible than style or shared values. Regardless of its source, your leadership development program has its own unique identity. Even if you modeled it on a very similar program, the personalities of the presenters and participants, as well as your own personality, will shape your program over time.

As an exercise in isolating the unique identity of your initiative, try using each of the adjectives listed below in the following sentence, "Our leadership program [center] is increasingly becoming known as the _____ Leadership Program [Center]":

creative	progressive
professional	resourceful
enlightened	adaptable
dynamic	future-oriented
values-oriented	goal-oriented
people-oriented	quality-oriented
conscientious	proactive
efficient	ambitious
cooperative	methodical
realistic	reliable
visionary	accelerated
friendly	unbridled
cutting edge	fearless
reflective	insightful
casual	enthusiastic
principled	inspired
inspiring	experimental
entrepreneurial	sophisticated
humanistic	humanitarian
philosophical	good-natured
welcoming	data-driven
integrated	multidimensional
state-of-the-art	managerial
executive	participatory
service-minded	unpretentious
appreciative	passionate
cosmopolitan	serene
joy-filled	intuitive
sincere	

Which adjective seems to fit what you do best? Which resonates most with you and your participants? Which serves as the best one-word or one-term summary of how you view your mission?

As you try out these various adjectives, you might notice several things happening. First, you may discover yourself attracted to synonyms or other closely related words. For example, if you cannot decide whether your program is best described as *welcoming, unpretentious,* or *casual,* it is clear that a distinctive feature of your program is that it is open to everyone and laid-back in its approach. That makes what you do very different from a program run by a director who feels equally attracted to the words *professional, goal-oriented,* and *methodical.* Second, you may find that you absolutely hate some of these terms. What does it tell you about your program if you laughed at or were repelled by such terms as *serene, reliable,* or *managerial?* Third, you may find yourself thinking something like, "I'm really attracted by the word *reflective* since our program focuses so much on how reflection can help administrators become better leaders. But I could never imagine us adopting the name 'The Reflective Leadership Program.'" That reaction is perfectly acceptable.

The point of the exercise is not to develop a new name for your leadership initiative (although that would be an acceptable outcome) but to give you insight into your program's true character and identity. If you do not like the name "The Reflective Leadership Program," do not use it. But remember that extensive use of reflection is a central part of what makes your leadership program special. Use that insight when you promote your program to potential participants, seek additional funding, or simply try to explain to others what it is that you are trying to do. It is this activity that sets you apart from other academic leadership programs and that serves as your key to comprehensive academic leadership.

Inclusive Academic Leadership

One quality that many academic leadership programs regard as integral to their identity is inclusivity. In fact, leadership development initiatives have long been at the forefront of promoting administrative diversity. As late as the 1970s the vast majority of managers attending leadership development programs were white and male (Ruderman and Hughes-James, 1998). Since that time, however, progress has been made in including women and faculty of color among the ranks of academic leadership. Several leadership development programs were designed specifically to meet the needs of underrepresented groups. Model programs include the Higher Education Resource Services (HERS) Summer Institute (www.hersnet.org/HERSHigherEducationResourceServices.htmsisihtm .asp?menu=HERS%20Institutes), which is offered at Bryn Mawr College; the American Dental Education Association Summer Program for Emerging

Academic Leaders (www.adea.org/Secondary.aspx?id=20829), which targets faculty of color; and the Association of American Medical Colleges Minority Faculty Career Development Seminar (www.aamc.org /members/gfa/64552/facultyaffairs_minorityseminar.html), which provides leadership training to junior faculty members from underrepresented groups. In the early 2000s, the Women in Engineering Leadership Institute held a number of influential workshops that were also designed to bring more women into leadership roles in a field historically dominated by men.

In 1992, Ann Morrison interviewed 196 managers and discovered six barriers experienced by all groups historically underrepresented in leadership roles (Morrison, White, Van Velsor, and Center for Creative Leadership, 1992):

1. Prejudice

2. Poor career planning

3. Poor working environment

4. Lack of organizational savvy

5. Greater comfort dealing with people similar to them as opposed to being from different backgrounds

6. Balancing career and family

Many of these barriers remain despite all the efforts that have been made in higher education to eliminate them. Moreover, to these six challenges, we add a seventh that is rampant in higher education: excessive service responsibilities because of the expectation that all committees have diverse representation. Overcoming these obstacles can provide a leadership development initiative with a clear focus and goal. While an emphasis on inclusive academic leadership certainly makes sense at single-sex institutions and historically black colleges and universities, those should not be the only schools that take on this mission. Opening the doors to leadership opportunities regardless of a person's race, gender, creed, national origin, marital status, sexual orientation, or political views can provide a program with a strong sense of purpose. It can be even more powerful to extend this mission further by basing the philosophy of your program on this conviction:

While few of us may be naturally born leaders, we all have the ability and deserve the opportunity to improve our leadership skills.

Final Thoughts

We began with this book with a question: Where have all the leaders gone? Throughout our study, we discovered that many excellent role models do exist and that there are a number of well-designed programs that help academic leaders do their jobs. Nevertheless, most administrators still come to their positions without any formal leadership training, prior executive experience, a clear understanding of the ambiguity and complexity of their roles, recognition of the metamorphic changes that await them, or awareness of the potential cost of their positions to their academic and personal lives (Gmelch, 2013; Green and McDade, 1994). In our research, we explored how campuses have been able to advance academic leaders effectively and then offered what we hope can serve as a blueprint for those who wish to establish or improve their own initiatives on campus.

One conclusion seems inescapable: trying to build an academic leadership program on the basis of what has proven to be effective in the corporate world simply does not work in higher education:

> Provosts who have tried using trainers or consultants from the corporate world for leadership development report that their services seldom translate well into the higher education context. Corporate sector approaches and strategies are often difficult to convert into the higher education environment, where shared governance and the tenure system can impede implementation. Additionally, any use of corporate jargon by presenters will cause faculty to quickly tune out. (Advisory Board, 2011, xi)

If comprehensive academic leadership is to be practiced more widely throughout higher education, colleges and universities will need to develop programs that make sense in their own environment for their own stakeholders. For example, the University of California, Berkeley, realized that in order to sustain its preeminence as a leader in public higher education, "the faculty administrators who lead departments, research units, and the campus itself must be excellent not only in research and teaching, but also in leadership, management, and administration" (*Preparing Faculty for Academic Management*, 2007, 5). Nevertheless, UC Berkeley found it had no comprehensive program to prepare faculty administrators or to support their professional development while in their positions. To address this gap, the university conducted an extensive study in this way:

1. Gathering and analyzing data from stakeholders to determine what skills and information faculty need in order to perform administrative roles

2. Interviewing campus academic leaders to assess what competencies, skills, and learning formats would be most useful to them in meeting their needs

3. Benchmarking faculty leadership development at six other University of California campuses, ten peer institutions, and two systemwide leadership development programs

4. Identifying available resources that could be used to help support leadership development on and off the Berkeley campus

The study concluded that most people preferred an informal approach (including mentoring, one-on-one meetings, resources available on demand, and small group discussions) to formal courses and workshops. In addition, they concluded that incentives must be provided to participants; otherwise most opportunities would not be used to their full advantage (*Preparing Faculty for Academic Management*, 2007).

While one of the report's main recommendations was further research into how the university can better compensate and motivate faculty administrators, many campuses cannot afford to wait until they develop the right package of incentives to encourage administrators in their leadership development. Too many studies can lead to paralysis by analysis. Often it is better to identify a need, develop a program to address it, and tweak the approach as challenges arise. Consider an example. A climate survey conducted by Centralia College in Washington State indicated that only 29 percent of employees felt that communication and relationships were "good" or "satisfactory" (Advisory Board, 2011). To address this problem, the college created a cohort-based leadership development program that would work to improve communication across campus. Unlike UC Berkeley, Centralia quickly launched this program without conducting a long study or needs assessment, with only minimal funds and the vice president for human resources heading the project. Adopting a build-as-you-fly strategy, the college began the initiative without even determining which topics would be addressed each month; the issues covered would be recommended by the participants as the program continued. The college relied on existing materials and other resources the organizers found online. The training cohort included representatives from academic affairs, student affairs, and business affairs, with an effort made to include a good cross-section of the institution. Within a year, institution-wide satisfaction with communication had increased by 10 percent. Five years later, after more than half of Centralia's leaders had been through the program, the organizers concluded that its original purpose had been served. Nevertheless, rather than terminating the initiative, the college decided to expand it in 2011 by partnering with two nearby peer institutions.

UC Berkeley and Centralia College represent two poles in developing comprehensive academic leadership programs: devoting major resources and research to getting it right from the start and figuring it out as you go along. No one approach is going to suit every institution, but there are exemplary programs from which other institutions can borrow effective practices and patterns of organization. The best example for you to borrow from may not be appropriate at all as a model at another institution. By choosing a broad range of programs to profile throughout our discussion and the appendix that follows, we hope each institution or university system will find practices that could work well in their own unique environments.

Developing faculty into academic leaders is both a privilege and a responsibility that institutions of higher education should eagerly embrace. The privilege comes from the opportunity to make a positive difference in the development of one's colleagues and successors, and the responsibility stems from the importance of developing higher education's most valued resource: its people. Through academic leadership programs, institutions benefit from making the most effective use of this resource, building connections across campus, promoting purposeful leadership diversity, tapping hidden talent, retaining campus talent, expanding people's potential, and ensuring institutional renewal, effectiveness, and efficiency. Achieving these benefits requires time, commitment, resources, and dedication. But the future of higher education depends on colleges and universities that are willing to answer the call to leadership with commitment and vision.

REFERENCES

Advisory Board. (2011). *Developing academic leaders: Cultivating the skills of chairs, deans, and other faculty administrators.* Washington, DC: Advisory Board.

Gmelch, W. H. (2013). The development of campus academic leaders. *International Journal of Leadership and Change, 1*(1), 26–35.

Green, M. F., & McDade, S. A. (1994). *Investing in higher education: A handbook of leadership development.* Washington, DC: Oryx Press.

Morrison, A. M., White, R. P., Van Velsor, E., & Center for Creative Leadership. (1992). *Breaking the glass ceiling: Can women reach the top of America's largest corporations?* Reading, MA: Addison-Wesley.

Peters, T., & Waterman, R. J. (1982). *In search of excellence: Lessons from America's best-run companies.* New York, NY: Warner Books.

Preparing faculty for academic management: Needs assessment and benchmark-ing. (2007). Retrieved from http://hrweb.berkeley.edu/sites/default/files /attachments/07academicmanagement.pdf

Ruderman, M. N., & Hughes-James, M. W. (1998). Leadership development across race and gender. In D. D. McCauley, R. S. Moxley, & E. Van Vel-sor (Eds.), *The Center for Creative Leadership handbook of leadership development*. San Francisco, CA: Jossey-Bass.

Stevens, M. (2001). *Extreme management*. New York, NY: Warner Books.

APPENDIX

RESOURCE GUIDES

THERE IS NO SINGLE correct way to organize an academic leadership center. Since each institution's needs will be different, the way in which it addresses those needs will be different as well. Throughout this book, we have profiled a number of successful leadership development initiatives, but they do not begin to cover the full variety of models that can work at colleges and universities.

The three following resource guides are intended to provide additional ideas for those who want to establish or improve an academic leadership program. It is simply not possible to outline all the programs that exist. New programs and centers are developed regularly. Some well-established programs are phased out when budgets are cut or directors retire. It was not even feasible to list current websites for these programs, since URLs change so frequently that any published list is out of date as soon as it appears. Instead, we have included a few select, representative programs of three different kinds: those that exist at the national, system, and institutional levels. We have intentionally omitted programs that we discussed in greater detail elsewhere in the book. But in order to provide some insight into the many different ways of organizing and focusing a leadership development initiative, we have analyzed a number of successful programs in terms of the 7-S model used throughout this book.

- ○ Strategy and shared values: What the initiative seeks to accomplish and why.
- ○ Structure and style: For whom the program is intended and why.
- ○ System: What format is used, including information about how often programming is offered and the delivery methods used.
- ○ Staff: Who organizes the program and provides content.
- ○ Skills: Which aspects of leadership the program tries to address. Since most programs seek to be comprehensive in nature, the skills listed in this column tend to be merely representative of a broader range of programming.

Academic Leadership Programs at the National Level

National Program	Strategy and Shared Values	Structure and Style
American Association of Colleges of Teacher Education (AACTE): Leadership Academy	To develop key leadership skills in administrators within colleges of education. To provide the training these leaders need in order to succeed and cultivate a network of supportive peers.	The program is designed primarily for new deans, department chairs, directors in schools of education, and other educational administrators. Emphasis is placed on both leadership development and networking.
American Council on Education (ACE): Fellows Program	To ensure that future leaders in higher education are ready to face real-world challenges. To build leadership capacity at colleges and universities.	Prospective leaders are nominated by their institution's president. Participants usually include a mixed group of emerging faculty leaders, department chairs, deans, and vice presidents. The programming is designed to prepare them for significant roles in the upper administration of a college or university.
The Chair Academy: International Leadership Conference	To provide the broadest possible range of leadership development. To offer opportunities for participants to	The Chair Academy offers several programs: the Foundation Leadership Academy for newer administrators, the

System	Staff	Skills
A four-day retreat held once a year with support faculty and national experts. The location varies.	The program is organized under the supervision of the AACTE president and chief executive officer, along with a board of directors and administrative staff. Programming is provided by a nationally renowned faculty.	Such topics as team development, leadership skills, conflict management, diversity, career planning, faculty development, time and stress management, personnel, financial management and development, and decision making.
An immersion experience at a host institution where participants shadow leaders and work on assigned projects. Periodic seminars with experts in the field, workshops, and other training opportunities are conducted for all participants.	The program is supervised by a senior program manager, working together with a program manager and program assistant. Since ACE is a large organization that offers a number of other leadership programs as well (including institutes for new presidents and chief academic officers, seminars for those considering becoming university presidents, workshops for chief academic officers and business officers, and leadership academies for department chairs), it is also able to draw on a large staff and network of contacts for programming.	Over the course of the program, participants are exposed to almost all aspects of college and university administration, including basic concepts of leadership, change management, strategic planning, financial planning and implementation, diversity issues, and the role of technology in education and research.
The International Conference runs for three days and includes multiple concurrent sessions in the form of roundtables,	Started as a grassroots movement in 1992 by Maricopa Community Colleges, the Chair Academy has become a large international	A broad range of academic, administrative, and organizational skills, including effective communication,

National Program	Strategy and Shared Values	Structure and Style
	integrate their leadership knowledge and skills.	Academy for Advanced Leadership for more experienced administrators, and the International Leadership Conference for administrators of all levels of experience. The International Conference offers both training and networking opportunities.
Kansas State University: Academic Chairpersons Conference	To train participants in practical approaches to academic leadership through presentations and workshops conducted by experts in their field. To create opportunities for participants to interact informally with these experts.	Primarily intended for department chairs, the program is also suitable for deans, academic vice presidents, program directors, and faculty development coordinators.
Higher Education Resource Services (HERS): Institute	To prepare women faculty and administrators for institutional leadership roles.	Participants in each institute typically hold mid- to senior-level positions, representing a broad range of ethnic and national groups, ages, and years of experience.
Harvard University: Harvard Institutes for Higher Education	To offer intensive and rigorous exposure to current theories and best practices related to academic leadership at each participant's appropriate level. To	Different institutes are offered depending on the type and extent of the participant's experience. The Management Development Program

System	Staff	Skills
skill-building workshops, informational sessions, and addresses by keynote speakers.	program. It is managed by a director and multiple boards (advisory, practitioners, editorial, and facilitation).	mentoring, dealing with conflict, managing change, and developing a personal leadership style.
Held once each year in a three-day format that includes concurrent sessions of papers, panels, roundtables, workshops, and full- and half-day leadership training sessions.	Organized and operated by the Division of Continuing Education at Kansas State University. The staff of that division provides logistical, technical, and administrative support, while presenters are experts in their fields from a wide variety of organizations and institutions.	Typically covers such topics as conflict management, leadership, evaluation and assessment, working with the dean, team building, promoting collegiality, decision making, and performance counseling.
An intensive twelve-day curriculum that is offered at three locations and in two residential formats. Programming consists of lectures, independent readings, group work, and individual assignments.	Operated by a president and executive director; several directors; coordinators in charge of communication, programming, and finance; and a board of directors.	Topics usually include understanding the higher education environment, planning and leading change, managing and investing strategic resources, and mapping the participant's own leadership development.
A two-week, highly intensive leadership development experience. Content is provided primarily through independent reading, actual case	Operated under the direction of Harvard's Graduate School of Education through its Division of Professional Education.	Approaches to leadership, developing strategy, evaluating the impact of change in higher education, realigning resources with mission

National Program	Strategy and Shared Values	Structure and Style
	apply principles of effective business management to the world of higher education.	is designed for administrators with three to seven years of experience, the Institute for Management and Leadership in Education for those with five to twelve years of experience, and the Institute for Educational Management for those with more than ten years of experience.
IDEA Education: Consulting Services	To provide support to the leadership development of administrators through one-on-one department consultation, coaching, and mentoring.	For administrators of all levels. The precise nature of the coaching or consulting service is arranged directly between the participant and the consultant.
Academic Conference of Academic Deans (ACAD): Annual ACAD Conference	To expose academic leaders to current issues in liberal education and provide those leaders with the resources they need for their success.	Designed primarily for deans, provosts, academic vice presidents, associate and assistant deans, and other academic leaders at institutions affiliated with the Association of American of Colleges and Universities (AAC&U). The style is that of a smaller, more intimate miniconference within the larger AAC&U conference.

System	Staff	Skills
studies, small group discussions, and interactive presentations. Seeks to apply the principles of business management to the world of higher education.		balancing internal and external leadership roles, analyzing financial data, and considering the ethical dimensions of academic leadership.
Of flexible length. IDEA Education recommends coaches based on their presentations at IDEA seminars or sponsored conferences, publication of IDEA papers, or service on IDEA Education's board of directors.	IDEA is a nonprofit organization with a mission to provide assessment and feedback systems to improve learning in higher education. The organization has a large staff, including a president, several directors and research associates, an administrative staff, and a board of directors.	A wide range of topics, including how to improve academic culture and effectiveness, increase administrator satisfaction, enhance each participant's professional life, expose participants to individualized improvement strategies, reduce staff turnover, and generally strengthen academic leadership in whatever area the participant most desires.
Once a year in January in conjunction with the annual conference of the AAC&U. The theme of the annual ACAD conference is tied to the broader theme of the AAC&U conference.	An executive director and a five-member board of directors, elected annually, including a chair, past chair, vice chair, and the chair of the governance and board development committee. Several other committees assist in planning the program and the organization's general operations.	Provides leadership development on a range of topics related to the ideals of liberal education.

National Program	Strategy and Shared Values	Structure and Style
American Association of Colleges of Pharmacy: Academic Leadership Fellows Program (ALFP)	To develop faculty members for roles as future leaders in academic pharmacy programs.	Faculty members are nominated by their deans. The participant's home institution continues to pay the participant's salary, tuition to the ALFP, and all travel expenses related to the program.
American Association of Colleges of Nursing (AACN): Leadership for Academic Nursing Program	To identify and prepare prospective leaders in nursing.	Intended for aspiring deans of nursing. Those interested participate in a competitive application process, with a class of about sixty fellows selected each year. Fellows have an opportunity to be mentored by an experienced dean.

System	Staff	Skills
ALFP is a year-long experience with four intensive sessions in residence throughout the year. Participants are also supported by ongoing informal mentoring and introduction to leadership.	The program is supervised by an associate director of academic programs and operated by the association's staff.	The four sessions include in-depth leadership development in such areas as team building, exploration of legislative and policy issues, and self and peer assessments. In addition, fellows engage in a collaborative group project. Overall the program seeks to cover personal and interpersonal competencies for leadership, practical management responsibilities, and administrative competencies of an academic pharmacy administrator, as well as leadership in the external arena of advocacy and the profession.
A year-long program that begins with a five-day intensive seminar. The seminar facilitates the establishment of a mentorship and allows follow-up activities with program faculty.	Supervised by the AACN's director of faculty development, with logistical support provided by association staff. Program facilitators are chosen from experienced leaders in the field of nursing.	A comprehensive program that includes assessment of the participant's current leadership style and skills, opportunities for strategic networking and case study development, consultation with experienced leaders to achieve long-term goals, and identification of key partnerships for the participant to develop.

National Program	Strategy and Shared Values	Structure and Style
Association of American Medical Colleges (AAMC): Executive Development Seminar for Interim and Aspiring Leaders	To provide leadership development opportunities for relatively new administrators in colleges of medicine.	Intended primarily for deans, aspiring deans, new department chairs, and associate deans at medical schools.
Council of Colleges of Arts and Sciences (CCAS): Leadership Development Programs	To prepare current and prospective leaders in academic units associated with the arts and sciences. To use realistic case studies to prepare participants to respond effectively in a wide variety of challenging situations.	CCAS sponsors separate leadership development programs for chairs and deans. Both formal training workshops and informal opportunities for networking and discussion are important features of all CCAS programs.
Center for Creative Leadership (CCL): Leadership Development Program (LDP)	To advance the understanding, practice, and development of leadership for the benefit of society worldwide.	The LDP, only one of many leadership programs run by CCL, is intended for midlevel managers who want to improve their effectiveness. Like all other CCL programs, it is not designed exclusively for those working in higher education. Other programs are designed

System	Staff	Skills
Three-day seminar designed to engage participants in exploration of organizational culture and management, interpersonal and interorganizational communication strategies, new leadership strategies for managing talent, and other critical leadership skills.	Jointly sponsored and organized by the AAMC and the University of California, San Diego, School of Medicine.	Managing interpersonal or organizational conflict, differentiating the role of a leader versus that of a follower, examining stress reduction techniques, exploring principled leadership (the concepts of integrity, authenticity, and commitment to something bigger than self), using meaningful data to improve organizational performance, and multiplying rather than diminishing the skills of organizational personnel.
Programs are two to four days in length and include presentations on practical topics by experienced administrators. In addition, the Deans Knowledge Base is a searchable database of resource documents of interest to deans.	CCAS programs are organized by an executive director, office staff, a president, president elect, past president, treasurer, and a governing board.	Topics typically include recruitment and retention, networking, fundraising, problem solving, promoting the liberal arts, and managing people and conflict.
A five-day program held at multiple locations around the world. CCL also offers white papers and other resources on many issues related to leadership.	CCL programs fall under the general supervision of the center's president and two governing boards: members (who have fiduciary responsibility) and governors (who set policy).	Topics include bridging the gap between senior management and the front line, collaborating across the organization to gain critical perspectives, managing organizational politics, coping with complexity to take advantage of rapidly changing conditions, leveraging

National Program	Strategy and Shared Values	Structure and Style
		for new leaders, senior leaders, women in leadership positions, human resource professionals, and so on.
Southeastern Conference Academic Consortium: Academic Leadership Development Program (ALDP)	To help develop the leadership skills of tenured faculty on campuses within the Southeastern Conference Academic Consortium who have demonstrated exceptional ability and leadership promise.	Members of the faculty and administration of the Southeastern Conference Academic Consortium are eligible to apply for the program. Those who are selected serve as fellows for a two-year term. During the second year, they serve as mentors to the new cohort of fellows. Applicants are expected to be tenured faculty members with demonstrated leadership ability, faculty members with administrative assignments and positions (such as department chairs or associate chairs), associate and assistant deans, deans or associate and assistant provosts.

System	Staff	Skills
		the participants' experience to increase their leadership effectiveness, and building resilience.
Workshops, presentations, and discussions at various institutions within the Southeastern Conference Academic Consortium. At most schools in the program, fellows also complete a leadership project during their second year. The program combines individualized training at each participant's campus and development on broader leadership issues through workshops conducted by sponsoring institutions within the consortium.	ALDP is organized by the offices of the provost at consortium member institutions. Each institution also has a coordinator who facilitates the applications process and communications between the program and the institution.	A broad range of topics, including communication skills, conflict resolution, emergency preparedness, organizational culture and change, creating a compelling vision for the future, accreditation, assessment, accountability, budgeting, and conducting faculty searches.

Academic Leadership Programs at the System Level

Systemwide Programs	Strategy and Shared Values	Structure and Style
Committee on Institutional Cooperation (CIC): **Academic Leadership Program (ALP)**	To prepare a diverse range of leaders for positions at all levels of research universities.	Institutions that are CIC members select their own fellows based on proven abilities or demonstrated promise and then nominate them to the ALP. The program is largely intended for those desiring to become deans, provosts, or presidents at flagship or research universities.
Committee on Institutional Cooperation (CIC): **Department Executive Officers Seminar**	To prepare heads of academic departments from CIC member institutions in effective leadership strategies and emerging issues in higher education.	Institutions that are CIC members select department chairs to attend. The process is coordinated by each institution's CIC liaison.
University of Texas (UT) System: **Leadership Institute**	To promote the value of leadership, model positive leadership behaviors, and improve academic leadership generally throughout the UT system.	Three programs exist for administrators at different stages of their careers: the System Overview for New Leaders for new deans and chairs in the UT system; A Day in the Life of a Department Chair for faculty members who are considering whether to become heads of departments; and A Day in the Life of a Dean for faculty members who are interested in a leadership role in higher education.

System	Staff	Skills
Three seminars hosted by three different CIC institutions. The seminars include a balance of informational and interactive sessions, opportunities for networking, and campus visits. Fellows are also sometimes expected to participate in on-campus activities at their home institutions throughout the academic year.	The program is overseen by an ALP chair with a board that serves as a liaison to the member institutions.	The three seminars are the Evolving University (the changing context of higher education), Internal and External Relationships (development of faculty and staff and engaging effectively with the larger community), and Money, Management, and Strategy (budgeting, fundraising, and alternative revenue streams).
A three-day workshop that includes presentations, group problem-solving sessions, exercises, and discussions.	The seminar is overseen by a program manager in cooperation with the liaisons at each member institution.	Typical programs include sessions on conflict resolution, time management, faculty development, performance reviews, and group problem solving.
The three systemwide programs are offered at various locations and times throughout the academic year in order to make participation in them more convenient for participants throughout the state. Format generally includes presentations combined with panel discussions. The Leadership Institute also offers customized programs and facilitation issues on a broad range of administrative topics.	The Leadership Institute serves all fifteen UT System institutions. It is led by a director who reports to the System Office of Academic Affairs and governed by an advisory group.	Topics generally include communication skills for academic leaders, external and governmental relations, delegation, diversity and inclusion, legal issues, operations, personnel management, resource management, and strategic planning.

Systemwide Program	Strategy and Shared Values	Structure and Style
Houston Community College System, Center for Teaching and Learning Excellence (CTLE): Instructional Leaders Program (ILP)	To offer practical development in instructional-oriented leadership.	Originally designed exclusively for department chairs, the ILP program is now open to academic leaders holding other positions within the Houston Community College System.

System	Staff	Skills
Each semester ILP offers ten to twelve workshops on various topics of concern to instructional leaders.	The program is organized by the CTLE within the Division of Academic Affairs. CTLE is the system's unit charged with developing faculty and staff in skills relevant to their positions.	Typical workshops include managing budgets and finance, hiring process and recruiting, faculty evaluation, program review, ethical and equal employment opportunity issues, annual planning, scheduling and faculty workloads, and orientation to duties and responsibilities.

Academic Leadership Programs at the Institutional Level

Institution Name	Strategy and Shared Values	Structure and Style
Pennsylvania State University: Academic Leadership Forums (ALFs)	To help academic leaders keep abreast of contemporary issues and topics so they can function at the highest possible level.	Admission to the ALF is by invitation only. Those invited are generally selected from Penn State department chairs, school directors, associate deans, and deans who have oversight of faculty.
Centralia College: Leadership Program	To improve communication skills and relationships among individuals across campus units.	Participants are selected from applicants. Each year's cohort contains approximately twenty participants, with one-third from each of the college's major divisions: academics, business, and student affairs.
University of Wisconsin, Madison: Chairs and Directors Workshops	To encourage and promote excellence through skill development in areas related to academic leadership.	Designed for department and program chairs, associate and assistant deans.

System	Staff	Skills
The ALFs are half-day sessions held once in the fall and twice in the spring with about ninety university leaders in attendance.	The program is organized by the vice provost for academic affairs, along with a planning committee and administrative staff.	Common topics include managing time and stress, performance counseling, legal issues, leading change, enhancing climate, survival skills, evaluating teaching effectiveness, building a diverse and inclusive environment, fundraising, mentoring, ethical leadership, conflict resolution and negotiations, and recruiting and retention.
The program takes place monthly, with ten four-hour sessions scheduled over the course of the academic year.	The program is organized by the vice president for human resources.	Typical topics covered throughout the program include leadership styles, trust and community, communication, motivating and leading others, organizational performance, teamwork, and problem solving.
A full-day training session is conducted for new chairs at the start of each academic year. Monthly half-day workshops are held, supplemented by an extensive Department Chair's and Director's Toolkit that is available online.	Organized as a joint effort by the Office of the Provost and the Office of Human Resources with sessions conducted by subject matter experts.	Typically topics include managing conflict, time, and stress; facilitating student success; strategic planning; dealing with legal issues; and institutional policies.

Institution Name	Strategy and Shared Values	Structure and Style
Ohio State University: Academic Leader Development Series	To create learning experiences for emerging and existing leaders that will enhance university effectiveness, build leadership skills, and improve relationships among institutional leaders.	Intended primarily for new deans, associate and assistant deans, school and center directors, and department chairs but open to all academic leaders who wish to attend.
Rice University: RiceLeaders	To offer comprehensive leadership development as a means of promoting institutional transformation.	A comprehensive program for cohorts of twenty-five leaders in each class. Intended largely for vice presidents, associate vice presidents, deans, chairs, and senior faculty members.
Michigan State University, Office of Faculty and Organizational Development: Organizational and Leadership Development Series	To offer effective leadership development opportunities to faculty members, new administrators, experienced campus leaders, and executive leaders.	Programs are designed for multiple academic audiences: faculty members who want to learn more about leadership; new administrators; and current deans, chairs, directors, and executive managers.

System	Staff	Skills
Seminars are scheduled in the late summer and/or beginning of the fall semester.	A joint effort of the Offices of Academic Affairs and Human Resources.	Topics typically include faculty review and development, critical legal issues, staff performance management, and financial stewardship.
Four two-day modules held throughout the calendar year; 360-degree assessments with executive coaches, action learning projects (teams of five), and a support system once the program is over.	Designed and supervised by the vice president for administration, with content provided by the university's executive education experts and external consultants.	Leadership concepts and instruments, managing and leading teams, creativity, and strategy implementation.
Orientation for New Administrators consists of three mandatory half-day workshops at the beginning of the academic year. The Leadership and Administrator Seminar consists of meetings with the president and provost and discussions of various issues of concern to academic leaders. The Executive Leadership Academy presents workshops on specific topics such as setting priorities, time management, and motivating others. Workshops for Faculty on Leadership and Academic Life are two- or two-and-a-half-hour programs on topics	The Office of Faculty and Organizational Development in the Office of the Provost directs multiple programs and prepares and organizes these programs. An associate provost/associate vice president for academic human resources is responsible for faculty development, leadership development, and organizational development programs. Administrative staff in the provost's office includes clerical personnel, an informational technology coordinator, and a budget director.	A wide range of issues are covered in this series, including policies and procedures specific to Michigan State University, general issues of leadership and management, and improving the efficiency of academic units.

Institution Name	Strategy and Shared Values	Structure and Style
Iowa State University: Emerging Leader Academy	To develop the leadership capacity of a diverse group of leaders in both academic and nonacademic areas.	A cohort of thirty participants is selected each year from academic and nonacademic units. Each applicant must be nominated.
University of North Carolina, Greensboro: Leadership Institute	To develop and promote a culture of innovation in leadership.	A cohort of twenty-five emerging leaders are selected across the institution from academic and nonacademic units. Some administrative experience is preferred but not required.
Tufts University: Academic Leadership Development Program (ALD)	To provide the tools and skills faculty members and administrators need in order to meet the numerous issues that arise with leadership roles.	The program is primarily intended for academic deans, department chairs, and program directors. Participants must apply to the program, and approximately sixteen to twenty leaders are selected to attend each program.

System	Staff	Skills
such as getting published and remaining active in research while pursuing an administrative career.		
Each month the academy offers a full-day workshop on a topic, along with panel discussions and participation in support groups.	The program is sponsored by the Office of the Senior Vice President and Provost and operates under the supervision of a director.	The academy introduces participants to leadership research, theory, and practice, as well as the university's strengths and challenges. It includes full-day sessions on organizational theory, culture, and context, interpersonal relations, approaches to leadership, communication skills, decision making, managing change and conflict, and university finance.
Eight all-day or half-day workshops with panels, action learning, project teams, and mentors. The program culminates with each student presenting a completed project to the university's chancellor and executive staff.	The institute is a joint project of the Office of Human Resources and the associate vice chancellor, with content provided by experts both within and outside the institution.	Sessions are devoted to the legislative process, boundary spanning, maintaining work-life balance, developing and leading teams, managing conflict, promoting entrepreneurial thinking, coaching others, improving diversity, and pursuing strategic initiatives.
A five-module program offered over three months in six half-day sessions.	The university's Office of Human Resources/ Organizational Development and Training, the Center for the Enhancement of Teaching and Learning, and the Office of the Provost coordinate to plan and provide the program.	The five modules in the program are the role of an academic leader, academic leadership styles, communication and conflict resolution, managing change, and the academic leader as a coach and mentor.

Institution Name	Strategy and Shared Values	Structure and Style
Rutgers University: Academic Leadership Program	To develop the leadership and managerial skills of faculty members who have demonstrated exceptional ability and academic promise.	A combination of programs and online resources intended to promote information sharing among academic department chairs, deans, and other administrators. Online resources include web pages devoted to such issues as addressing discrimination and harassment, promoting health and safety, and understanding university regulations.
Emory University: Academic Leadership Program (ALP)	To provide development for the university's academic leaders, improve their performance and effectiveness, and establish a leadership pipeline for succession planning.	Open to current and future chairs, deans, division leaders, and other senior faculty leaders.

System	Staff	Skills
Regular sessions are held throughout the academic year to examine critical issues and share effective practices among administrators. Typical sessions are seventy-five minutes in length and are presented in a lecture/discussion format.	The program is sponsored by the Center for Organizational Development and Leadership (ODL), the Graduate School, and the Office of the Executive Vice President for Academic Affairs. The Academic Leadership Program is cochaired by an associate dean of the graduate school and the executive director of ODL. Staffing also includes a program coordinator and an administrative assistant.	The program addresses theoretical and practical problems of academic leadership, assessment and accreditation, workplace violence, emergency management, sharing effective practices across disciplines, managing transition, and creating a collaborative network of administrators and faculty members charged with providing academic leadership for the institution.
A year-long strategic program of case studies, leadership development training, skills sessions, financial management planning, and hands-on projects related to faculty matters at the university.	The ALP is offered by the Provost's Office and organized by the Office of the Senior Vice Provost for Academic Affairs. Facilitators include both Emory faculty and national experts in leadership development, financial management, faculty recruitment, promotion, and retention, and other academic leadership areas.	Sessions include development in leading change, understanding leadership styles, maintaining work-life balance, project management, interviewing skills, recruiting faculty, leading effective meetings, faculty development, faculty review, strategic thinking, mentoring faculty, and fundraising.

INDEX

Page references followed by *fig* indicate an illustrated figure; followed by *t* indicate a table.

Center for the Study of Academic Leadership

Originally founded in 1988 as the Center for the Study of Department Chairs in collaboration with the University Council for Educational Administration, the center advanced its research into the study of deans, associate deans, and other academic administrators. Over the years, the center has directed two national studies of 1,600 university department chairs in the United States, one study of 1,580 Australian department heads, another investigation of 1,000 community college chairs, and an international study of 2,000 academic deans in Australia and America.

The center has conducted research and written extensively on the topics of leadership, team development, conflict, and stress and time management, producing over two hundred articles, twenty-seven books and monographs, and numerous scholarly papers in national and international journals. Some of the books the affiliated authors have published include *Chairing an Academic Department* (2004), *Leadership Skills for Department Chairs* (2011), *Productivity Teams: Beyond Quality Circles* (1984), *Coping with Faculty Stress* (1993), *Beyond Stress to Effective Management* (1982), *The Department Chair as Academic Leader* (1999), *College Deans: Leading from Within* (2002), *The Dean's Balancing Act* (2002), *The Changing Nature of the Deanship* (2001), *Seasons of a Dean's Life* (2011), and *The Life Cycle of a Department Chair* (2004).

Over the past twenty-five years, the center has conducted professional development seminars for universities, colleges, deans, and department chairs throughout the United States and internationally. The topics have included:

- Team development
- Stress management
- Effective time management
- Conflict management
- Working with difficult colleagues
- Strategic leadership
- Effective decision making
- Balancing personal and professional trade-offs
- Life cycle and development of deans and department chairs

For further information regarding publications and professional development, contact:

Walter H. Gmelch, Ph.D., Director
Center for the Study of Academic Leadership
Department of Organization and Leadership
University of San Francisco
2130 Fulton Street
San Francisco, CA 94117
415-233-3611
E-mail: whgmelch@usfca.edu

ATLAS: Academic Training, Leadership, & Assessment Services offers training programs, books, and materials dealing with collegiality and positive academic leadership. Its programs include:

- Time Management
- Work-Life Balance
- Conflict Management
- Promoting Teamwork
- Promoting Collegiality
- Communicating Effectively
- Mentoring Faculty Members
- Positive Academic Leadership
- The Essential Academic Dean
- The Essential Department Chair
- Best Practices in Faculty Evaluation
- Change Leadership in Higher Education

These programs are offered in half-day, full-day, and multiday formats. ATLAS also offers reduced prices on leadership books and distributes the Collegiality Assessment Matrix and Self-Assessment Matrix, which allow academic programs to evaluate the collegiality and civility of their faculty members in a consistent, objective, and reliable manner. The free *ATLAS E-Newsletter* addresses a variety of issues related to academic leadership and is sent free to subscribers.

For more information, contact:

ATLAS: Academic Training, Leadership, & Assessment Services
4521 PGA Boulevard, PMB 186
Palm Beach Gardens FL 33418
800–355–6742; www.atlasleadership.com
E-mail: questions@atlasleadership.com

If you enjoyed this book, you may also like these:

Positive Academic Leadership: How to Stop
Putting Out Fires and Start Making a Difference
by Jeffery L. Buller
ISBN: 9781118531921

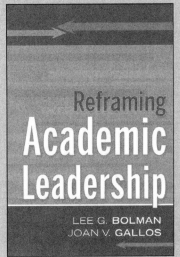

Reframing Academic Leadership
by Lee G. Bolman and
Joan V. Gallos
ISBN: 9780787988067

Want to connect?

Like us on Facebook
http://www.facebook.com/JBHigherED

Subscribe to our newsletter
www.josseybass.com/go/higheredemail

Follow us on Twitter
http://twitter.com/JBHigherED

Go to our Website
www.josseybass.com/highereducation